BREAKING RANKSII™:
Strategies for Leading High School Reform

With a foreword by Theodore R. Sizer

THE
EDUCATION
ALLIANCE
BROWN UNIVERSITY
PROVIDENCE, RI

NATIONAL ASSOCIATION
OF SECONDARY SCHOOL
PRINCIPALS
RESTON, VA

NATIONAL ASSOCIATION
OF SECONDARY SCHOOL
PRINCIPALS
promoting excellence in school leadership

1904 Association Drive
Reston, VA 20191-1537
nassp@principals.org
www.principals.org

Keith Taton, President
Cynthia Rudrud, President-Elect
Gerald N. Tirozzi, Executive Director
Lenor G. Hersey, Deputy Executive Director
Rosa Aronson, Director of Advocacy and Strategic Alliances
Michelle C. Lampher, Director of Marketing, Sales, and Publishing
John R. Nori, Director of School Leadership Services
Robert N. Farrace, Associate Director for Publications
Tanya Burke, Associate Director for Graphics Services
James R. Rourke, Principal Author
Julie Phillips, Technical Editor
David Fernandes, Production Manager

Design by EEI Communications
Cover design by Tanya Burke

Contents

Preface

The National Association of Secondary School Principals is proud to publish *Breaking Ranks II,* which represents the template upon which to improve our nation's high schools. It is built on the foundation laid by *Breaking Ranks: Changing an American Institution,* which was published in 1996. *Breaking Ranks II* outlines 7 cornerstone strategies and 31 recommendations for school leaders ready to take on the challenge of reforming their high schools. NASSP offers *Breaking Ranks II* as a handbook that all schools can use, regardless of their size, geographical location, or where they are on the school improvement continuum. The handbook offers research-based successful practices, real-life examples of high schools at various stages of reform, a step-by-step approach to change, obstacles to avoid, and resources from which to draw.

In his widely read book, *Good to Great,* Jim Collins starts with a striking assertion: "Good is the enemy of great." The author analyzes what makes an organization, including schools, improve from doing well to doing better. For the most part, secondary schools have done a good job of educating most of our students. We have been reasonably successful at educating the most diverse population in the world. These accomplishments have been achieved in the face of dwindling resources and increasing mandates. However, school leaders must ask, "Have we done enough to reach and engage each student who enters our school system, regardless of socioeconomic status, ability level, or ethnic background?" Most people would agree that we must do better. Being a less-than-average high school is simply not acceptable; being a good high school largely represents a commitment to the status quo; being a great high school should be the individual and collective resolve for all who toil in the vineyards of secondary education.

Leadership is not a spectator sport; it requires active and continual engagement. School leaders continue to be a significant force in the struggle for better schools and to take charge of school reform. Let us reclaim the reason why many of us have chosen to serve in education: to level the playing field for young people whose future rests in our hands. To assist secondary school leaders who want to dramatically reform the American high school, we offer *Breaking Ranks II* as the resource needed to achieve this goal. In effect, NASSP is optimistic that our new publication will assist you in your efforts to "break ranks."

Gerald N. Tirozzi, Ph.D.
Executive Director
NASSP

Acknowledgments

Many people and organizations deserve our thanks and acknowledgment for their efforts to ensure that *Breaking Ranks II* supports fundamental changes within high schools:

- The Education Alliance at Brown University, and its *Breaking Ranks II* project team, for contributions to the development of *Breaking Ranks II* in both concept and content based on the experience and the technical assistance they have provided to schools adopting *Breaking Ranks* as a framework for change.

  Joseph DiMartino, Director, Center for Secondary School Redesign (CSSR),
  The Education Alliance at Brown University, Providence, RI

  Patricia Smith, Assistant Director, CSSR,
  The Education Alliance at Brown University, Providence, RI

  Robert McCarthy, Senior Consultant, *Breaking Ranks*

  John Clarke, founding member of the Education Alliance at Brown's Secondary School Network,
  and Professor Emeritus, University of Vermont–Burlington

  Denise Wolk, Program Assistant, CSSR, The Education Alliance at Brown University, Providence, RI

- The NASSP High School Task Force for helping to define the scope of the project and making the final product a useful tool for principals and their leadership teams. Their assistance and feedback during preliminary meetings was particularly helpful in limiting the universe of areas to be covered and in keeping the project focused on the practicality of implementation.

  Sharon Buddin, Principal, Ridge View High School, Columbia, SC

  Luis Ray Burrola, Principal, Robert H. Goddard High School, Roswell, NM

  Ryan D. Champeau, Principal, Waukesha (WI) North High School

  Joseph A. DiMartino, Director, Center for Secondary School Redesign,
  The Education Alliance at Brown University, Providence, RI

  Kimberly Bellum, Principal, Watertown (SD) High School

  Irving C. Jones, Sr., Executive Director, Secondary Education, Richmond (VA) City Schools

  James W. Jordan (Chair), Principal, Chapin (SC) High School

  Robert J. Kemmery, Executive Director of Schools, Baltimore County (MD) Public Schools

  Sara E. Landgren, Associate Principal, Lincoln (NE) Southwest High School

  Mark D. Muxen, Principal, Kiona-Benton High School, Benton City, WA

  Diane Payne, Principal, Broughton High School, Raleigh, NC

- The *Breaking Ranks II* National Commission for their thoughtful feedback on the drafts and for other contributions to the content.

  Martin Blank, Director of Community Collaboration, Institute for Educational Leadership, Washington, DC

  Gene Bottoms, Director, High Schools That Work, Atlanta, GA

Betsy Brand, Co-Director, American Youth Policy Forum, Washington, DC

Julie Brilli, Principal, Pulaski (WI) Community Middle School

Anne Bryant, Executive Director, National School Boards Association, Alexandria, VA

Kermit Buckner, Professor and Chair, East Carolina University, Greenville, NC

Robin Calitri, Consultant and Development Team Member for Re-Engineering Schools Project, Halesite, NY

Mike Cohen, President, Achieve, Inc., Washington, DC

Linda Darling-Hammond, Professor of Education, Stanford (CA) University

David Ferrero, Program Officer, The Bill and Melinda Gates Foundation, Seattle, WA

Dennis Sparks, Executive Director, National Staff Development Council, Oxford, OH

Tim Westerberg, Principal, Littleton (CO) High School

Ronald Wolk, Founding Editor, *Education Week* and *Teacher Magazine*

- Theodore R. Sizer for his work on the Foreword and his inspiring efforts to foster high school reform.

- The Bill and Melinda Gates Foundation for providing a grant that will make it possible to disseminate *Breaking Ranks II* across the country, including a free copy of this report to each high school principal in the United States. Particular thanks to Ray McNulty, Education Program Director, and Tom Vander Ark, Executive Director, Education.

- The many high schools who have provided us with examples of practices to profile in *Breaking Ranks II*. The works of three schools in particular—Littleton High School, Noble High School, and Wyandotte High School—are profiled extensively. The principals and other members of their teams deserve our thanks for pulling these profiles together. Their experience—successes and enduring challenges—will inform implementation for other schools across the country.

- The Pathways to College Network for nominating schools to be featured in the "Strategies and Recommendations in Practice" section at the end of this handbook.

- The Northwest Regional Education Lab, especially Robert Blum, for nominating schools to be featured in the "Strategies and Recommendations in Practice" section at the end of this handbook.

- NASSP staff members (Rosa Aronson, John Nori, and others) for their tireless efforts to keep the project focused and on time.

- James R. Rourke, writer, consultant, and former NASSP editor and program manager, for his ability to compile and distill the thoughts of so many individuals and groups into a concise "field guide" for principals and leadership teams.

NASSP

The National Association of Secondary School Principals—the preeminent organization and the national voice for middle level and high school principals, assistant principals, and aspiring school leaders—provides its members the professional resources to serve as visionary leaders. NASSP promotes the intellectual growth, academic achievement, character development, leadership development, and physical well-being of youth through its programs and student leadership services. NASSP sponsors the National Honor Society, the National Junior Honor Society, and the National Association of Student Councils.

The Education Alliance at Brown University

For the past 25 years, the Education Alliance at Brown University has been a leading advocate for equity for public school students who are traditionally underserved. Additionally, since Ted Sizer joined the Education Department at Brown two decades ago, Brown has been recognized as a national leader in the movement to create more personalized settings in high schools. When the Education Alliance was granted the contract to become the Northeast and Islands Regional Educational Laboratory, it was afforded an excellent opportunity to merge these two important initiatives and further promote and support the creation of student-centered learning environments in both urban and rural settings. The Alliance develops products and services for school administrators, policymakers, teachers, and parents in New England, New York, Puerto Rico, and the Virgin Islands.

The projects of CSSR at the Education Alliance share two fundamental principles: the research-based premise that student-centered learning contributes to high school students' academic success, and the assertion that more needs to be known about how to make student-centered learning a norm in public high schools. The goal of the CSSR program is to develop, apply, and disseminate research-based knowledge and practices that enhance the capacity of districts and schools in the region to create high-performing, student-centered learning environments that engage high school students and effectively prepare them to achieve high academic standards. The *Breaking Ranks* study investigates the effects of a framework for transforming urban high schools and is complemented by other work developed to closely examine and strengthen key features of the design model.

Through the *Breaking Ranks* project, the Education Alliance provides technical assistance to high schools that are implementing a research-based process based on recommendations of *Breaking Ranks* designed to build leadership and school capacity to increase student-centered learning in high schools. This project has allowed the Alliance to develop a process that assists 23 high schools in 11 districts throughout the Northeast. Each school works closely with a veteran educator acting as a change coach to guide staff toward implementation of components of systemic reform based upon creating high standards for all students, smaller and more personalized learning environments, collaborative leadership structures, and the use of data to support continuous improvement.

Foreword

Breaking Ranks II is not "just another report."

It is a working document—a detailed resource with suggestions for principals on how to proceed with improvement of the work of their schools, even with the *rethinking* that may be necessary prior to substantial *reform.*

It does not just exhort its reader to look hard at his or her school. It provides strategies for action, drawn from almost a decade of experience since the release of *Breaking Ranks: Changing an American Institution.*

It focuses on the well-established facts that many teenagers are disengaged from the hard intellectual work expected by their schools and the larger community and unprepared for the harsh world beyond those schools. We are not doing as well as we want and as well as we should, not only for low-income youngsters, or for non-English speakers, or for adolescents with special needs, but for all of us. Good enough for yesterday will not serve as good enough for tomorrow—in every community, rich and poor, across the country.

It implicitly addresses the extraordinary political climate in which high school principals and their colleagues find themselves in 2004: an atmosphere of distrust, affront, and impatience, and an expectation that they will be judged by the performance of their graduates rather than merely on the basis of "delivering services."

It does not argue with the naysayers. It is not defensive. It takes the necessary high ground. It focuses on what we must do to improve what we do, to give it focus, to make it work well, to allow our secondary schools to graduate young people with the skills, habits, and convictions that are required in the rapidly changing American culture and global workplace.

It clusters its recommendations around three touchstones for effective secondary schools. These three drive all else.

First: The principal is the principal *teacher,* the first among many—part of a team of professionals. His or her job is to gather this community, to find its special genius, to press it hard, to nurture it, to depend on it. Learning is done child by child; our work is, by necessity, highly decentralized. We all will do well with it if we collaborate. Principals lead—better, *orchestrate*—this collaboration, encouraging the strengths and addressing the weaknesses within the adult community. This is no cop-out, no shifting of responsibility by the principal onto an amorphous "faculty" where the buck never stops anywhere. It is the relentless and sensitive pressure to get the best out of the community. It is more than a simple command such as *follow me* or *do as I say.* It is far subtler, far more respectful. It is reflected in the statement that "this is *our* school," not "this is *my* school."

Second: It is inconvenient that no two students are exactly alike and that no individual student stays exactly the same over her or his travel through the high school years. Batch processing does not work, at least for most adolescents. *Personalization* is a necessity, if for no other reason than the fact that each individual student takes that state test, meets that required standard, performs in that demanded fashion, sinks that basket, sings that solo, writes that essay, solves that problem—one by one. A good school emerges from the creative weaving of distinctive parts into a whole cloth rather than from a mindless assemblage of discrete programs, each protecting its independence.

Third: While our students differ in wonderful (and sometimes exasperating) ways, we serve them well by taking a "core mission" and playing it out in teaching and assessment in ways that reflect each student's strengths and weaknesses, learning styles, and special needs. That mission has to be lean and focused; the necessarily rich variety emerges from individual students' interests, abilities, and weaknesses, as these wax and wane over time. It requires that each student be known well. Student "anonymity" has been the most consistent criticism of America's high schools. It must end, whatever it takes.

Breaking Ranks II titles these three touchstones: "Collaborative Leadership and Effective Learning Communities," "Personalization," and "Curriculum, Instruction, and Assessment." As the reader dips into the rich detail of this report, he or she must keep these three essences clearly in mind. Get these right for *a* school—not *all* schools in some kind of predigested "model," but *our* school, the one that reflects the best of its setting, its community's values, its community's highest aspirations, and that prepares its students for a demanding world, one full of hazards and opportunities that none of us can fully predict.

"Breaking ranks" was the metaphor selected in 1996 to represent clearly the need to break from the all-too-familiar and often unproductive patterns of the past. *Breaking Ranks II* sets a fresh standard, a pattern around which we can now *close ranks*.

Theodore R. Sizer
Chairman Emeritus, Coalition of Essential Schools;
University Professor Emeritus, Brown University;
and Visiting Professor of Education, Harvard and Brandeis Universities

Breaking Ranks Revisited

> *Good ideas serve only as fodder for intellectual debate if they are not put to use. And so it is with school reform, a topic about which millions of words have been written…. lifting words off paper and putting them into operation in the nation's high schools remains the most difficult and important part…. Leadership requires that some people have the will and ability to act.*
>
> —Breaking Ranks: Changing an American Institution

Principals Set Course for Reform

With the goal of contributing to the success of all students, *Breaking Ranks: Changing an American Institution* joined the school reform debate and entered the lexicon of practitioners and policymakers interested in transforming high schools into zones of achievement, high expectation, and continuous improvement. Its debut in 1996 signaled the beginning of a new opportunity for high school principals and their school leadership teams to tackle the thorny issues involved in reform.

The product of nearly two years of deliberation by the Commission on the Restructuring of the American High School, a panel composed of principals, assistant principals, teachers, and students, *Breaking Ranks* provided a statement of principles and a template for action. The commission's work was accomplished with the support of the National Association of Secondary School Principals (NASSP) and the Carnegie Foundation for the Advancement of Teaching. Unique to the effort was the fact that the document was not primarily a research document; rather, it was a set of principles designed by practitioners keenly aware of the day-to-day realities of education.

Although the amalgamation of so many practitioners' perspectives may have been unique to *Breaking Ranks,* many of the recommendations evolved from the groundbreaking work of other practitioners and researchers who had tackled the topics individually or espoused various models of reform. Anyone familiar with the work of the Coalition of Essential Schools (CES), and Theodore Sizer's writing on the study of high schools, specifically, *Horace's Compromise* (1984), would immediately discover commonalities in the areas of personalization, school and class size, instruction, and assessment. The influence of Ernest Boyer's (1983) work, *High School: A Report on Secondary Education in America,* relating to the interdisciplinary nature of curriculum, can also be seen in the recommendations. In addition, *A Nation at Risk* (National Education Commission on Time and Learning, 1983), *Prisoners of Time* (National Education Commission on Time and Learning, 1994), and *Turning Points* (Carnegie Council on Adolescent Development, 1989) all served to galvanize the debate around the need for reform and established substantive areas in which to undertake that reform.

As a roadmap for reform, *Breaking Ranks,* and the more than 80 recommendations it contained, has provided direction for high school principals around the country in making schools more student-centered by personalizing programs, support services, and intellectual challenges for *all* students. Clearly, the emphasis on a practitioner's view of reform struck a chord with principals and policymakers alike. Federal, state, and local policymakers, as well as accreditation organizations, have embraced many of the concepts and recommendations in *Breaking Ranks.*

Legislation, standards development, and other policy and structural initiatives are essential to systematic school improvement; however, addressing and implementing the necessary reforms clearly falls upon the shoulders of educators—teachers, aides, assistant principals, principals, the central office, and many others. Yet, within the school building, the principal bears ultimate responsibility for schoolwide implementation. *Breaking Ranks II* is a field guide for the principal and the school leadership team wishing to face this responsibility head-on by implementing the recommendations established in *Breaking Ranks.* However, the implications of *Breaking Ranks* reform go well beyond the high school campus. High school improvement teams will need to form much closer relationships with their elementary and especially middle school counterparts to ensure that high expectations and rigorous curriculum are the standard in earlier grades. High school teams also may learn from the well-tested middle school personalization practices. Just as high schools work with earlier levels of education on high expectations, high schools also need to establish closer relationships with higher education institutions to align curriculum and ascertain the expectations of colleges—and whether high school graduates are meeting those expectations.

To help principals accomplish whole-school reform, *Breaking Ranks II* focuses on the **implementation of those *Breaking Ranks* recommendations in which principals have a significant role.** Given this emphasis and the fact that many of the original recommendations were statements of principle addressing policymakers, many of the original 82 recommendations are beyond the purview of this publication. *Breaking Ranks II: Strategies for Leading High School Reform,* will revisit the *Breaking Ranks* recommendations through the eyes of ordinary principals and teachers undertaking extraordinary reform initiatives consistent with those recommendations and offer strategies for school leadership teams to consider and adapt in accord with local conditions and expectations.

Why Reform Now?

Given the challenges of reform, why would a principal or school undertake *Breaking Ranks*-style reform? The answer has two components—mandate and enticement.

■ First, the mandate: Public high schools in the United States are at a crossroads. Federal and state legislation have established benchmarks intended to improve achievement for all students—including those who in the past were accepted as part of the "normal" failure curve. Standardized testing will be one measure of whether or not the benchmarks have been met. In addition, an emphasis on raising achievement in subgroups of student populations, such as English language learners and special education students, will require a more comprehensive review of disaggregated data to ensure that all students are receiving the benefits of education. What will be judged is the percentage of students who meet the standard overall and within the subgroups, not—as has been the case—the average performance of the entire school.

This mandate will not be consistently met by schools if current conditions persist. *Breaking Ranks* championed the cause of *all students* achieving at high levels; federal and state legislation will require it. Equity of participation, the status quo, must be forced aside as equity of outcomes comes to the fore. *Breaking Ranks II* provides strategies to help all students achieve at high levels.

■ Second, and most important, the enticement: Realizing the educator's dream means realizing each student's dream. Most principals and teachers took their first step down the path to educating the nation's children because they wanted to make a difference in the lives of individual students by helping them acquire a love of learning. Unfortunately, that dream is not being realized by all students. The promise of *Breaking Ranks* reform is to promote a culture of continuous improvement in order to help each student become part of a community in which all students have the opportunity to achieve at high levels. In so doing, principals and teachers will make a deeper and more equitable difference in the lives of many more students and reap the rewards for fostering student learning.

Clearly, many high schools and the principals who lead them have been undertaking reforms to improve student achievement. Their success has shown policymakers that success on a grander scale is possible. Many schools, however, have failed to undertake reforms that could have resulted in higher student achievement. Time is of the essence; not only must federal and state benchmarks be met, but, more important, each minute wasted means less time is spent addressing the needs of students not achieving at acceptable levels. More than 13 million students currently in high school rely on principals and teachers to help them fulfill their dreams, to reach heights never before imagined, and to embrace a lifelong love of learning. Failure in these, the most important of life's courses, is not acceptable.

If the day after reading *Breaking Ranks II*, you see your work as being the same as what you did the day before, be assured that nothing of substance will change very much for very long. On the other hand, if you begin to see *yourself* differently in your work and in the way you help others see the wisdom of change, your school will change. Principals, in conjunction with their school leadership teams, have the choice of either raising the white flag of surrender or aggressively beginning the conversations to extricate themselves from adverse circumstances. *Adversity spawns discussion, discussion informs ideas, ideas **may** lead to change, the Changing of An American Institution.*

From *Breaking Ranks* to *Breaking Ranks II*

Although this publication is designed to stand alone and does not require prior knowledge of *Breaking Ranks: Changing an American Institution,* the comprehensive nature of first volume and the depth and breadth in which it discusses necessary changes in high schools complement the present implementation tool. This publication is intended to assist principals in the following manner:

■ Provide strategies for implementing the recommendations

■ Illustrate possible entry points or areas in which to begin reform

■ Profile the successes, challenges, and results of schools implementing the recommendations.

To provide a practical, more manageable implementation tool for principals, several modifications to the original *Breaking Ranks* structure were necessary:

- By focusing on only those recommendations over which principals have significant sway, *and* by combining recommendations with similar content, the number of recommendations contained herein have been reduced and condensed from the 82 in *Breaking Ranks* to 31. Although the original 82 recommendations remain important, repeating the recommendations over which principals have very little control could prove daunting to a principal who is confronted with the question: With which one of the 82 should I start?

- Each of the 31 recommendations has been "clustered" or assigned to one of three core areas:

  1. Collaborative Leadership and Professional Learning Communities (Chapter 2)
  2. Personalization (Chapter 3)
  3. Curriculum, Instruction, and Assessment (Chapter 4)

These three core areas or clusters have evolved from the themes outlined in *Breaking Ranks* (NASSP, 1996, p. 5) "emphasizing that better education depends on personalizing the high school experience for students, lending coherency to their education, organizing time differently, using technology at every opportune point, revitalizing the ongoing professional education of teachers and administrators, and enhancing leadership at every level at which it can affect teaching and learning."

Organization of *Breaking Ranks II*

Recognizing that principals and others may not be able to steal enough time to read this guide in one sitting, or as one integrated unit, its organization becomes particularly important. This handbook has been organized with a three-step progression in mind: realize that your school needs to change if it wants to serve each student, help others to see that need, and implement the practices that support each student's improved performance.

Step 1: Realize the need. Schools are often told to change but rarely are asked whether they believe they need to change. Chapter 1 asks by way of a series of questions—questions not often asked by many schools—whether *your* school is doing all it can to reach each student. Following the school assessment is a vision for a fictional school that is attempting to reach each student. If you are not satisfied by your answers to the questions and would like to set your own vision for reaching each student, cornerstone strategies capitalizing on the interdependence of the 31 *Breaking Ranks II* recommendations are proposed. Thus, as an *intended* consequence, schools can adopt the cornerstone strategies and be well on their way to implementing the entire set of 31 recommendations.

Step 2: Help others see the need to change. Once you have taken the assessment, you may realize that your school must change. But how? Fundamental to the success of making the necessary changes is providing a collaborative process in which others also see the need for, and participate in, implementing the changes. Chapter 2 outlines the necessary steps to involve others in the change process through collaboration, review of data, and professional development. Skipping this step of the process may result in reforms that are either unsustainable or not well implemented.

Step 3: Promote improved student performance by providing opportunities for students to build relationships within the school and between themselves and what they learn. Chapters 3 and 4 discuss these relationships in detail, including the strategies and barriers to implementation of various practices.

For practitioners using this as a reference tool, the following may be helpful. If you are looking for:

- The seven cornerstone strategies, see page 6.
- The 31 *Breaking Ranks II* recommendations, see pages 17–18.
- Benefits, strategies, and challenges of implementing the recommendations, see the tables at the end of Chapters 2, 3, and 4.
- Resources to support implementation of the strategies and recommendations, see pages 149–161.
- Examples of specific schools implementing changes consistent with *Breaking Ranks*,

> Chapters 2, 3, and 4 contain an extended profile of a school's reform efforts written from the school's perspective—three profiles in all.
>
> In Strategies and Recommendations in Practice (pages 133–148) a variety of schools are highlighted along with specific practices consistent with *Breaking Ranks* recommendations. (Note that many schools other than those profiled in this section and at the end of Chapters 2, 3, and 4 have taken significant steps to change their approach to improving the performance of all students. The schools profiled are examples of schools that have made an effort to reach all students, some with greater success than others. Finally, as each of the schools in the extended profiles will attest, efforts are ongoing—reaching the promise of a more student-centered school with more personalized programs, support services, and intellectual rigor remains a goal on the horizon.)

For a reader tempted to "pick and choose" a single strategy or section from the handbook or focus on one chapter that discusses a specific area of interest, remember that implementing one or two recommendations is merely tinkering around the edges of school reform, and therefore ill-advised. Substantive reform will only be successful and sustainable if it is continuous, involves an ongoing and rigorous analysis of the entire school's needs, and takes into account the interdependence of elements within a learning community. A best practice implemented in isolation may not be sustainable over time if it relies on other changes that are never implemented. Those who take this handbook to heart must know and be prepared to face the challenge first voiced in *Breaking Ranks*, the challenge our profiled schools have begun to take on, the challenge lurking in the hallowed halls of tradition's estate:

> The cause of reform is hobbled by the inclination of educational institutions to resist substantial change. The rituals of high school, whatever their shortcomings, appeal to many people who suspect that substantial reform would undo the essence of teenhood. David F. Donavel, reflecting on the failure of restructuring in the high school in Massachusetts in which he worked as an English teacher, said: "The school, especially the high school, is nothing if not traditional and so has become the means by which people in our culture come to know who they are. Thus, any attempt at change violates our sense of who we are." What passes as change is frequently no more than tinkering around the edges. *Plus ça change, plus c'est la même chose.* (The more things change, the more they remain the same.) And so it is with America's high schools: The more they change, the more things seem to remain the same. It is not by accident that this report titles itself *Breaking Ranks (NASSP, 1996, pp. 4–5).*

1 On the Road to Changing an American Institution

There are many themes throughout this work, but if one theme could be extracted that is overarching and paramount, it is a message that the high school of the 21st century must be much more student-centered and above all much more personalized in programs, support services, and intellectual rigor.
—Breaking Ranks: Changing an American Institution, Executive Summary

Why Break Ranks?

A quick turn through the evening news channels, eavesdropping on a dinner-party conversation, or a scan through the latest national education reports provides enough grist for the "why change" mill. Yet the frequency and often abstract nature of these assaults can also have a numbing effect. Furthermore, they tend to point out problems that "some other" school might face. As a consequence of highlighting worst-case scenarios—high dropout rates, the deplorable structural conditions in some schools, violence, poor performance on standardized or state tests, and other indicators—"above average" schools have often said:

"We'll compare our performance to any of the surrounding high schools."

"We have some of the best test scores in the state/country."

"That could never happen at our school."

"Our dropout rate is less than 5%."

"Our school is above average in every standardized measure."

Clearly, measures of low, average, and high performance can be useful for some comparative analyses and setting benchmarks. The real measure of performance, however, is how well your school is meeting the academic needs of each student within it. If 90% of your student population ensures that you are ahead of local, regional, state, and national benchmarks but the other 10% of the student population remains unchallenged, then it may be time for your school to break ranks—not only because the 10% are being ill-served, but because, more than likely, a large portion of the 90% could be performing at higher levels if schools knew the strengths and weaknesses of each student and tailored instruction accordingly.

Schools featured in the worst-case-scenario news stories and schools performing below average on state or national assessments *may* see the obvious—a need to change. Schools operating above those benchmarks or the schools that, *on average,* perform well enough to be highlighted in more positive local news stories often don't have the "negative pressure incentive" to review how things could be better. In fact, these schools often are under pressure from the community to "leave a good thing alone." Below is a list of questions that you as the principal, in conjunction with your school leadership team, may want to consider to assess how well your school is meeting the needs of individual students. If, after contemplating the answers to, and implications of, each question, your team decides each answer is satisfactory, then perhaps you have already broken ranks from the pack and have created a school more personalized in programs, support services, and intellectual rigor. The experience of principals undertaking reforms consistent with *Breaking Ranks* recommendations, however, belies the possibility of ever having completely "broken" ranks—because it is a process of continuous improvement.

How Well Does *Your* School Serve Each Student?

1. How many of the students who enter your school in ninth grade graduate in four years?

2. What percentage of your graduates must take remedial courses in college or a community college? What percentage of those finish college?

3. Does your leadership team successfully interact with "hard-to-reach" parents with activities such as home visits, weekend meetings, and meetings outside of regular business hours?

4. How many low-income and how many minority students are enrolled in advanced courses?

5. How many teachers from different disciplines work together on a regular basis?

6. Are the aspirations, strengths, and weaknesses of each student known by at least one faculty member or other member of your staff? How do you ensure that the staff member uses that information appropriately to help the student become successful in all classes and activities?

7. What percentage of the classes per week at your school are primarily lecture-driven?

8. Aside from student government, do students have a voice at your school?

9. Were you able to answer these questions and support the responses with data?

If you have completed this assessment and any complementary assessments that your school uses, and are satisfied that your school is doing everything it can for each student, then yours is a school that should be profiled in subsequent publications. If, on the other hand, you see room for improvement, setting a vision for that improvement is your next step.

What Might Your School Look Like After *Breaking Ranks*?

Defining a vision for your school should be a product of many thoughtful conversations within your school and within your community. There is no template of what a *Breaking Ranks* school might look like because school values differ from community to community. However, in the interest of spurring conversation within your school, the letter below from a fictional principal attempts to paint a picture for students, school board members, school staff, the superintendent, and the larger community—and thereby get them involved. It details what the school might look like when the reforms have been implemented. This text may form the basis of a conversation among your leadership team and beyond about the vision for your own school.

Our *Breaking Ranks* high school will be a learning community that reflects a culture born of respect and trust, where the spirit of teaching and learning is driven by student inquiry, reflection, and passion. Our efforts to cultivate that spirit will begin well before students enter freshman year or before they transfer into our school with a feeder schools–to–high school transition program—so that when students join us, they understand that each of them is expected to achieve to his or her highest potential. Before walking in the door the first day of school, each will have investigated the opportunities available and each will have already met with a teacher or other member of the staff to lay the groundwork for building a personal connection to the school.

Rather than leave a student's high school experience and the outcome of that experience to pure chance, we believe we have the obligation to understand a teenager's personal needs and to challenge them by meeting those needs intellectually, socially, and personally. Some students have little problem finding a voice, but others struggle well into adulthood to find a productive voice. By providing a variety of structured experiences in which students can be actively engaged, we believe we can address a student's need to:

- *Express personal perspectives*
- *Create individual and group identities*
- *Examine options and choose his or her own path*
- *Take risks and assess the effects*
- *Use his or her imagination*
- *Demonstrate mastery.*[1]

Chance is not a game that should be played with a student's life. High schools have been able to address some of these needs for some of their students since schooling began. We endeavor to entice each student to fulfill each of those needs.

How often is it that only a few students express themselves—even though in theory all are "allowed?" Does that mean others don't want to? Are afraid to? Some would say, "part of growing up is finding the ability to express oneself, and if someone can't, then that's life." But what happens if one never learns that skill? Is that life? We think not! We will provide several arenas in which each student can express himself or herself in one-on-one and group settings—through our advisory program, our activities program, student exhibitions and presentations, and within each classroom.

How often do students fall into the wrong cliques only because they want to belong to something? Although we cannot dictate friendships, clearly we have an opportunity to provide groups (project groups, advisories, etc.) in which each student feels a sense of belonging and perhaps where friendships will be fostered.

[1] Developmental assets noted by Clarke & Frazer (2003).

How often does each student have the opportunity to demonstrate mastery of a subject, a concept, an instrument, a sport? The "A" students, the valedictorian, the lead in the play or the band, the star on the football team all have those opportunities—and well deserved at that. But what about the students who haven't been working on a skill for as long, or who try just as hard and don't quite "make the cut?" We're not talking here about equality of rewards or giving everyone a star, but rather that each student should be encouraged to excel and should receive recognition for it—individually, and if appropriate, in a group setting. Our school has designed the practices to make this a reality in the classroom, in advisory settings, and through our student activities program. Students will be creating, developing, and publicly exhibiting projects that demonstrate their mastery of learning on a regular basis and will also be able to demonstrate their unique talents through a student activities program and a service-learning program tied directly to skills and knowledge needed to meet the larger learning goals for each student.

Our efforts to meet the needs of students are not made simply so that we can develop friendships with students and make them feel better about themselves. The business of education is about learning and achievement for each student. We believe that without these personal connections and our understanding of the motivations, aspirations, and learning styles of students, most students will never become engaged in their own learning and never really achieve their potential. The statistics about students who never complete high school—at least a quarter of all students—tell only a small part of the tale. What about those students who graduate, never having been challenged, and then go on to college only to drop out? Or those students who are bored day in and day out? Or those top-notch students who could have been seriously challenged by taking more challenging courses, or pursuing an internship or in-depth research project, or being mentored by an expert in the "field of their dreams," or taking courses at the nearby college or online, but instead are left to stare out the window and wait for the bell to ring while the teacher reviews materials the student has already mastered?

We need to reach each of these students their first day, their first week, their first month, and throughout high school. We can't wait until graduation to say, "she has a lot of potential—I hope she has an opportunity to use it in college." Our school will get to know the potential of each student through our Personal Adult Advocate program. Our emphasis on decreasing the total number of students per teacher will allow teachers more time to confer with parents and mentors to personalize each student's educational experience, and to be able to effectively advise a small group of students. Each advocate will work with students to develop and monitor individual Personal Plans for Progress that will detail the academic, social, and other aspirations and needs of students. The adult advocate will work with students, their parents, and their teachers to ensure that each student's potential is being realized in the classroom, on the field, in the community, and, most important, in the mind of the student.

Academic achievement in our school will be driven by students being engaged in classes, seminars, and lessons designed by teams of teachers who integrate the curriculum. Students will be encouraged to write in all classes and to attack challenges from various perspectives using their own strengths while addressing their weaknesses. There will be no tracking of students. Instead, students will be grouped heterogeneously and include educationally challenged and culturally diverse students in all classes and students will have multiple opportunities to redo their work until the work meets the established standards. The school will support personal drive and aspiration by providing a rigorous curriculum, AP courses, the International Baccalaureate (IB) program, college-credit courses, internships, and service-learning opportunities to all who are willing to take on the challenge. All students will have access to honors programs and students will earn honors credit by their distinctive performance.

Our school will be dramatically different from the traditional American high school, and that difference will be obvious to even the casual observer. Upon entering our "Breaking Ranks" high school, the level and intensity of questioning and listening by students and the teachers who are encouraging more questioning and listening will set our school apart from others.

At graduation, the teachers and administrators who joined the profession and have made their own sacrifices to make a difference in the lives of young people, the parents who have supported, cajoled and inspired their sons and daughters—now young men and women—and the students who have spent four years of their lives and are now preparing to leave home for perhaps the first time should ever have to say, "We missed an opportunity to challenge ourselves." At our school, those words will never be uttered because the work of each student and his or her portfolio will be the proof for everyone at graduation to see that at every step of the way, each student was challenged.

The vision you set for your school may differ significantly from that above, but a vision will remain simply a vision unless your school is willing to embark on significant changes to make that vision come to life. The success of "all" students lies at the heart of many contemporary goals within the education profession. However, at the heart of a family's vision, there has always been one constant—not the success of the amorphous "all students," but the success of "our son," "our daughter." Reaching that vision will require a strategic plan for change.

What Should We Change First?

Let's assume that you are convinced that your school can do a better job of improving student performance. Let's further assume that the observations made thus far and your own experience have convinced you that improving student performance is inextricably tied to student engagement, and engagement for each student can be accomplished only through a more personalized academic and intellectual program. Finally, let's assume that you see a need for significant change in your school. Where do you begin? Which should you change first: School culture? School structures? Instruction?

Scholars, school leadership teams, and management experts have long struggled with this question with few definitive answers. Some argue that most high schools are structured in a way that will not allow the change in culture necessary to adjust instruction to meet the needs of all students. Changing structures *can be* the first step in changing instruction and culture (although not the ultimate step). Others argue that the culture of the school has to change before anything else can be accomplished. Without minimizing the importance of the debate, for the purposes of this handbook, suffice it to say that the three are highly interconnected, change is needed in all three areas, culture change must occur before change truly becomes effective, and each school will approach the challenge from a different perspective based on factors specific to the school's situation. Although the approach may vary from school to school, there are a number of common strategies that have proven effective in supporting efforts to improve student performance.

Seven cornerstone strategies have been gleaned from the experiences of schools implementing strategies consistent with *Breaking Ranks* recommendations. The strategies are designed to give your school possible "entry points" to pursue fundamental changes—clearly, your school's priorities and stage of reform may require different entry points or you may develop different strategies. This is merely one model of simplifying implementation by providing strategies that address more than one recommendation at a time. In other words, by implementing the strategy, you will have also implemented one or more *Breaking Ranks* recommendations. The strategies, not in any particular sequence in terms of implementation priority, are listed below.

Break Ranks:
Seven Cornerstone Strategies to Improve Student Performance

1. Establish the essential learnings a student is required to master in order to graduate, and adjust the curriculum and teaching strategies to realize that goal.

2. Increase the quantity and improve the quality of interactions between students, teachers, and other school personnel by reducing the number of students for which any adult or group of adults is responsible.

3. Implement a comprehensive advisory program that ensures that each student has frequent and meaningful opportunities to plan and assess his or her academic and social progress with a faculty member.

4. Ensure that teachers use a variety of instructional strategies and assessments to accommodate individual learning styles.

5. Implement schedules flexible enough to accommodate teaching strategies consistent with the ways students learn most effectively and that allow for effective teacher teaming and lesson planning.

6. Institute structural leadership changes that allow for meaningful involvement in decision making by students, teachers, family members, and the community *and* that support effective communication with these groups.

7. Align the schoolwide comprehensive, ongoing professional development program and the individual Personal Learning Plans of staff members with the content knowledge and instructional strategies required to prepare students for graduation.

Together, these seven cornerstone strategies, if implemented effectively, will form the foundation for improving the performance of each student in your school. The seventh strategy, regarding professional development, underpins all others—and in most cases is required for each of the other six strategies to be adequately implemented. Too often, professional development programs do not have a coherent or strategic purpose; instead, they relate to the interests of individual teachers. Placing professional development last allows the reader to see what the focus of the professional development program must be: acquiring the skills, knowledge, and disposition to implement the six previous strategies.

The strategies cross the somewhat artificial boundaries that have been established for the three clusters of recommendations (Collaborative Leadership and

Professional Learning Communities; Personalization; Curriculum, Instruction, and Assessment). Although the recommendations within those three clusters align with the seven cornerstone strategies, the recommendations themselves are somewhat discrete and may be more easily implemented through a strategy that takes into account the interdependence of changes within a school—hence, the seven cornerstone strategies. Furthermore, even though each strategy has broad implications, from an appearance standpoint, seven strategies are considerably more palatable to discuss as first steps than are dozens of individual recommendations. (Imagine for a moment attempting to get your leadership team, your faculty, your school board, or your superintendent to discuss, adopt, and take ownership of 31 recommendations—all in one sitting.)

Let's take a closer look at the seven strategies to see how you can adopt them in your school.

---

1. **Establish the essential learnings a student is required to master in order to graduate, and adjust the curriculum and teaching strategies to realize that goal.**

Actions to support this strategy include:

- Devise a process to formulate essential learnings that takes into account state standards and the standards set by individual disciplines and the school community. Although state standards are often beyond your control, the process related to identifying the school community's essential learnings might be similar to the one outlined in *Providing Focus and Direction Through Essential Learnings* (Westerberg & Webb, 1997). [See Chapter 4 of this handbook for a possible model process for developing essential learnings in your school.]

Once the essential learnings have been established, actions to support adjusting the curriculum and teaching strategies to help students master the essential learnings might include:

- Focus on mastery, not coverage; focus on what is learned, not simply what is taught. Use student exhibitions, portfolios, and senior-year or capstone programs to demonstrate mastery and learning rather than focusing on seat time or the Carnegie unit.

- Raise the level of academic rigor in all classes. (See Appendix 1 for a school self-assessment tool that your team may want to use to assess perceptions about the level of rigor at your school; review the academic-rigor planning pyramid to pursue some activities to make your program more rigorous; and review a model graphic for reporting your attempts at rigor to the community.)

- Open honors, AP, and IB classes to all students.

- Initiate interdisciplinary instruction, teaming, and an appropriate emphasis on real-world applications.

- Reorganize traditional departmental structures to integrate the school's curriculum to the extent necessary and emphasize depth over breadth of coverage.

- Teach literacy across the curriculum.

- Insist on heterogeneous grouping of classes.

- Align student activities, service learning, and internships with essential learnings.

This strategy emphasizes the concept of "backward design," or beginning with the end in mind. Once a school has determined what it is that students should know or be able to demonstrate in order to graduate, the school can decide on the actions to take to ensure that students acquire the essential learnings. Development of challenging essential learnings is fundamental to providing a rigorous curriculum.

---

2. Increase the quantity and improve the quality of interactions between students, teachers, and other school personnel by reducing the number of students for which any adult or group of adults is responsible.

Actions to support this strategy include:

- Reduce a large school into smaller units (houses, school-within-a-school, thematic units, ninth-grade academies or other exclusive structures) under the direction of teaching teams who can get to know the strengths and weaknesses of each student...

- Reduce the number of students for which an individual teacher is responsible (in some cases, this may mean reducing class size, but often more important is reducing the total number of students a teacher has during a semester/term/etc.)...

- Create and implement interdisciplinary teams of both teachers and students that encourage shared responsibility for student learning...

- "Loop" teachers with students so that a group of students and teachers are teamed together for more than one year (e.g., groups of teachers would remain with the same group of students for ninth and tenth grades).

Reducing the size of the school and reducing the number of students for which a teacher has responsibility may not, by themselves, automatically improve student performance, but they may have an effect on the school environment and level of distraction and the number of disciplinary infractions. A change in student performance is more likely if these initiatives are combined with other efforts that take advantage of the reductions. Debate will continue into the foreseeable future about the ideal school size and the ideal class size; however, few would argue with the premise that improving the quantity and quality of interactions between students and teachers is a good idea. Moreover, one might ask, "How many parents would contend that their son or daughter is receiving *too much* attention from teachers to address academic challenges?"

Although downsizing in and of itself is not a panacea for student improvement, recent research has made a compelling case for establishing smaller learning communities to set the conditions for improved student performance. In her analysis of the research, Cotton (2004) highlights the following benefits of smaller learning communities:

- **Achievement**—"Those attending small schools achieve at higher levels than do students in larger schools, both on standardized achievement tests and other measures.... Researchers observe that the effects of smallness on achievement are indirect, being mediated through such other small-school features as quality of the social environment and students' sense of attachment to the school."

- **Equity**—Poor and minority students have "notably higher achievement in small learning environments."

■ **Affiliation/Belonging**—Students and teachers have the opportunity to get to know and care about each other. In a large school population in which there are often more than enough students to participate, it may go unnoticed that many students never participate, but in small learning communities (SLCs), student participation in school activities is genuinely needed.

■ **Safety and Order**—"An obvious benefit of student affiliation and belonging is increased order and safety. The full range of negative social behavior—from classroom disruption to assault and even murder—is far less common in small schools…."

■ **Truancy and Dropouts**—"School attendance and graduation rates are higher in small schools generally and better still in deliberately small schools."

■ **Preparation for Higher Education**—More college-bound students are graduates of SLCs.

■ **Cocurricular Participation**—While "in small schools generally, levels of cocurricular participation are higher, and students report both having more important roles…and deriving more satisfaction from those activities," many SLCs participate with the larger school in the activities program.

■ **Teacher Attitudes and Satisfaction**—Teachers "feel in a better position to make a real difference in students' learning and general quality of life … [and] have closer relationships with students and other staff; experience fewer discipline problems, and are better able to adapt instruction to students' individual needs."

■ **Curriculum Quality**—Detractors of smaller schools stress that larger schools have more curricular offerings. Cotton's review of the research points out that in the core areas, SLCs are comparable to larger schools, and that in the larger schools, other offerings are often taken advantage of by a very small percentage of students. Furthermore, Cotton says, "Gladden (1998) takes the typical curriculum argument and turns the tables: 'Instead of being a deficit, the inability of small schools to differentiate students by offering a diverse curriculum seems to be an advantage. It forces small schools to teach a core academic curriculum in heterogeneous classes—and this factor is associated with a higher and more equitable level of achievement among students.'"

■ **Costs**—Cotton counters the argument that small schools are not economical:

   • Required disciplinary and other administrative personnel required for larger schools "are so costly that, past a certain point, per pupil cost goes up—and keeps going up as the school grows larger."

   • Researchers in a large-scale study of small schools in New York City "reasoned that a more useful comparison than cost per student is cost per student graduated, and by this measure they found that small schools, with their much higher graduation rates, are the most economical schools of all."

3. Implement a comprehensive advisory program that ensures that each student has frequent and meaningful opportunities to plan and assess his or her academic and social progress with a faculty member.

Actions to support this strategy include:

■ Beginning with incoming students (either ninth graders or "transfer" students), institute a comprehensive transition program between the "feeder schools" and the high school. This specialized program can be done in conjunction with the larger advisory program—or it can be a separate program—but it must provide an opportunity for an adult to get to know each student well so that the adult can continually assess whether the academic and school activities programs of the school are meeting the needs of the student.

■ Establish a development program for advisors as well as a calendar, guidelines, and a proposed list of topics to be discussed in a small-group advisory setting or in an individual setting between an advisor or Personal Adult Advocate and an individual student.

■ Provide opportunities for students to lead discussions about their own progress and their accomplishments in the advisory setting and in adviser/teacher/family progress checkups.

■ Provide resources and time for students to research and investigate college opportunities and career choices.

■ Require each student, in conjunction with his or her adviser *and* family, to prepare a Personal Plan for Progress that might include:

  • Reflections on personal aspirations and an academic courses plan and school activities strategy that may lead to realization of those aspirations

  • A review of personal learning styles

  • Areas of strength and areas for improvement

  • Specific products or portfolio items demonstrating accomplishment and progress in academic areas, school activities, sports, and school or community leadership. [See model Personal Plan for Progress in Appendix 2.]

Many schools either have an advisory program or have tried them in the past. Often these have been little more than "homeroom," opportunities to distribute paperwork, or time for school announcements. Effective, well-planned advisory programs can offer much more. In *Changing Systems to Personalize Learning: The Power of Advisories,* Osofsky, Sinner and Wolk (2003) reviewed the research and found the following beneficial effects of an effective advisory program:

■ Academic achievement was improved, failing grades were reduced, and test scores increased

■ More students took college entrance exams

■ Forty-six percent [of teachers] believed they influenced several of their advisees to improve their grades

- Student attitudes improved significantly (75% by one measure)
- Student-teacher relations improved
- Number of dropouts declined
- Transition to high school was eased
- Liaison for the parents was provided.

(See Appendix 3 for five key dimensions of an effective advisory program.)

---

4. Ensure that teachers use a variety of instructional strategies and assessments to accommodate individual learning styles.

Practices to support this strategy include:

- Conduct inventories of instructional strategies through observations to discover whether or not teachers are using a variety of strategies. (See Appendix 4.)

- Allow students to construct knowledge. In an example offered by *Breaking Ranks,* teachers offer a list of key questions to guide this inquiry or provide students with the titles of books and articles that are pertinent to uncovering the knowledge. A student is then responsible "for unlocking the knowledge, analyzing it, synthesizing it, and presenting it as a body of material for which he or she has taken possession."

- Provide development and teaming opportunities so that teachers learn how to incorporate seminars, inquiry-based learning, cooperative learning, debates, field experiences, independent study, laboratories, reflection, and project-based learning into the traditional repertoire of lectures, question-and-answer periods, etc.

- Use standards-based assessments.

Many schools incorporate some of these practices to a limited extent, but how prevalent are they across the curriculum? How many teachers still rely on lecturing for every class? Do you have a way to assess how often teachers are using a variety of strategies? What systemic ways does your school assess students' individual learning styles? These are just a few of the questions that should be addressed as you review the practices associated with this strategy—practices proven to increase students' level of engagement and improve academic achievement.[2]

In addition to the benefit that learning is more memorable for students who are involved and engaged, the Education Alliance has found that schools with which they work that implement this strategy have:

- Fewer students dropping out
- Improved class attendance rates
- Fewer discipline referrals
- Improved teacher attendance
- Improved test scores.[3]

[2] Valerie E. Lee and Julia B. Smith's "High School Restructuring and Student Achievement" (as cited in *Breaking Ranks: Changing an American Institution,* 1996).

[3] Education Alliance at Brown University, Roundtable discussion of benefits, July 2003.

5. Implement schedules flexible enough to accommodate teaching strategies consistent with the ways students learn most effectively and that allow for effective teacher teaming and lesson planning.

Actions to support this strategy include:

- Increase the time allowed for sustained learning by adjusting the length of class periods

- Adjust length of school day

- Adjust length of school year—trimesters or year-round school

- Institute a.m/p.m. structures—mornings for class instruction, afternoons for work- and community-based learning, student activities, professional development, and integrated team planning

- Integrate the curriculum to allow for more instructional time

- Implement teacher and student teaming

- Increase the frequency and improve the opportunities for common planning time for teachers

- Take advantage of community-based learning opportunities aligned with essential learnings (taking classes at local college, internships, independent study, etc.)

- Create small units to improve the quantity and quality of student-teacher interaction.

This strategy purposefully incorporates several concepts: flexible time, individual learning styles, and preparation for implementing effective teaching strategies. Flexible scheduling should support instruction; it should not be a goal in and of itself. Implemented in isolation from other instructional changes, flexible schedules will simply permit teachers to teach the same way they always have *for longer periods*. Without preparing faculty for flexible scheduling and without a comprehensive understanding of the use of various strategies to accommodate individual learning styles, flexible scheduling will not achieve its intended results. Conversely, done properly, "flexible scheduling and faculty teamwork allow for a level of depth and an interdisciplinary approach that provides students with a much richer educational experience." (Fine & Somerville as cited in Cotton [2004, p. 22.]) In general, flexible scheduling can also lower the overall frenetic pace of the school: students aren't racing from class to class (and don't need to be encouraged to do so, thereby eliminating opportunities for unnecessary confrontation), teachers have more than a three-minute time frame to switch their mindset from 9th-grade algebra to tenth-grade geometry, and roll call and other administrative tasks do not occupy such a high percentage of what should be learning time.

The Vermont High School Task Force, in its review of the research, discovered these additional benefits of flexible scheduling (2002, p. 34):

- "Students can concentrate on a smaller number of courses at one time, typically four instead of the usual six or seven;

- When teachers are responsible for smaller numbers of classes and students, they are able to establish closer relationships with their students, which has been found to be one of the most important influences on student motivation;

- Longer classes allow teachers to design and implement better project- and work-based learning opportunities.

- Collaboration among teachers and with business partners is facilitated."

---

6. Institute structural leadership changes that allow for meaningful involvement in decision making by students, teachers, family members, and the community *and* that support effective communication with these groups.

Actions to support this strategy include:

- Formalize participation of students, teachers, family, and community members in site-based decision making teams, school leadership councils, strategic planning and school improvement teams, etc.

- Develop a program to support Personal Plans for Progress that allow students to plan their learning and the activities to support it.

- Institute conferences in which the students lead the discussion (e.g., students would lead the discussion about strengths and areas of improvement in the parent/teacher/student conference).

- Provide student government and other leadership forums with opportunities to be included in discussions of substantive issues.

- Offer families significant opportunities to monitor student progress on a regular basis (i.e., report cards are not enough).

- Encourage family and community members to become involved in curriculum and fiscal conversations.

- Meet with families on weekends, at home, or accommodate work schedules in other ways.

Schools should not underestimate the power that gaining the trust of families and parents can play in gaining the trust of students. Despite the research indicating that students whose parents stay involved tend to fare better academically and socially than others, families become less and less involved as students progress from elementary to middle school to high school. This disconnect has happened for any number of reasons but, as *Breaking Ranks* advises, commitment from both families and students is essential to improved student engagement:

> People more readily commit themselves to an institution that accords them a measure of influence over its operations…. [There is] merit in including students on various committees that determine policies that affect discipline, grading standards, and participation on sports teams. A high school that follows such a philosophy will do all it can, for example, to foster a viable student government. It will also convene forums in which students can share ideas about school reform and equip students with mediation skills so that they can help resolve problems in the school. Young people learn how to exercise responsibility by having the chance to do so. Students should know that things do not just happen to them; that they can act to affect outcomes. (p. 32)

7. **Align the schoolwide comprehensive, ongoing professional development program and the individual Personal Learning Plans of staff members with the content knowledge and instructional strategies required to prepare students for graduation.**

Actions to support this strategy include:

■ Align the schoolwide professional development program with the essential learnings, content and performance standards, and instructional strategies established in strategy 1.

■ Ensure that each educator creates a Personal Learning Plan that addresses his or her need to grow, stressing knowledge and skills related to improved student learning and aligned with the school's essential learnings. Just as each student's Personal Plan for Progress provides opportunities for a student to reflect upon goals and progress toward reaching those goals, *Breaking Ranks* proposes that the Personal Learning Plan for each staff member will facilitate self-appraisal and that "self-reflection becomes more effective when pursued in a formal and systematic way." The plans should draw on

   • Portfolios that teachers maintain of their teaching activities

   • Observations by supervisors and colleagues

   • Appraisals that students make of teachers

   • Teachers' own professional reflections.

■ Institute a formal, comprehensive orientation program for new and transfer teachers.

■ Provide opportunities for teachers to teach teachers what they have learned from various professional development seminars, conferences, etc.

■ Develop a mentoring process.

■ Align the hiring process and subsequent professional development to ensure that skills of new teachers can meet the challenges incumbent in instituting the first six cornerstone strategies.

■ Encourage frequent teacher-to-teacher observation with feedback tied to providing a specific course for professional development.

■ Ensure that professional development is continuous and that each development opportunity is reinforced with follow-up activities.

As previously noted, professional development is critical to the success of the other six strategies: establishing and implementing essential learnings, improving the quality of interactions in your school, instituting an effective advisory program, using a variety of instructional strategies and assessments, implementing flexible schedules, and increasing the substantive involvement of families, students, and the community. How to support a comprehensive, ongoing professional development program in the context of building a professional learning community and bringing about changes in your school systematically through effective school leadership are discussed in greater detail in the next chapter.

Seven Strategies: A Good Beginning

Before proceeding to the "how-to" of change, a look at the comprehensive and interdependent nature of "what" must be changed is necessary. The seven strategies are just a beginning—albeit a complex and intensive beginning. *Breaking Ranks* reminds us that

> As a complex institution, the high school comprises many interlocking parts. Alter one element and you affect others. Thus, the recommendations that we offer… are best viewed as a series of connected proposals that in many instances depend on implementation in one area for success in another… Piecemeal change may lead to some positive results, but it is not apt to be as effective as efforts that reach into the various parts of the system, in other words, systemic reform. High schools need more than tinkering (p. 6).

The seven strategies outlined in this chapter provide a means for implementing the 31 recommendations gleaned from *Breaking Ranks*. Assigning the recommendations to three clusters as we have done may simplify implementation and "digestion" of the material, but it is important to understand the interdependence of the recommendations. The following diagram listing an abbreviated version of the 31 recommendations within the three clusters provides a graphic illustration of that interdependence. (The complete text of each recommendation can be found immediately following the graphic.) Discussion of the three clusters and the recommendations supporting them are the focus of the remainder of this handbook.

On the Road to Changing
an American Institution

Connecting *Breaking Ranks II* Recommendations in High School Renewal

Collaborative Leadership/ Professional Learning Communities

Principal: Vision, Direction & Focus

Site Council

Staff Collaboration

Redefine teacher role

Personal Learning Plans for Principal & Teachers

Political/Financial Alliances

Five-Year Review

Small Units
Flexible Scheduling
Democratic Values
90-Student Maximum

Higher Education Partnerships
Celebrate Diversity
Coaching Students

Improved Student Performance

Personal Plans for Progress (PPPs)

Personal Adult Advocate

Families as Partners

Caring Teachers
Activities/Service Tied to Learning
Community Learning
Critical Thinking
Learning Styles
Youth Services

Essential Learnings
Alternatives to Tracking
Integrated Curriculum
Real-World Applications
Knowledgeable Teachers
Integrated Assessment
K-16 Continuity
Integrated Technology

Personalizing Your School Environment

Curriculum, Instruction, and Assessment

Diagram by John Clarke, Steering Group, Vermont's "High Schools on the Move."

Breaking Ranks II
Recommendations

Breaking Ranks II **Recommendations**

Collaborative Leadership and Professional Learning Communities

1. The principal will provide leadership in the high school community by building and maintaining a vision, direction, and focus for student learning.

2. Each high school will establish a site council and accord other meaningful roles in decision making to students, parents, and members of the staff in order to promote student learning and an atmosphere of participation, responsibility, and ownership.

3. A high school will regard itself as a community in which members of the staff collaborate to develop and implement the school's learning goals.

4. Teachers will provide the leadership essential to the success of reform, collaborating with others in the educational community to redefine the role of the teacher and to identify sources of support for that redefined role.

5. Every school will be a learning community for the entire community. As such, the school will promote the use of Personal Learning Plans for each educator and provide the resources to ensure that the principal, teachers, and other staff members can address their own learning and professional development needs as they relate to improved student learning.

6. The school community will promote policies and practices that recognize diversity in accord with the core values of a democratic and civil society and will offer substantive ongoing professional development to help educators appreciate issues of diversity and expose students to a rich array of viewpoints, perspectives, and experiences.

7. High schools will build partnerships with institutions of higher education to provide teachers and administrators at both levels with ideas and opportunities to enhance the education, performance, and evaluation of educators.

8. High schools will develop political and financial relationships with individuals, organizations, and businesses to support and supplement educational programs and policies.

9. At least once every five years, each high school will convene a broadly based external panel to offer a public description of the school, a requirement that could be met in conjunction with the evaluations by state, regional, and other accrediting groups.

Personalization and the School Environment

10. High schools will create small units in which anonymity is banished.

11. Each high school teacher involved in the instructional program on a full-time basis will be responsible for contact time with no more than 90 students during a given term so that the teacher can give greater attention to the needs of every student.

12. Each student will have a Personal Plan for Progress that will be reviewed often to ensure that the high school takes individual needs into consideration and to allow students, within reasonable parameters, to design their own methods for learning in an effort to meet high standards.

13. Every high school student will have a Personal Adult Advocate to help him or her personalize the educational experience.

14. Teachers will convey a sense of caring so that students feel that their teachers share a stake in student learning.

15. High schools will develop flexible scheduling and student grouping patterns that allow better use of time in order to meet the individual needs of students and to ensure academic success.

16. The high school will engage students' families as partners in the students' education.

17. The high school community, which cannot be values-neutral, will advocate and model a set of core values essential in a democratic and civil society.

18. High schools, in conjunction with agencies in the community, will help coordinate the delivery of physical and mental health and social services for youth.

Curriculum, Instruction, and Assessment

19. Each high school will identify a set of essential learnings—in literature and language, writing, mathematics, social studies, science, and the arts—in which students must demonstrate achievement in order to graduate.

20. Each high school will present alternatives to tracking and to ability grouping.

21. The high school will reorganize the traditional department structure in order to integrate the school's curriculum to the extent possible and emphasize depth over breadth of coverage.

22. The content of the curriculum, where practical, should connect to real-life applications of knowledge and skills to help students link their education to the future.

23. The high school will promote service programs and student activities as integral to an education, providing opportunities for all students that support and extend academic learning.

24. The academic program will extend beyond the high school campus to take advantage of learning opportunities outside the four walls of the building.

25. Teachers will design high-quality work and teach in ways that engage students, encourage them to persist, and, when the work is successfully completed, result in student satisfaction and their acquisition of knowledge, critical thinking, and problem-solving skills, and other abilities valued by society.

26. Teachers will know and be able to use a variety of strategies and settings that identify and accommodate individual learning styles and engage students.

27. Each high school teacher will have a broad base of academic knowledge with depth in at least one subject area.

28. Teachers will be adept at acting as coaches and facilitators to promote more active involvement of students in their own learning.

29. Teachers will integrate assessment into instruction so that assessment is accomplished using a variety of methods and does not only measure students, but becomes part of the learning process.

30. Recognizing that education is a continuum, high schools will reach out to elementary and middle level schools as well as institutions of higher education to better serve the articulation of student learning and to ensure that at each stage of the continuum, stakeholders understand what will be required of students at the succeeding stage.

31. Schools will develop a strategic plan to make technology integral to curriculum, instruction, and assessment, accommodating different learning styles and helping teachers to individualize and improve the learning process.

2 Sowing the Seeds for Change: Collaborative Leadership, Professional Learning Communities, and the Strategic Use of Data

The fact that the captain of the ship can clearly see the port is of no use if the crew continues to paddle in different directions.

—*Author Unknown*

Memo
from the principal's desk

To: **All Staff**
Date: **May 31**
Subject: **Significant Change**

A week ago, I attended a meeting with several principals from neighboring high schools. They have had great success with several programs in their schools. After much thought, I have developed a plan to implement those programs in our school.

In September, we will implement a **Personal Adult Advocate** program and a **Personal Plan for Progress** for each student, and we will **reorganize our traditional departmental structure** to meet the needs of a more integrated curriculum. I realize this school year is almost over, but please be prepared to implement the attached plans upon your return for the next school year. The roles and expectations for each staff member are specified in the attachments. Please feel free to ask any questions. My door is always open!

Have a great summer!

Imagine for a moment being on the receiving end of a memo like this. A short G-rated list of thoughts entering the recipients' minds and spilling out their mouths for the benefit of peers might include:

- "Changes like this he just announces—and in a memo?!?"
- "Our school isn't anything like those schools."
- "Don't we even get a chance to discuss how to implement these changes?"
- "I'd love to see the data about how effective these changes were in those schools."
- "We don't know how to do any of those things. When do we get training?"

Taken directly from the pages of "How *Not* to Bring About Successful Change," this fictional memorandum—and the potential resistance it would fuel—demonstrates the importance of a school leadership team understanding the change process, using data to justify the need for change, getting others involved in the process, and, finally, providing the necessary professional development to implement, assess, and sustain the change. Implementing *Breaking Ranks* recommendations regarding personalization, curriculum, instruction, and assessment first requires cultivating collaborative leadership to ensure that the school is fertile for change.

Who Will Lead?

The idea for comprehensive change may not begin in the principal's office, but it most assuredly can end there through either incomplete planning, failure to involve others, neglect, or failure to create conditions so that a new order of things can emerge in the high school. Creating those conditions is often the first challenge—and sometimes it must start within the principal's own thinking and interactions with people. Usually, when the status quo is found wanting, our initial impulse is to seek to change the world around us. From the students to parents, to teachers, to school boards, to districts, to communities, to states, to the nation itself—if only something were different! Then, we

---

Assumptions About Change

1. Assume that the view others have of change differs from your view.
2. Assume that conflict and disagreement are fundamental elements of successful change.
3. Assume that people will often require a degree of pressure to change, even though they will benefit from the change.
4. Assume that change takes time. It is a work in progress.
5. Failure to implement change or an initiative is not always an outright rejection of a change.
6. Do not expect all people to change. Progress occurs when we take steps that increase the number of people affected.
7. No amount of knowledge will ever totally clarify what action should be taken (analysis paralysis).
8. Assume that change is a frustrating, discouraging process. If all or some of the above assumptions cannot be made, do not expect significant change to be implemented.

Source: Fullan (1991) as cited in NASSP (1998).

---

think, "I could have a better school." As you begin to think about change—and how you must change your own thinking—silently remind yourself of these words often in your interaction with others, "I cannot change you—I can only change how I respond to you."

Since the principal's is typically one of the first names uttered when the topic of accountability comes to the fore, principals have a great deal at stake and might want to charge forward; however, interpreting the comprehensive changes called for by *Breaking Ranks* as an opportunity for single-minded leadership will undoubtedly undermine reform efforts. If for no other reason—and there are plenty—time commitments alone require principals to pursue a more collaborative and shared leadership style.

Comprehensive reform requires an extraordinary level of support from the community, the school board, the superintendent, families, teachers, and students—not only in approval of the reforms but also in their implementation. Simply getting the conditions right for improvement will require significant planning and strong leadership. Properly cultivated teacher, family, and student leadership—all within the framework of a cohesive collaborative leadership plan embraced by the principal—will bring the implementation of *Breaking Ranks* recommendations much closer to reality.

As important as bringing reform to reality, or perhaps more so, is the need for continuity and sustainability of the reform. Reform driven solely by the principal is not only less likely to succeed, but also less likely to provide long-term results. Additional justification for principals to embrace collaborative leadership arises from continuity of leadership issues. Retirements within the profession and a dearth of people seeking to take on the complex and demanding responsibilities of the principalship have produced a shortage of highly qualified principals in some areas. This shortage, and various accountability adjustments, have increased the mobility of some principals and put additional strain on reforms requiring continuity.

Leaders of Change

The fictional principal who wrote the memo at the beginning of this chapter was on the mark from one standpoint: the importance of beginning a conversation about change. Unfortunately, the principal started the wrong conversation. Enabling others to shape and take ownership of a vision for change is fundamental to its success. Developing the skills necessary to facilitate change requires a principal to understand the principal's and the leadership team's own strengths and weaknesses, including the challenges associated with various leadership styles. Shortcomings are inherent in all leadership styles:

Visionary change leaders view change as necessary and tend to be supportive of change efforts. However, visionary change leaders are often overly optimistic and tend to make global assertions about a change prior to a thorough analysis of all the possible effects.

Technocratic change leaders emphasize hard and quantifiable results while neglecting the concerns of the people who are affected by a change. The process and the concerns and emotions of those affected are viewed as barriers that need to be overcome in order to achieve a desired outcome. Short-term gains are accomplished at the expense of long-term resentment.

Sympathetic change leaders focus on the concerns of the people who are affected by a change but they neglect the hard and quantifiable results. The concerns and emotions of people are viewed as the primary target of change intervention. As a result, change efforts often stall or move excessively slowly. Source: Breaking Ranks Leadership (NASSP, 1998, p. 11).

A synthesis of these three leadership styles will no doubt be required to successfully implement significant change. As you, the principal, begin to look closely at your own leadership style and as your leadership team begins to discuss possible entry points for change and setting the conditions for change, the following should be considered (NASSP, 1998, p. 31):

- Look outward at the environment to diagnose what needs to change rather than trying to impose your idea for change on the system

- Challenge beliefs and assumptions by creatively rearranging certain realities to create something new (e.g., *propose* subject-oriented heterogeneous grouping to challenge beliefs that tracking is appropriate and necessary)

- Shape changes or innovations into a vision over time and then facilitate the sustaining of the dream

- Maintain persistence and resist giving up early.

Finally, do not underestimate the power that simply creating the opportunities for conversation about change can have on the process. To include others in the process:

- Build coalitions; convince, enlist, and involve others; and assess and use the powerful tools of information, resources, and expertise

- Work through teams

- Make everyone a hero, share the glory of each success, and ensure that credit is given to all who contribute to the effort.

Without engaging in these conversations and defining a vision, the recommendations provided throughout this handbook may become merely a "To-Do List"—one that will never be done and may even prove counterproductive. Many of the charts, diagrams, worksheets, and supporting materials in this handbook are intended to encourage conversations or to be used in text-based conversations. They are not prescriptive plans that must be followed to the letter. Indeed, your school may decide upon a much more appropriate formula to improve student performance—but you may never know unless the conversations begin. Time is of the essence—hundreds of students in your school await. The four-step change process outlined in the succeeding pages should provide myriad opportunities for conversation.

A Sample Process: Four Steps to Change

Many schools have already begun the process of change; however, for those having difficulty with change, those considering change, or those looking to complement their own plans for change, the process outlined in the succeeding pages (adapted from Gainey & Webb, 1998[4]) is designed to align with *Breaking Ranks* change.

1. **Establish the action planning team**

2. **Use data to identify opportunities for improvement**

3. **Assess conditions for change and develop the action plan**

4. **Report the results.**

[4]The process outlined here was originally a 10-step process. Several stages of the process were adapted and combined for length and clarity purposes for inclusion in this handbook.

Step 1: Establish the Action Planning Team

Whether a school uses an existing school improvement team to investigate a specific change or forms a new team for that purpose will depend on local circumstances. In NASSP's *Engaging Teachers in the School Improvement Process,* Painter and Valentine (1999) highlight the importance of effective participation in implementing changes within the school:

> Teachers are typically expected to be involved to various degrees in their school's improvement processes; however, teachers are too often expected to implement plans they did not have any part in writing and may not even support or understand. The success of change initiatives lies in the meaningful involvement of teachers: if teachers are invited and even expected to be part of decision-making processes, they are more likely to be committed to successful implementation. (p. 3)

Assuming that these teams are critical, and that a school does not currently have one established, how would a school select members for the team? Painter, Lucas, Wooderson, and Valentine (2000, p. 4) cited several options proposed by Maeroff (1993):

■ Teachers sign up for the team until enough have volunteered to fill the available slots

■ An election is held, and those who get the most votes are put on the team

■ The principal consults with other leaders in the school before designating members to fill the team

■ Members of an existing group, such as a faculty advisory council, become the team

■ Any combination of the above…

The following may inform your decision about which selection process or processes to choose. As noted in *The Use of Teams in School Improvement Processes* (Painter et al., 2000, p. 4), potential members should possess:

■ A commitment to growth and development

■ A reputation for innovation

■ An ability to make things happen

■ Evidence of energy and persistence

■ Demonstrated leadership ability

■ A willingness to work

Indirect Benefits of School Improvement Teams

■ The use of teams helps to forge a sense of community and shared commitment among teachers, contrasting with the culture of isolation and uncertainty often found in schools.

■ School improvement teams empower teachers and establish them as instructional leaders, so that they can stimulate change in multiple classrooms by serving as role models and mentors to other teachers in the building.

■ Members of the team, including the principal, often develop personal relationships that would not be formed under other circumstances. Such relationships advance collaborative school cultures where all members, including administrators, are supportive of each other (Maeroff, 1993; Painter & Valentine, 1999).

Source: NASSP (2000, p. 3).

- Patience
- The respect of the faculty
- Small and large group communication skills.

More specifically, they recommend (pp. 4–7):

1. "Teams typically consist of 4 to 6 members, including the principal, although these numbers can be adjusted to reflect the size of the faculty."

2. Attempt to include those in the building already serving in leadership roles or who "have the greatest promise of becoming leaders."

3. All members of the faculty must "understand the change processes and realize their potential roles in the process."

4. "Members must serve out of conviction, not simply because they are asked, elected, or ordered to do so."

5. "If a team is to be successful, change efforts 'should begin, at least in part, with those most inclined toward and most sympathetic to breaking with the status quo' (Maeroff 1993, p. 41)."

6. "To help ensure faculty acceptance of the team, team membership should reflect the faculty as a whole.

   - Members' ranges of experience in teaching should be similar to the ranges of experience of the entire faculty.

   - Diversity of gender, race, and ethnicity should be considered.

   - Natural divisions in the school—grade levels, teams, subject areas, core and exploratory assignments—should be taken into account.

   - Special attention should be given to the cliques or subcultures that often exist in schools.

   - New members should be rotated periodically into the leadership team— both to invigorate it and to enhance support from the whole faculty."

7. "Only faculty members who are apt to remain in the building for several years should serve on the school improvement team." (Meaningful change takes years to accomplish.)

8. "The involvement of community members, non-teaching staff, and parents is important within school communities, but these stakeholders should not necessarily be members of school improvement teams. (Maeroff 1993). Members of the school improvement team are charged with engaging the rest of the faculty in change efforts—a difficult role if the team is comprised of individuals not part of the teaching staff. The school improvement team is a working group, often meeting formally and informally during school hours, making it difficult for community members to be an integral part of the team."

9. "Be wary of including only 'yes' individuals or uncritical optimists." Healthy skepticism among team members can be productive. "Team members who ask the tough questions and challenge processes can help a team to progress purposefully and thoughtfully."

10. "[A] Team should include a principal but the principal should not assume the role of team leader…. Each individual on the team should assume a liaison role, develop an awareness and expertise about a particular topic such as school culture

or teaching and learning, and share his or her expertise with members of the team and faculty."

Several of these recommendations may not be appropriate for your school. Your individual situation will dictate the appropriate composition. For example, some will wonder where students or families or new teachers might fit into the team. Other schools may require some type of teacher union representation. In other situations the school may feel it's important to have the principal be the team leader—though if you think this is the case in your school, consider this action's effect on the openness of conversations.

Although the number of people involved on the team itself may be limited, a critical aspect of the team's charge is to involve others in the decision making. The level of involvement and the groups involved (parents, teachers, students, the school board, the superintendent, the central office, community members, businesses) will be decided by your school's initiative(s). The process outlined is a framework that can be replicated or amended: your action planning team may not be able—or best suited—to bring to fruition whole-school reform without the creation of other "subteams" focusing on issues such as guidance and advisement, curriculum, data, and assessment.

Define the Vision

If a clear vision for the school has not been established, one of the first actions of the team (or perhaps the site council or other group) will be to define the purpose, future, and vision of the school. As Painter and Valentine remind us in *Engaging Teachers in the School Improvement Process* (1999, p. 6):

the foundation of the school improvement plan—the basis on which all decisions are made—is the list of shared values and beliefs.

The school improvement team must engage the faculty in activities that generate:

- A brainstormed list of values and beliefs

- A more-focused list encompassing values and beliefs supported by a majority of the faculty

- A prioritized list of the values and beliefs that are at the heart of what the faculty believes to be true.

The development of values, beliefs, and mission statements is critical to subsequent pieces of the improvement process. These statements reflect what school members hold closest to their hearts and what they believe to be their purpose. These concepts feed into and guide the organization's vision, which provides a look at what the organization will be like in the future.

Developing your vision will require an understanding of the culture of your school as well as an understanding of changes in the culture of the United States:

- Demographics (aging population, diversification of the family unit, transition from a nation *with* minorities to a nation *of* minorities)

- Transition in the economic base of the United States (i.e., from the durable goods of the industrial age to the entrepreneurial services of the postindustrial age)

- Impact of technology on all aspects of our lives.

As your team works on these and other activities, use the list below to gauge team effectiveness and to prevent significant challenges in later stages.

If you have not already incorporated team-building activities and established effective dialogue practices in the team's process, some of these warning signs may prompt that reaction. It is advisable, however, to pursue team-building and dialogue exercises before the warning signs develop. Once you are satisfied that the team is up to the challenge, your next step is to use data and research to identify more substantively the opportunities for improvement.

Early Warning Signs of Teams in Trouble

- Team members cannot easily describe or agree upon the team's purpose
- Meetings are formal, stuffy, or tense
- Broad participation produces minimal accomplishment
- There is talk, but not much communication
- Team members air disagreements privately after meetings
- The leader makes all decisions
- Members are confused or disagree about roles or work assignments
- Key people outside the team are not cooperative
- The team does not assess its progress or processes.

Source: Parker (1990), as quoted in Painter et al. (2000, p. 8)

Step 2: Use Data to Identify Opportunities for Improvement

At this stage the team should outline opportunities. Often, data will be the first indicator that there is a problem, but there may be other ways in which it is identified. Regardless of how it comes to your attention, after the problem is identified, data should be collected that will help the team understand it better and guide the necessary changes. Research should also be conducted on best practices and to see whether other schools have encountered similar challenges, the reforms they implemented, and the results. This research will inform your strategies and help ensure that your expectations of outcomes are reasonable and that the strategies you choose are the best for the situation.

Gainey and Webb offer the following advice:

- Formulate a statement of what you hope to achieve: describe the situation in the school environment that will be addressed by your efforts.

- If rectifying a problem, indicate what is wrong that will be addressed.

- If the intervention is seen as an opportunity to improve some aspect of the school operation, frame the opportunity in the form of question(s).

- Develop an introductory statement and then list the questions that will be addressed in your action plan. State the problem or opportunity in one or two sentences. If you have trouble doing this, there is a possibility you have not crystallized the focus of your efforts.

- Ask yourselves: Is this a serious problem or is this a good opportunity? If so, are you likely to be able to do anything about it? If the answer to either question is "no," find another opportunity.

Collect the Data

Underestimating the critical nature of data could dampen the prospects of success—even at a school with few *perceived* problems. As Gainey and Webb remind us,

> Public polls consistently indicate that people believe the improvement of education is and should continue to be a national priority, but that their local high school is doing a good job of educating its students. Thus, if you expect to gain support for your change initiatives, you will need to provide data that illustrates that the school can do a better job for its students. (p. 6)

As noted in *Using Data for School Improvement* (NASSP, 1999), data serve critical functions in justifying and evaluating improvement initiatives:

> Data collected at the beginning of a school improvement initiative can serve as baseline information to assess progress toward the school's long-term goals. Periodic data thereafter provides insight on the realization of the goals established from the school's vision and as a formative assessment of continuous change within a school.

> Data are also essential to understand the disparity among current practice, current perceptions, and best practice. For many principals and teachers who believe their school is functioning flawlessly, data—particularly valid observation data—may challenge their convictions. Reflecting on the data may result in a number of different reactions. The most common initial reaction is denial: "I don't know who took these surveys, but they aren't talking about our school." Another reaction is resignation: "Yes, that's our school, but we don't need a survey to tell us how bad it is, we work here." (p. 1)

If a school cannot measure the effects of change, how does a school know the impact on students? How can a school justify its reform actions without the accompanying data? As noted in *Personalized Learning: Preparing High School Students to*

Grading Schools: Perceptions of "Our" Schools vs. Perceptions of the Nation's Schools

What grade would you give the public schools nationally—A, B, C, D, or FAIL?

A:	2%
B:	24%
C:	52%
D:	12%
Fail:	3%
Don't know:	7%

What grade would you give the school your oldest child attends?

A:	29%
B:	39%
C:	20%
D:	8%
Fail:	4%

Source: The 35th Annual Phi Delta Kappa/Gallup Poll of the Public's Attitudes Toward the Public Schools

---

Create Their Futures, "What we have learned from decades of school improvement efforts is that focusing more on the process of change without a concurrent focus on results does not lead to any significant impact on student achievement." (Lachat, 2002, p. 214)

Deciding Upon What Data to Collect

To assist your team in determining the appropriate data to collect, a conversation might begin by focusing on the following passage:

> Most schools have easy access to existing data such as student and staff attendance, discipline referrals, suspensions, participation in school activities, student grades, and student standardized achievement tests. However, most readily available data are ignored, and when they are used, they are often misused. For example, most schools review standardized achievement data annually. Some schools even analyze long-term patterns of achievement over several years. Such analyses tell very little about the true quality of the school. Is the school effectively meeting academic needs of all students? Do we know which segments of our student body we most effectively serve? Only by way of purposeful disaggregation of the data can we develop an understanding of our students' academic successes and failures. Analyses by ethnicity, socio-economic status, gender, prior achievement, participation or non-participation in school-sponsored activities are some of the obvious and important ways to study achievement data. Disaggregated data analysis takes time, yet it is essential. (Quinn, Greunert, & Valentine, 1999, p. 3)

Data on culture, climate, instructional practices, and student attitudes will be quite helpful as you focus attention on personalizing the learning experience (Middle Level Leadership Center [1998], as cited in Quinn et al., 1999, p. 10). Disaggregating these data could point to challenges not yet recognized, as well as guide the team toward strategies to address the challenges. Gainey and Webb (1998, p. 7) recommend that a team's strategy should take into consideration the following three areas:

- "Discrepancy data related to the problem (e.g., trend data that show the situation has been occurring for a period of time). Review any data that show the measurable difference between the present situation and the desired state."

- "Data that show the impact of the problem on the entire educational enterprise in your setting (i.e., poor reading skills will have an adverse impact on student learning in virtually all curricular areas)."

- "Data regarding factors in the setting that could possibly cause the discrepancy(ies). This type of data may be evident in your school or may be suggested by the literature."

Local circumstances as well as the identified problem or opportunity will dictate the necessary data a school should collect. For example, an effort to improve student achievement might focus on instructional strategies. (See Appendix 4, which provides a rubric to help assess instructional strategies. In *Using Data for School Improvement,* Quinn et al. (1999) also recommend several specific instruments that can be used to collect information on variables such as student perceptions, culture, and instructional strategies. (See Appendix 5 for an extensive list of variables.)

The Center for Resource Management, Inc., a partner of the Education Alliance at Brown University, has developed a list of guiding questions for data-driven improvement (Lachat, 2003, p. 221):

1. How are specific groups of students performing on multiple assessments over time?

2. How are students who are engaged in new and more promising learning opportunities performing on multiple measures and performance indicators?

3. How are students in different school clusters or learning communities performing?

4. To what extent are students enrolled in specific course offerings or program opportunities demonstrating proficiency on state assessments or other external measures?

5. How do factors such as absence or mobility affect student performance?

6. What are the proficiency levels of various student groups in specific content and skill areas?

7. Are there knowledge and skill areas where there are notable gaps in student performance by gender, race/ethnicity, or language proficiency?

8. What is the correlation between the grades or performance benchmarks given to students and their scores on state assessments and other standardized measures?

9. To what extent are students enrolled in Special Education, Bilingual Education, ESL, or School-to-Career programs achieving positive results on multiple measures over time?

10. What is the participation rate of specific groups of students in higher level courses?

11. Do grading patterns suggest inconsistencies in grading criteria across learning communities, subject areas, or course offerings?

12. What students appear to be at risk of school failure due to excessive absence?

13. What are the characteristics of students with high absence or discipline rates, or who drop out of school?

14. What is the longitudinal performance of specific cohorts of students?

Again, many potential data sources exist. The job for your team is collecting the appropriate data. The options given so far should get you well on the way.

Collecting data is essential to identifying and tracking opportunities for improvement. The *Breaking Ranks* recommendations and the seven cornerstone strategies provide direction to address these opportunities once identified. However, before embarking on implementation of the recommendations, your team should establish a baseline that will indicate how important the staff feels each of the recommendations is and to what extent the staff feels your school already practices each recommendation—if at all. A sample survey instrument is included in Appendix 6 to guide your efforts in setting this baseline of perception data. The instrument can also be adapted to the seven strategies.

An example from the survey is provided below. In this example, teachers (or other groups that the team feels it important to survey) are asked to what degree they believe a Personal Plan for Progress is important for each student. The survey then asks about the level to which Personal Plans for Progress have been implemented/practiced within the school. The improvement team would then compile the results of all respondents into mean scores and (in the far right column) provide the numerical difference between the perceived level of importance and the perceived level of practice.

Breaking Ranks Recommendation	Rate IMPORTANCE of recommendation (1 is LOW 5 is HIGH)	Rate the Level this recommendation is PRACTICED (1 is LOW 5 is HIGH)	Difference between Perceived Level of Importance and Level of Practice.*
Each student will have a Personal Plan for Progress that will be reviewed often to ensure that the high school takes individual needs into consideration and to allow students, within reasonable parameters, to design their own methods for learning in an effort to meet high standards.			

*Column at right for demo purposes—not to be on survey.

Collecting this information is important for several reasons:

■ A high disparity between perceived level of importance and perceived level of practice will highlight areas for improvement or attention

■ The survey itself will acquaint the staff with the language of the *Breaking Ranks* recommendations and provide opportunities to ascertain the level of understanding of the recommendations

■ It may allow your team to prioritize implementation of the recommendations

■ Comparing these ratings with ratings in later years will provide information on how well the faculty perceives the practices/recommendations to have been implemented

■ Taking the survey results seriously will be another way to demonstrate the action planning team's interest in reaching out to various stakeholders and addressing the perceptions and reality of individuals and groups

■ If the survey shows that a *Breaking Ranks* recommendation is not perceived as important by the staff, then the action planning team can use that as an opportunity for conversation around the meaning and implications of a recommendation and an opportunity to provide examples, research, and data on the importance of the recommendation; or, the team can use the responses to discuss why the staff or other group does not feel the strategy or recommendation is a priority.

What Should the Team Do with the Data?

Summarizing the data, perhaps the most important element of data collection, is the team's next challenge. The summary's importance lies in its ability or inability to identify causes contributing to the problem—a step toward convincing the various stakeholders that change is necessary and that the causes may be addressed. Without this connection, "research and common sense tell us that data will not automatically motivate people to change what they are doing. Change begins with acceptance that there is a need to change. Data can serve as the basis for understanding and accepting that need." (Quinn et al., 1999, p. 2)

Parents, teachers, students, and others will want to know why an improvement team is proposing a change. A well-devised summary of the data will offer answers, begin to form the conceptual basis of the argument for developing an action plan, and convey an urgent belief that something has to be done.

Your action planning team may have done all its homework up to this point, compiling the data and research to support change, but unless the team assesses how prepared the school is for the change, then that homework may be all for naught. The next step is assessing the conditions for change.

Step 3: Assess Conditions for Change and Develop the Action Plan

Development and implementation of an action plan must take into account your school's "organizational readiness" for accepting the plan. *Breaking Ranks Leadership* (NASSP, 1998), a manual developed for a *Breaking Ranks* implementation training program, offers the following five areas of organizational culture (adapted from Dalziel & Schoonover, 1998) that must be considered when preparing any organization for change:

1. **An organization's previous experience in accepting change** is often the most accurate predictor of successful change implementation. Those who previously have had positive experiences with change are likely to have positive experiences with change in the future. Likewise, those who have had negative experiences with change are likely to have negative experiences in the future unless change leaders:

   • Gather all pertinent information regarding past changes

   • Spend extra time talking about the proposed change

   • Provide ongoing feedback

   • Arrange for an immediate positive outcome from the change

   • Publicize successes.

2. **The clarity of expectations** regarding the impact and effects of a proposed change is a major consideration for change leaders. Change leaders need to scrutinize the varying expectations from diverse work groups and various levels of the organization to define and emphasize common interests.

3. **Leaders must also consider the origin of an idea or problem,** or where in the organization the idea for change originated. Consider the fundamental law of change (i.e., the greater the distance there is between those who define a change and those who have to live with its effects, the higher the probability that problems will develop).

4. **The support of district- and school-level management** is especially critical during the initial phases of change and remains an important consideration throughout the change process. In the most successful change efforts, top management is highly visible and actively participates throughout the entire project. In less successful projects, top management functions in a less visible role as "provider of capital."

5. **The compatibility of a change with organizational goals** describes the degree of agreement between the proposed change and the current organizational situation. Whenever possible, changes should be integrated into the organization's overall goals and mission to facilitate the transition between old and new and start the change in an accepting environment.

In developing the action plans, teams must also address each of the following challenges (Gainey & Webb, 1998, pp. 2–3):

- "Resistance to change is consistently reinforced by the majority of people who tend to be satisfied with their school, although they generally concede that there may be some aspects of the school that can be improved."

- "A number of stakeholders, while not necessarily opposed to the plan, may be undecided regarding one or more components. Most of these individuals will be looking for reassurance that the proposed course of action will benefit all students."

- "Not only should you be prepared for opposition, you should not be surprised if some opposition comes from stakeholder groups who have traditionally been supporters."

- "Expect the degree of opposition to be positively correlated to the degree of change you hope to implement."

- "Anticipate where the opposition will come from and do not take for granted any one group as supporters."

- "Keep in mind the political reality…. Regardless of how sound a proposal might be from an educational perspective, it would take courage for policymakers to endorse an intervention that has strong opposition from key stakeholder groups."

The Action Plan

Given the wide variations in local circumstances and resources (fiscal, human capital, social capital, and time), it is impossible to provide a single comprehensive action plan for implementing the seven cornerstone strategies or the 31 *Breaking Ranks* recommen-

---

Why Teachers Resist Change:

- Administration mandated the change
- If it ain't broke, don't fix it
- Fear of rejection or the perception of incompetence
- Tried it before, and it didn't work
- Don't have the time
- If I need to change, then I must be wrong—I believe what I am doing is right
- Lack of knowledge and understanding of different methods
- Basic insecurity

Source: Middle Level Leadership Center (1998), quoted in Quinn et al. (1999, p. 2)

---

dations profiled in this handbook. If a plan could be provided, then there would be no need to assess the conditions for change at a particular school—the plan would be inflexible. A prepackaged plan would not only be inappropriate for all schools but, by providing a plan, the critical stage of getting others involved in developing a plan unique to an individual school would be forgotten. For similar reasons, your team should suppress the urge to have the team do all of the planning—despite the best of intentions (Painter et al., 2000, p. 9). If your team includes others in the development of the plan and ties the strategies to the defined problem, the research, the data, and the specific circumstances of the school, the overall plan will be better defined and will more likely be defensible before any challenges.

Gainey and Webb (1998) cite several critical components to address in a successful plan:

- Describe in clear terms the expected benefits and how you will attempt to "close the gap between what is and what the shared vision indicates should be."

- Provide milestones tied to the strategies.

- Develop indicators related to the quantitative or qualitative data that served as the basis for the intervention. Project incremental gains—immediate results are not realistic.

- Do not attempt to implement something beyond your team's scope of influence.

- Recognize that the time line will probably need to be revised.

- Indicate how others will be involved and "how you will motivate and sustain the efforts of key stakeholders."

- Assess and address the influence of the following:

    - **Rules**—formal and informal policies, and contracts that will foster or impede implementation.

    - **Roles**—formal and informal leadership characteristics. Who makes things happen? Under what circumstances? Identify roadblocks or bottlenecks within the bureaucracy.

    - **Relationships**—understand the potential for the various formal and informal relationships between individuals and groups to foster or impede your efforts.

    - **Responsibilities**—existing rules may govern exactly how much responsibility you and your team will have and will be able to give to others.

- Monitor the plan regularly to help justify expenditure of resources and build momentum and participation, be prepared to respond to questions, adapt the plan where necessary, and recognize and celebrate the incremental successes as they occur.

Professional Development Fundamental to the Action Plan

To effectively implement and assess an action plan, principals, teachers, and other staff members need appropriate professional development. As important, and perhaps more so given the breadth and depth of change called for in *Breaking Ranks,* is developing a school community in which learning is not a *task for students,* but rather, a *goal for everyone.* The action plan will be just another sterile document for the circular file if it does not promote a school community in which all members of the community are interested in learning.

The level of complexity in transitioning from many traditional practices to those recommended in *Breaking Ranks* requires significant professional development. For example, using multiple instructional strategies and multiple forms of assessment, transitioning from the traditional subject-specific courses to interdisciplinary instruction, and identifying individual learning styles require more than a one-day workshop. Follow-up, practice, opportunities to reflect, an assessment of how well the practice is implemented, and its effects on students are just some of the variables that should be included in a comprehensive professional development strategy. Because of the degree required to adequately address comprehensive professional development and the volumes of literature addressing the topic, here only the following aspects are covered as they relate to an action plan:

- Supporting a professional learning community

- Standards and practices of professional development that may help your team prepare a comprehensive professional development strategy to implement your action plan

- The need for each principal and staff member to have a Personal Learning Plan that takes into account the skills and knowledge each staff member must acquire to implement the action plan.

Learning Communities

How effective have you, as a school, as a principal, been at establishing a community that respects learning for all—students, staff members, families, and community members? By reviewing activities associated with a healthy learning community, (the left column in Figure 2.1), your team can better devise instruments to:

- Evaluate whether teachers and other staff members are prepared to implement strategies in the action plan

- Ascertain the type and level of professional development needed

- Gauge progress toward establishing a community of learners in your school by establishing a baseline.

This list can be a valuable tool used to include the faculty and others in evaluating how much your school is like a learning community. Once identified, any weaknesses can be addressed in the comprehensive professional development plan and aligned with your strategies for change.

Align Comprehensive Professional Development Plan With Action Plan

Figure 2.2 provides a conceptual framework to guide your action planning team as it assesses the professional development required to support the strategies, processes, and programs detailed in your action plan. Your team could develop a similar chart outlining the content, objectives, activities, and evaluation of the professional development program.

As your team develops the action plan, it should ensure that the "Activities" align with national standards. The National Staff Development Council (NSDC) provides such standards to ensure that quality professional development is tied to improving learning for all students. Several of those standards are highlighted below (visit the NSDC Web site at www.nsdc.org for a complete list of the standards as well as an assessment tool to help ascertain your school's level of adherence to the standards):

Staff development that improves the learning of all students:

- Uses disaggregated student data to determine adult learning priorities, monitor progress, and help sustain continuous improvement

- Uses multiple sources of information to guide improvement and demonstrate its impact

- Prepares educators to apply research to decision making

- Uses learning strategies appropriate to the intended goal

Figure 2.1

How Is My School Like a Learning Community?

Learning Community Activities	Direct Benefits
Using shared planning to develop units, lessons, and activities	Divides the labor; saves time because no-one has to do it all; increases quantity and quality of ideas
Learning from one another by watching each other teach	Provides concrete examples of effective practices; expands the observer's repertoire of skills, stimulates analytical thinking about teaching
Collectively studying student work to identify weaknesses and plan new ways to teach to those weaknesses	Increases quantity and quality of insights into student performance; focuses efforts on "the bottom line"—student learning; increases professionalism and self-esteem of learning community members
Sharing articles and other professional resources for ideas and insights; conducting book studies of books on teaching and learning	Expands pool of ideas and resources available to members of the learning community
Talking with one another about what and how you teach and the results your teaching produces	Decreases feelings of isolation; increases experimentation and analysis of teaching practices; increases confidence of teachers; provides teachers with greater access to a range of teaching styles, models, and philosophies
Providing moral support, comradeship, and encouragement	Enables teachers to stick with new practices through the rough early stages of learning to use new skills; decreases burnout and stress; increases team members' willingness to try new methods and to share ideas and concerns with other members of the learning community
Jointly exploring a problem, including data collection and analysis; conducting action research	Improves quality of insights and solutions; increases professionalism
Attending training together and helping each other implement the content of the training	Helps learning community members get more out of training; enables them to go to one another with questions or to get clarification about what was presented during training
Participating in continual quality improvement activities	Creates more efficient use of time; takes advantage of particular talents or interests of learning community members
Using collective decision making to reach decisions that produce collective action	Improves quality of instruction, student performance, and school operations
Providing support for "help-seeking" as well as "help-giving"	Makes a strong statement of shared responsibility and commitment to one another's learning
Sharing the responsibility for making and/or collecting materials	Helps learning community members feel secure in asking for help and advice; enables the giving of assistance and advice without establishing one-up/one-down relationships

* Note: Most of these learning community activities cost nothing to implement.

Source: Collins (1998). Reprinted with permission.

Sowing the
Seeds for Change

- Applies knowledge about human learning and change

- Provides educators with the knowledge and skills to collaborate

- Deepens educators' content knowledge, provides them with research-based instructional strategies to assist students in meeting rigorous academic standards, and prepares them to use various types of classroom assessments appropriately

- Provides educators with knowledge and skills to involve families and other stakeholders appropriately.

School teams are encouraged to use the standards as a checklist against which to judge all professional development offered for school faculty.

Designing your comprehensive professional development plan to align with *Breaking Ranks* changes requires the development of an evaluative mechanism or instrument. How will you measure whether or not the professional development provides the intended results? Developing the measures prior to offering the professional development is critical. Figure 2.3 provides questions and a sample grid to guide you in the evaluation process. Making the connection between the need identified in the action

---

Figure 2.2
Overview of the Planning Process

Component	Primary Decisions	Sources of Information
Content	What knowledge, skills, strategies, and/or values and beliefs need to be studied?	• Analysis of students' work or performance • Teacher self-assessment • School or district programs or practices • National standards
Objectives	What will participants know and/or be able to do as a result of their participation in professional development activities? What is the desired impact on student learning?	• Analysis of students' work or performance • Professional growth goal-setting • School or district programs or practices • National standards
Activities	What will participants do to achieve the identified objectives?	• Five models of professional development • National Standards
Evaluation	How will results of the professional development activities be measured?	• Changes in knowledge, beliefs, values, skills, or practices of participants • Changes in student achievement, behavior, attitudes and other characteristics

Source: Collins (1998). Reprinted with permission.

plan and the need the professional development activity will address is essential to ensuring that development is tied to the goal of improved student performance.

Thus far, we have discussed professional development from the macro or schoolwide perspective as it relates to bringing about changes consistent with *Breaking Ranks* recommendations. Yet the impact must be made student by student, class by class—which requires a focus on individual teachers.

Creating a Personal Learning Plan

In the end, the effectiveness of a comprehensive professional development plan is measured by each staff member's awareness of the skills they require to improve student performance—and in their ability to acquire those skills. If comprehensive reform is to be achieved, each staff member must reflect upon his or her development needs as they relate to the action plan and create and continually update a Personal Learning Plan

---

Figure 2.3
Evaluating the Impact of Professional Development

Sample Grid
Key Questions to Guide the Evaluation of Professional Development Activities

Target or Group	What need will this activity address?	How was this need measured?	What change is this activity intended to produce?	How will this change be measured?
Teachers	Teachers need training and practice in strategies proven to be effective in improving reading achievement for at-risk students.	A survey was conducted in which teachers prioritized their professional development needs. Training and practice in reading strategies for at-risk students was the highest-rated need.	Teachers will be able to use the identified strategies with a high degree of effectiveness.	A large sample of teachers will be interviewed using the "Levels of Use" instrument from the "Concerns-Based Adoption Model" materials.
Students	Student achievement in reading among at-risk students has declined for three of the past four years.	A norm-referenced achievement test is given to all students each spring. Scores for at-risk students were broken out and analyzed to reveal this trend.	Reading achievement of at-risk students will improve.	The same norm-referenced test will continue to be given each spring and the results broken out to reveal the achievement for at-risk students as a sub-group.
Organization	The school needs to be responsive to the needs of all students.	Test scores of at-risk students declined while scores of other groups improved or remained stable.	The school will improve its awareness of and responsiveness to the needs of all students.	Test scores will be disaggregated, and the performance of all sub-groups will be identified and analyzed.

Source: Collins (1998). Reprinted with permission.

consistent with the action plan. (The information below regarding creation of Personal Learning Plans has been adapted from *Personal Learning Plans for Educators* [Webb & Berkbuegler, 1998].)

Creating a Personal Learning Plan, especially in the context of the changes we have proposed in this handbook, requires a review of what students need to know, as Sparks and Hirsh (1997) remind us:

> Rather than basing the Personal Learning Plan solely on the teacher's perception about what he or she needs (e.g., to learn more about classroom management), the plan should consider what students need to know and be able to do and work backward to the knowledge, skills, and attitudes needed by the teacher if those student outcomes are to be realized. (p. 27)

Approaches to self-evaluation include:

- Quantitative tools such as rating scales, checklists, or self-rating forms.

- Videotaping a classroom performance. "Videotaping allows evaluatees to see themselves as others see them and reduces the subjectivity that is normally involved in evaluating one's own performance." (Webb & Norton, 1998, p. 390).

- Portfolios.

- Peers and students should not be overlooked. Peer-to-peer classroom observations, peer review of lesson plans, handouts, or worksheets, and student evaluations can provide valuable feedback. Research even refutes the criticism that evaluations by students are nothing more than popularity contests, grade dependent, or of limited value because of the inexperience or immaturity of student evaluators (Follman, 1995). "Using student evaluations demonstrates to students that their opinions are valued and may encourage them to become more involved in the learning process" (Herbart, 1995).

The model in Figure 2.4 provides a valuable tool to help teachers and principals in the process of self-assessment.

Many of the seven cornerstone strategies and/or the 31 *Breaking Ranks* recommendations outlined in Chapter 1 could easily be adapted and plugged into the model in Figure 2.4—specifically in the top right box: "Ideal Teaching Practices."

Matching Type of Professional Development to the Personal Learning Plan

After reviewing professional needs, staff members must decide on one of five basic models of staff development (Hirsh, 1997, as cited by Webb & Berkbuegler, 1998) to meet each need. The breadth of *Breaking Ranks* reforms will require several, if not all, models be pursued:

- **Inquiry**—Teacher inquiry…be it a solitary activity or the collaborative project of a small or large group. It can be formal or informal and can take place in a classroom (action research), at a teacher center, or as a part of a formal educational program. As a result of engaging in the research process (defining a problem, reviewing the professional literature, and collecting, analyzing, and interpreting data), teachers not only develop their research skills and acquire knowledge but can use the results of the research to improve their own skills and/or improve practice in the school.

- **Training programs**—Training, specifically in-service training, historically has been the most common approach to professional development for teachers. Too

Figure 2.4

Self-Assessment and a Self-Directed Change Model

Steps in Using Self-Assessment	Components of a Self-Directed Change Model
1. Identify practices to be studied. 2. Identify standards or criteria for judging targeted practices (these criteria describe ideal teaching practices). 3. Identify methods for collecting information about targeted practices. 4. Collect information. 5. Compare real practices with standards or criteria for ideal practices. 6. Identify priority areas for more in-depth study and professional growth. (What are the most significant differences between the real and the ideal?) 7. Identify the desired outcomes of the professional development activities. 8. Plan the professional development activities, including follow-up activities, that will address the targeted practices. 9. Implement the plan; assess and monitor its progress periodically. 10. Use feedback to determine the extent to which the professional development activities achieved the desired outcomes; continue or modify the activities as necessary or identify new practices for study.	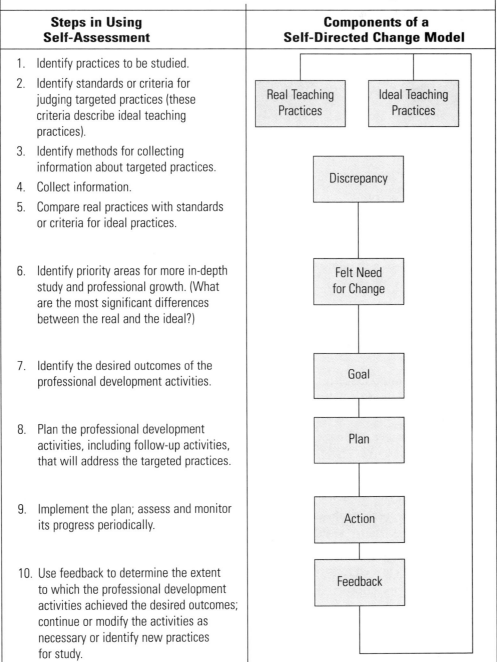

Source: Collins (1998). Reprinted with permission.

often, it is of the "one-shot" mode where some expert is brought in before the school year starts to give a one or two-day workshop where participants "sit and git." Typically, little or no follow-up or support for implementation is provided. However, if properly conducted, with a clear set of learning objectives, training can be an effective process for improving skills and knowledge. Research does suggest that a combination of components (exploration of theory, demonstration of a skill, practice of the skill, feedback on performance, and coaching in the workplace) are necessary if the outcome is skill development. Research by Sparks and Loucks-Horsley (1989) also suggests that:

- Training sessions be spaced one or more weeks apart so that content can be "chunked" for improved comprehension and so that teachers have opportunities for classroom practice.

- Teachers prefer their peers for trainers: When their peers are trainers, teachers feel more comfortable exchanging ideas, play a more active role in workshops, and report that they receive more practical suggestions (p. 48).

■ **Involvement in a development/improvement project or process**—Teachers are commonly asked to engage in curriculum design, development, or revision, or to engage in systematic school improvement efforts aimed at improving the curriculum or classroom instruction. Participation in these projects may require the teacher to acquire specific knowledge and skills through reading, discussion, training, observation, or trial and error.

■ **Observation and assessment**—Research and the experience of hundreds of school districts support the fact that when properly conducted, observations, including pre- and postconferences, can yield valuable and valid information about teacher performance. This model is based on the assumption that teachers will reflect on and analyze the feedback information to improve instruction and student learning.

■ **Individually guided activities**—The teacher determines his or her staff development goals and selects the activities that will result in the achievement of the goals. The model assumes that teachers are in the best position to determine their own learning needs, are self-initiated, and will be most motivated when they select their own relevant learning activities. The types of activities teachers engage in (workshops or conferences, university courses, reading, action research, etc.) are determined by the teacher's preferred learning style.

As Figure 2.5 demonstrates, each of the five strategies has its advantages and disadvantages.

Different strategies and recommendations will require different models, but they all require continual revision of the Personal Learning Plan. The principal, the leadership team, and the action planning team must (Webb & Berkbuegler, 1998, p. 6):

■ Clearly express a vision "with measurable objectives stated in terms of student outcomes."

■ "Create an environment in which teachers will experiment, take risks, discuss their weaknesses, and share their successes and failures without feeling threatened."

■ "Practice what they preach."

Figure 2.5

Effectiveness Estimates for Five Models of Professional Development

Desired Outcome	Individually Guided	Observation/ Assessment	Development/ Improvement Process	Training	Inquiry
Mastery of a simple, specific teaching skill	Medium: requires more time to plan than other models	High: adding peer coaching can increase application to 80%	Low: better suited for broader outcomes	Highest: recommended components make it very effective	Medium: less efficient than other models
Implementation of a complex set of teaching strategies	Medium: less efficient than other models	Medium: harder to observe complex strategies	Medium: less efficient than other models	Highest: more complex outcomes make follow-up more important	High: adding peer coaching can increase application to 90%
Gaining insight into how students learn	Medium: includes professional reading, observation of students	Low: focuses on observing teachers' behavior, not students'	Medium: less efficient than other models	Medium: less efficient than other models	Highest: effective in testing hypotheses
Mastery of new classroom management skills	Medium: less efficient than other models	High: adding peer coaching can increase application to 90%	Low: better suited for broader outcomes	Highest: recommended components make it very effective	High: adding peer coaching can increase application to 90%
Implementation of new assessment procedures	Medium: includes collaboration with others	Medium: assessment procedures are not always observable	Medium: less efficient than other models	Highest: recommended components make it very effective	High: effective but time-consuming
Solving a complex problem dealing with improving student achievement	High: flexibility allows activities to be designed specifically for this outcome	Low: better suited for giving feedback than problem-solving	Medium: can be adapted to problem-solving tasks	Low: better suited for supporting implementation than creating new knowledge	Highest: effective in solving complex problems, generates a great deal of learning
Acquiring group leadership skills/ working as a team to solve a problem	Medium: allows group members to learn what they need, when they need to know it	Low: these skills developed outside the classroom, less observable	Highest: leadership opportunities abound in this model	Low: better suited for supporting implementation than building leadership skills	Medium: less efficient than other models
Increasing knowledge of content or subject matter	Medium: include professional reading and contact with subject matter experts	Low: focuses on teacher's behavior, not content knowledge	Highest: important element is acquiring new knowledge to solve a problem or meet a specific need	High: effective in helping teachers acquire new knowledge, especially in applying it	Medium: less efficient than other models; focus is creating new knowledge, not acquiring knowledge

Source: Collins (1998). Reprinted with permission.

- "Provide the atmosphere, organization, and structure that allow teachers the freedom, time, and resources to explore and experiment."

Once you have assessed the conditions for change in your school, developed an action plan aligned with the seven cornerstone strategies or the *Breaking Ranks* recommendations (depending on your school's stage of change), provided the proper professional development to implement the strategies, and then implemented the action plan, you're done, right? Not quite. Everyone wants to know whether the plan was successful—the good, the bad, the undecided. On to step 4.

Step 4: Report the Results

All too often, new programs are planned, announced with great fanfare and ceremony, and never implemented as intended or, if implemented, never evaluated…. They more or less seem to have a life of their own and continue to operate, whether effective or ineffective, until a new program comes along. However, the various stakeholders in schools are becoming much more suspect of new programs than in the past. If *Breaking Ranks* is going to serve as the catalyst for changing an American institution, then the results of the various efforts to implement the recommendations contained in *Breaking Ranks* will have to be reported to the various stakeholders, many of whom are reluctant to change the American high school (Gainey & Webb, 1998, p. 15).

Just as report cards for students are important for identifying areas of strength, weakness, and accomplishment, reporting the results of reform strategies should be given high priority. An effective report of the action plan and the results should be clear, concise, cogent, correct, and compelling enough that it will be read, yet detailed enough to indicate how the efforts support the improvement of student learning. Include:

- An overview of the action plan
- The methodology employed
- The chronology of activities
- The results of formative evaluation that occurred during the operational phase, describing what was accomplished, how it occurred, and who was involved, as well as any changes or modifications made as a result of monitoring the implementation
- A discussion of the summative evaluation used to measure program effectiveness
- A summary and conclusion that not only reports the effectiveness or ineffectiveness of the intervention, but any constraints on the intervention, as well as limitations on the "generalizability" of the results
- The implications for theory and practice.

This report can be shared in any number of ways, including creating opportunities for the principal or the staff to share the results with community, parent, and student organizations.

A Tool for Leaders to Assess Their Own Need to Change

To help school leaders assess their own skills and to begin that "deep change" to which Dennis Sparks, executive director of the National Staff Development Council refers (see sidebar), NASSP has developed a rating form for principals and other school leaders to enable them to assess their strengths and weaknesses in the following areas:

- Setting Instructional Direction
- Teamwork
- Sensitivity
- Judgment
- Results Orientation
- Organizational Ability
- Oral Communication
- Written Communication
- Development of Others
- Understanding Own Strengths and Weaknesses

A form with detailed questions about individual practices within each of these categories is provided in Appendix 7. This form and a similar instrument to help others observe and rate your areas of strength and opportunities for improvement can also be found on the NASSP Web site at www.principals.org/CPD/self/developmental_assessment.cfm.

**The Importance of Leadership:
A Conversation with Dennis Sparks, Executive Director,
National Staff Development Council**

Q: *You have said that school reform depends on a leader's ability to address the personal and emotional aspects of change. Can you elaborate on that point? What are specific successful strategies or practices you have encountered that help leaders address these issues and how can a leader manage these over time?*

A. Leading school reform is intensely interpersonal. Instructional improvement and culture-building are relationship-intensive and emotionally demanding. They require the application of sophisticated communication and problem-solving skills as well as the rational and technical processes of planning, applying research, and assessing progress.

Some methods of interacting with others have proven more effective than others in addressing such issues. School leaders can develop clarity regarding their purposes and values, become more powerful speakers and writers, learn to listen deeply and with empathy to others in the spirit of dialogue (which is particularly challenging when they feel unfairly attacked), acquire the ability to stay focused on possibilities rather than falling prey to resignation and dependency, and develop the resourcefulness to generate multiple pathways to the attainment of goals. The NSDC has conducted pilot programs that have demonstrated that these are teachable skills that can improve the results achieved by even experienced, sophisticated leaders.

Individualized support can take the form of mentoring for new leaders and of "executive coaching" for veteran administrators of the type that has become increasingly prevalent in businesses. Such support can provide leaders with the insights and wisdom of successful, experienced educators and offer opportunities for leaders to clarify their intentions, strengthen their planning and problem-solving capacities, develop stronger communication and interpersonal skills, and maintain energy and enthusiasm for their critically important work. Such efforts will also contribute to the long-term retention of leaders who feel that the challenges they face are understood by their employers, who believe that they are being adequately supported in meeting those challenges, and who perceive that their efforts are truly making a difference. The ultimate success of school reform, I believe, will be determined to a large extent by our ability to support leaders in addressing these demanding interpersonal challenges.

Q: *If, as you believe, significant change begins with significant change in leaders, what are the steps a leader must take to change himself/herself? How does a leader know when he or she is prepared—has undertaken his or her own personal change journey?*

A. Significant changes in schools begin, I believe, with significant changes in what leaders think, say, and do. As someone once observed, if you do what you've always done, you'll get what you've always gotten. To that I would add, if leaders continue to think and speak in the same ways, they'll continue to produce results that are consistent with those they previously produced.

Change in thought begins with deep understanding of important issues and the adoption of beliefs aligned with the leader's goals. Deep understanding typically requires that we elaborate our learning through processes such as discussion, writing, applying it in real-life circumstances, teaching the subject to others, and reflecting on the results of our actions. A change in beliefs requires placing ourselves in situations that produce cognitive dissonance. One of the most powerful means is dialogue through which we make our assumptions known to others and open ourselves to being influenced by the beliefs of others. A great deal more on this subject can be found in the September 2003 issue of *Transformational Professional Learning*, which is located on the NSDC's Web site (www.nsdc.org). At this Web site, you may also download *Designing Powerful Professional Development for Teachers and Principals*. (Both publications are provided free to educators as part of the Council's efforts to dramatically improve the quality of professional learning for all teachers in all schools by 2007.

Change in speech means that the leaders consistently represent their intentions, values, and beliefs as they interact with students, teachers, parents, and other members of the school community. Such representation typically begins by developing clarity through processes such as writing, group discussion, or the type of one-to-one assistance described above.

The demonstration of new behavior reveals a leader's personal commitment to change and provides an impetus for such changes in others. Some have called this "walking the talk." It is also a way that leaders bridge the "knowing-doing gap" (the gap between what we know and the actions we consistently take), a barrier to significant change within schools.

Q: *You have said that teachers who work in isolation, rather than experiencing strong bonds of professional connection with other teachers, may be less able to create classrooms and schools in which students feel connected to other students and to adults. What are indicators of strong bonds of personal connection with other teachers? What are successful practices you have seen that help to form these bonds? And most important, can you elaborate on why you believe there is such a strong connection between the two—that is, a connection between teachers connecting with colleagues and students connecting with each other and adults?*

A. A high level of interpersonal trust is at the core of productive adult relationships within schools just as it is at the core of successful classrooms. This trust, in turn, is based on candor, integrity, and the honoring of commitments. And, because leaders set the agenda for relationships within schools, the establishment of trusting relationships begins with them.

Many schools operate as "pseudo-communities"—they are marked by surface congeniality that masks important differences in views regarding teaching and learning, the capacity of particular subgroups of students to achieve at high levels, the role of parents in promoting students' learning, and other significant topics. Although few leaders enjoy conflict, it is often the door through which a school must pass if is to become a productive learning community that truly benefits all a school's students.

Some of the most important forms of professional learning occur in daily interactions among teachers in which they assist one another in improving lessons, deepening understanding of the content they teach, analyzing student work, and examining various types of data on student performance. Consequently, ongoing high-quality teacher-to-teacher communication about teaching and learning is one of the most powerful yet underused sources of professional development and instructional improvement.

Therefore, one of the most important responsibilities of principals is the development of a high-performance culture in which productive relationships can thrive. Because culture is the sum total of interactions among community members and the beliefs that they bring to those interactions, the creation of such a culture means establishing norms and practices that lead to trust and mutual respect, continuous improvement, team-focused collaboration, clarity of thought, candid expressions of views, and interpersonal accountability for the fulfillment of commitments.

The learning and relationships we desire for our students are preceded, I believe, by similar depth of learning and quality of relationships among the adults in schools. Deep learning and trusting, caring relationships among adults are the cognitive and affective centerpieces of the proposals offered in *Breaking Ranks II.* Those qualities begin with deep change in school leaders that are manifested each day through their thoughts, words, and actions. Leaders truly matter.

In Their Own Words...

Below is the first of three profiles about school changes consistent with Breaking Ranks*–style reform. Each of the profiles has been written from the personal perspective of a member of the team responsible for implementation. The profiles are designed to show the comprehensive and interdependent nature of the reforms your school is being called upon to undertake. Although not all of the changes each school has instituted will be appropriate for your school, the perspective of your colleagues should nevertheless be valuable and may form the basis of a text-based discussion for your team.*

Noble Challenges: Breaking Ranks for Equity, Rigor, and Personalization

by Pamela Fisher

Introduction

Ten years ago, during a visit to Noble High School with some of his Brown University graduate students, Ted Sizer commented to a group of teachers, "you have to change enough, quickly enough, so that gravity cannot drag you back." Although not a slogan for Noble's evolving plan to reinvent the school, at the time the process felt like a dizzying array of changes to those involved and particularly for parents. However, the changes were systemic, coherent, and had students at the center. To reinvent a school to be equitable, rigorous, and personalized for all learners, every practice, structure, and policy was held to a new standard. Constructing these standards and matching them to organizational structures and practices was the real challenge. Within three years, the changes dramatically impacted student learning. Test scores escalated, the number of students attending college nearly doubled, and 10 years later, the rural school community of 1,200 students lives in a new building designed for 15 small, independent learning communities. The new programs and structures have persisted after several changes in leadership at all levels in the district. Today, they are how Noble defines itself. They are no longer "changes." They are Noble's vision of an Essential School.

Profile
Noble High School
North Berwick, ME
Rural
1,200 students
http://knight.noble-hs.sad60.k12.me.us

Practices to look for include:
- *Teacher leadership*
- *Small units/integrated teams of students and teachers*
- *Heterogeneous grouping*
- *Reorganization/elimination of traditional department structure*
- *Variety of assessments*
- *Professional development*

The small, rural southwestern Maine communities served by Noble are not where you would expect to see the launching of a major school renewal initiative. In 1990 the school was comfortably tracked, with a traditional array of courses and programs aligned with tiers of expectations, based upon career or academic pathways, and generally by socioeconomic status of the students. It was, and still is, an all-white population of youth. Anyone who attended high school in the 50s or 60s could identify with the culture and traditions of the school. Teachers worked hard, with some teaching as many as 130 students during the fast-paced eight-period day. All but a few still drive in from more prosperous suburban towns to educate other people's children. Students attending college are still mostly "first generation." The three towns serving the schools are geographically dispersed, with many students traveling an hour by bus. The district receives considerable subsidy from the state due to the level of income and property valuation.

In 1990 a group of teacher leaders designed and launched a plan to change. The goal was to define and build a democratic and equitable learning environment for all students, from the underserved to the presumed elite, to raise the aspirations of all students, and to guarantee that every student would leave the high school with a transcript that would open doors to higher education. This account documents the change: the shift in beliefs, the shift in organizational structures and practices impacting equity, and the construction of a school governance plan to ensure democracy and equity for faculty and students. The Noble story is a story of the human side of school change, a successful story of the endurance of core beliefs over 13 years, that now can be told with the benefit of reflection. It is clear evidence that our existing public schools can be transformed into places that celebrate the gifts and promise that exist within every child who walks through our school doors. From the teachers who led the changes at Noble to the new crop of interns coming in each fall, teachers work hard to stay grounded in the core principles and practices around which they designed the first school in Maine to become a member of the Coalition of Essential Schools (CES). The journey of change, with its bumps and potholes, affirms for both teachers and students the values of the Efficacy Institute: think you can, work hard, succeed. Schools that believe in the promise of every student have the capacity for equity and will leave no child behind.

Beginning the Journey

"We don't track kids here. Kids choose to take the level of course they want so they can experience success. We don't want to set them up for failure." This quote could come from almost any traditional high school. When I interviewed, individually, every Noble faculty member and employee in the summer of 1990, having been hired to be the new principal, this message was an undercurrent. Most teachers were eager to serve all youth well; others were convinced they were doing well enough already. However, student achievement data did not back up the school's sense of success. That summer, I reviewed the grades of all 690 students and was immediately struck by the degree to which the "final exam," when averaged with the quarter grades, lowered the overall grades of two-thirds of the students. Other summer insights revealed a schedule of favoritism for some faculty, discriminatory (in my opinion) practices regarding room and course assignments for students, and a long history of a department-head structure. The schedule was an eight-period day consisting of 40-minute sound bites. The "honors" students loaded their schedules with eight classes. Other students had three to four "study halls" each day! Nearly 30% of the students spent 30% of their high school careers in study hall! Parent interviews revealed dissatisfaction with the school. Mothers told stories of their sons or daughters being channeled into programs because they "were not college material." Other parents worried about discipline and drugs. School had not yet begun.

To begin the new year and to begin to build connections with the community, I invited any interested teachers to help plan a freshman orientation program for the fall of 1990 that would be a positive start to the year. Several teachers planned a barbecue for freshmen and their parents, with entertainment and older students engaging new students and parents in welcoming and informational activities. The evening was a great success, culminating with the faculty singing a Simon and Garfunkel tune to the parents. With high expectations, but with no real strategy, I was ready to learn more about Noble and to understand why so many students were not achieving.

Thinking About Equity

Wandering around on the first day of school, checking into classes and getting acquainted with the students, I filled my day with painful "ahas." My first stop, just down the hall from my office, was the "Latin room." Seated at tilted, side-arm desks, neatly lined up and crowded in the small room, students were struggling to keep racks of test tubes and beakers from sliding off the desk-tops. These were the "general bio" kids. Their class met for one period (out of the eight-period day) in length and could not be scheduled into the lab because it was already booked by the college prep and honor bio students. The teacher greeted me and pumped up the kids by telling me what a great group they were. Hmm. Not good enough for a real biology lab, I thought. I continued down another hall and exited the back of the building to a beautiful summer day. Hearing loud voices from a closed metal door (the former grounds equipment room), I ventured in. There, in a room without windows, was the "behavioral room," a special education class, consisting of a dozen or more disengaged kids, a harried teacher, and outfitted with furniture that deserved to be at the town dump. As the day wore on, I discovered several more "self-contained" special education rooms, a collection of math courses ranging from business consumer to general math, being held all over the building and consisting of collections of kids whom no one assumed would ever learn math. I saw freshman science classes of 25 students and physics classes of 6. There were two AP courses in the school. Course requirements and expectations were different for different kids and only made sense to those who were convinced that they could identify who could learn, who wanted to learn, and who deserved to learn, with great accuracy. At the end of the day, at the first department-head meeting, comments were made about seeing "too many hats," some kids not dressed properly, and kids coming in who just wanted to "stay warm for the winter." I went home to reread *Horace's Compromise,* and to wonder if anyone saw the injustices that made up this place called public high school.

By November, I shared my personal vision for a good school with the faculty. I had worked every day to build trust, had engaged in daily conversations about the school we wanted for our kids, and had filled teacher mailboxes with educational articles. I asked that whoever was interested in making some significant changes for students and teachers meet with me for a day-long retreat and begin to plan. Nearly 30 teachers showed up— more than half the faculty. During the session, a veteran Noble teacher commented, "if not in our schools, where else should democracy and equity thrive? We need to completely change the way we've been doing things." This was a turning point. The teachers, first called the strategic planning team and later the faculty council, were empowered to develop 5-year and 10-year action plans, including professional development and community engagement activities, that would reinvent the concept of schooling to ensure equity of opportunity for all kids to learn and to be successful.

Learning to Be Small

During this 1990–1991 planning year, teachers came forth with a plan to change organizational and structural practices to begin to address equity, rigor, and personalization, and what they considered to be injustices in the way students were labeled and sorted. The plan involved phasing in integrated 9th-grade teams consisting of an English, a science, a social studies, a math and a special education teacher, and a guidance counselor. The teams would have common planning time and a core group of 80 students. Twelve teachers coming from all grade levels and who were at times targeted as "born-again teachers" volunteered to take the lead. The program would be a heterogeneously grouped core curriculum, would include all special education students within the classrooms, and would require all students to take algebra as their first high school math course. The Freshman Core was born. On the same night that former President Bush announced the beginning of the Gulf War in January of 1991, Noble faculty stood before more than 200 parents in the cafeteria and were challenged to explain why the school would ever consider having "those" kids sit in the same classroom with their kids. On that evening, our own tracking war began. Meetings with the superintendent over concerns about moving too quickly for the community assured faculty that we could not afford to lose another generation of students. Parents, teachers, and I continued to meet in small groups over the winter months. A respected researcher from the University of Southern Maine facilitated a "Parent Assessment Advisory Group" charged with evaluating every aspect of this new idea, and the school board gave approval for a "trial period" for the Freshman Core. The school overcame the tracking concerns with its own data-tracking system, by inviting parents into any and all classrooms, by including parents in the evaluation of the program, and by not giving up when the going got tough.

Since 1991, we have learned much about what happens to teaching and learning when teachers begin to work in heterogeneously grouped, integrated teams in our high schools. The Noble teachers experimented with many projects and thematic events as their allegiance shifted from their department to their teaching team and to the students. The teams, although on a fast learning curve, always conveyed an open-door policy to the parents, who, by the end of the year, felt much more comfortable with the concept. The evaluation data provided the hard evidence for concerned parents. One teacher, as part of her research for her master's degree, did a study of achievement among special education students taking algebra and general math. She proved that, at the end of the year, students who had struggled in an algebra class performed better on a general math exam than students who had taken general math for yet another year. This example is one of many in which the school continued to gather and assess student achievement and other data to make the case for change. Politically astute, teachers awarded an "honors" grade (a practice phased out over time) within the classroom for students who contracted to do differentiated, more challenging work. Note that students entered high school teams from a junior high school that was highly tracked at the time, making the shift more challenging for the community.

The next year, the sophomore teams were instituted (three teams of four teachers in English, Biology, American History and the World—Part II, and Geometry. Students advanced in math could take Advanced Algebra with the juniors.) The very act of having half the school involved in integrated teams, with a core curriculum, created an even more interesting situation with the junior/senior teachers. First, teachers who were not interested in teaming, or getting involved with change, were beginning to trickle up. Untracking half the school led the other half to topple quickly. At the same time, talented, veteran teachers were taking the lead in increasing graduation requirements for all students, making four years of rigorous mathematics and four years of science, including chemistry and physics, required. At all levels, the school was redefining and raising its standard of excellence to include all learners. Today, all students are required to meet the standards in heterogeneously grouped chemistry and physics classes. Courses are mostly organized within the integrity of the academic discipline, but as part of a team structure, common schedules and teacher planning time provide multiple opportunities for integrated, project- and community-based learning. This core curriculum allowed flexibility for many AP courses to grow and is an early college option open to any student willing to give them a try.

The lessons learned from teaming include:

- Given the opportunity to work and plan together, teachers will create a more customized, personalized environment for students. For example, teachers are able to help kids get the support they need within the team, such as going back to hear a lesson a second or third time. Teachers also adjust for learning styles by providing assessment choices and students help to design scoring rubrics. Teaming gives kids a small team of teachers that know them well.

School Profile 1:
Noble High School

- Experimenting with new ideas is imperfect at best, but teachers and students thrive in an environment where it is safe to take great leaps.

- Using student data is essential in communication with, and building confidence in, parents and community about change.

- Although it is essential to build a common vision for the schools, it is okay for groups of teachers to take on new challenges while others watch for a while.

- The mere acts of teaming and heterogeneously grouping does not ensure rigor or equity. Some kids need to hear the algebra lesson three times. Others need more time to write an essay. To be successful, various support structures need to be in place to ensure that every student is able to achieve a high standard. Today, this includes a paraprofessional on every team, independent learning time during the day for extra support, and after-school and summer support (Appendix 8).

- Teachers need to learn how to team effectively. It's all about the students, but time spent working on engaging curriculum is of most importance.

- Teams are SLCs, which, given the opportunity to carve out their own identity, can become a safe haven for kids and can generate a great sense of belonging.

- Heterogeneous teams are more equitable for teachers, too. Everybody teaches everybody. There is no tilting the hat to the veteran regarding who gets "the best kids."

- Integrated teams are a great first step to creating small autonomous schools within a large school because allegiance to teachers within common disciplines is greatly reduced when traditional departments are abandoned.

- None of this works unless every teacher believes all kids can learn and learn much more than they have ever learned before.

Leadership and Professional Learning Communities

A relatively poor rural school is challenged to be creative in finding resources for professional development. Early on, the school tapped into those provided by the CES, becoming a member in 1993, adopting the then nine common principles and engaging in every opportunity provided by CES. Our aim was to grow a school of professional learning communities. Any teacher could become a member of the faculty council. Students were invited to participate in all committees. Faculty planned and led full faculty meetings, which were designed to be learning experiences. Faculty read common texts, engaged in study groups, and currently all participate in Critical Friends Groups. The idea of collaborative leadership began when the department-heads structure dissolved. The fabulous veteran teachers faced some challenges in this change in traditions, but the critical notion that every teacher is a leader and that the principal is the head learner is essential for the school to be a vibrant learning community. Teams of teachers take charge of their own learning by reading articles and beginning team meetings with a text-based discussion. These habits build slowly and must be reinforced and supported as part of the regular work of school.

The inclusive school governance structure developed an alternating-day block schedule for the school to accommodate long blocks of team time, the concept of the student seminar that involves every student, the senior project (originally named senior celebration), a new grading system, and ideas important to students, such as a unique lunch program designed to allow students to visit with their friends on other teams.

Evolving Practices

Curriculum, instruction, and assessment practices continue to evolve and are aligned not only with the CES, but with the core principles of *Promising Futures* (Maine Commission on Secondary Education, 1998), Maine's seminal document calling for high school reform that closely aligns with *Breaking Ranks,* and the Maine Learning Results, Maine's standards for learning and award of the diploma.

All Noble students are required to meet the standards of the core curriculum. This is assured by the new grading systems, common assessments, and the senior project. All students work on the senior project for up to two years. The project is presented to a panel, along with the student's portfolio, at the end of the senior year. Students who attend vocational centers during the day are engaged in core curricula in the afternoon. Whether a student is involved with an internship, a mentorship, or early college options, the core curriculum is required. What that means continues to evolve as the school uses common assessment, the state tests, and classroom assessment to grow the required Local Comprehensive Assessment System. An important point in this, one with which every school needs to wrestle, is the traditional grading system and report card. Noble students, parents, teachers, and school board members got together 10 years ago to address the impact of "number averaging" on grades and students attitudes and engagement over the year. Final exams were abolished in 1990 by the administration—not a democratic decision, but one made to allow new ideas to evolve and to abolish inequitable results.

Grading systems impact equity, the school culture, and the core beliefs of the school community. Noble did not have a history of weighted grades, which made the discussion of the grading system more inclusive and probably less divisive. In the early 90s, Noble's grading system involved the common practice of awarding four quarter grades. Two quarters were averaged to give a semester grade. Each semester was averaged to give the final grade for a full-year course. This system is well known to most high school folks. (Final assessments were done within the quarter grade because of the huge impact they had on the overall grade averaging in the past. There is no "exam" period taken out of the regular school calendar.) The Report Card Committee examined data provided by the principal, including exercises in averaging and dialogue about the meaning of "assessment" in our new world of standards-based teaching and learning. It was apparent that teachers were assessing students differently in their classrooms but were recording grades on the basis of old practices. Parents were concerned about GPA, rank in class, and having the report card look like something they could understand. What was needed was something that worked for parents, but was better for students and more representative of what was happening in classrooms. Everyone recognized the silliness of having a new struggling freshman earn a 70 in the fall, work hard, earn a 95 by winter, then end up with something in the middle that was supposed to represent learning. Many kids were being held hostage by early struggles. Others would slack off at the end of the year because their third-quarter "average" would carry them. Instead of beating ourselves up to figure out how to keep kids on task in May, we needed to change the system and change our classrooms!

The Report Card Committee came up with a plan that was adopted easily by the school board and a bit more hesitantly by the teachers. However, it has persisted for a decade. Here is the model, which has had a significant impact on the culture of the school:

School Profile 1:
Noble High School

> Grades are awarded on an A, B, C, Novice, No Credit system. The first four are aligned with the standards of the Maine Learning Results and standards set forth by the common course teachers, and are printed in the program of studies for all to understand from the outset. Grades are awarded at the end of each semester only. There is no averaging. Teachers send home several narrative reports during the semester, engage in student-led conferences with parents, and have a host of other activities to keep parents up to speed on student progress. The mantra became "it is more important where you end up, than where you began." This is complicated in our world of wanting to keep every child accountable for every moment in school. The simple structure that Noble implemented keeps kids engaged in learning over the course of the year. It provides teachers and kids the freedom and flexibility to teach and learn without worrying about summative assessments every nine weeks.
>
> Semester grades are not "averaged" and credit is awarded when the grade is earned (1/2 credit per semester). If a student does not meet the standards in a semester and thus loses "credit"—an idea fast fading in Maine and no longer required for graduation by 2007—there are multiple opportunities to demonstrate that the standard has been met. Because of the teaming structure, students are not removed from a course, or "put back" to repeat a course later with a younger group of students. During the semester, students are given additional opportunities to meet the goal should they persist in falling short.

The change in grading system is a snapshot of how a few simple ideas can change the culture of a school. The common idea that students should "repeat" freshman English if the course average is below a specific number or grade has never worked. It is demeaning; the course never takes into account the needs of the struggling learner. Additionally, this causes discipline issues, poor role-modeling for younger students, and is frustrating to teachers. This snapshot is also an example of how professional learning communities develop confidence in faculty to engage parents and community in the challenging issues of equity.

Today Noble High School lives in a new facility consisting of 15 small learning communities (SLCs). Designed by a teacher-led Future Planning Team, and having the advantage of a philosophy for teaching and learning firmly in place, the school space liberates teachers to maximize the potential of SLCs. The school teams are aligned as three "vertical learning communities," becoming small schools with some looping of grade-level teams.

Students have the opportunity to be part of small teams and communities, and they have the advantage, in very rural areas, of participating in a vast array of opportunities in the arts, athletics, and AP programs. The onsite health center and other services address a huge need and are able to be provided because of an economy of scale. Noble is a relatively large school of 1,200 students learning to be small in a variety of ways. The effectiveness of personalized environments and curriculum are a product of and contributor to equity in design. There is no such place as a personalized, tracked school.

The building was designed to be led by a leadership team, as opposed to one principal. Each principal of the school must struggle with carving out his or her role in a very challenging and energizing environment. What is autonomous among the communities and teams? What must be the same? A large school with a strong common vision, designed as small autonomous environment, can be very successful. The key is common grounding in core principles and beliefs for all students.

Lessons Learned by School Leaders and Teachers Involved in Whole-School Change

As the school principal charged with helping to lead whole-school change, there are many lessons learned. Large, existing public schools can change. Most teachers are wonderful people who truly want the very best for all students. Leaders need to believe in their capacity to change, to mobilize commitment guided by clarity of common vision. To change our existing public schools, to ensure that they are equitable, democratic, inspiring learning communities for all students and teachers, there are some essential elements and practices that must be in place:

1. Essential to planning for whole-school change is establishing a culture safe for experimentation, one that celebrates the talents of all teachers, and one that agrees upon and can articulate a common vision and mission.

2. For the core beliefs of the school to be anchored in improving students and practice for students (not focused on the needs and wants of the teachers), schools leaders must guide the professional development. This may be as simple as reading common articles or texts weekly, or hosting forums and seminars to engage parents and teachers in common dialogue.

3. Faculty will gravitate more easily to changes that tinker—such as interpreting personalization by adding an advisory program—as opposed to personalization of pedagogy in the classroom. Putting the student at the center of changes in classroom practices, including curriculum, instructions, and assessments, is the starting point.

4. Changing structures can change beliefs. Many teachers will not believe that heterogeneous grouping will work until they get involved. Once involved with teams, teachers never look back to departmental structures; teachers value the opportunity to create unique learning structures and to celebrate their individual talents.

5. We need to provide for teachers the same benefits that we want for our students: equity of opportunity to learn and to work in an environment that ensures success. Any practices that tilt the hat to favoritism for veterans, or put new teachers in untenable situations, is discriminatory and professionally unsound. Every teacher, new or old, veteran or "green," needs to be able to participate in the gov-

ernance and leadership of the school, contribute to key decisions about the school, and share in the development of curriculum.

6. Every student deserves to be taught by a person who is passionate about the content. Although integrated teams may provide a rich diversity of integrated learning experiences, students deserve to be taught to write by teachers who are passionate and skilled in writing, and taught mathematics and science by those skilled in the concepts and principles of these disciplines. Integrated learning communities need not dissolve the integrity of disciplines, but when taught by the highest qualified teachers, allow for an even richer, more rigorous experience and expectations for all learners.

7. Teachers may be skeptical of collaborative teams and SLC environments for a number of reasons. For some, it is the first time they have had to share their practice. There is fear of making mistakes. Perhaps there is fear of accountability for student achievement, or fear of lacking the skills to teach in a heterogeneous environment. Teachers need to be supported in both the good times and the bad. Teaching all kids to a rigorous standard is never easy. Noble teachers have published the past techniques for working with heterogeneous groups. It is *not* about teaching to the middle!

8. It is important to be clear about models for change. Teams have been targeted as being squishy and too much like the "touchy-feely" middle school model. Or, classrooms are looking too much like elementary schools. The mission of the school is to attend to the diverse learning needs and styles of young adolescents. Making best use of technology, an array of models beyond school walls, and many other learning options are needed to enrich the resources of the local school. This includes anchoring the student in a SLC that knows him or her well, taking charge of the learning plan, and shepherding the student toward success.

9. The more teachers have an opportunity to articulate the vision, the more it becomes part of the life and breath of the school, and the better the vision sticks. It's part of the nature of leaders to protect the faculty from local controversy (their job is to take care of the students in the classroom). Just as the role of principals change, teachers need to be included in public advocacy and be able to lead parent groups and speak at community events regarding the practices of the school. Change happened at Noble in large part because a trusted veteran spoke perfectly at school board meetings, facilitated groups for anxious parents, and spoke at the local civic clubs. Teachers are the best folks to assure parents and students that they do not turn into poor teachers overnight by trying out a new idea!

10. There is no place for a poor or uncommitted teacher to hide in a small team or learning community. In a traditional structure, a poor teacher in a department may be given the "low groups" where they do the least damage.

11. To build programs and curricula for all learners, the school has to be equitable by design. There are not a lot of bells and whistles in the program of studies because of the commitment to a core program for all learners. The key to the success of the school is the support structures and range of opportunities students have to demonstrate knowledge.

12. There are structures in our schools that are absolutely guaranteed to impede change and limit students: persistence in tracking students, department-head structures,

traditional grading practices, school schedules of short learning periods, and teachers working in isolation.

13. Finally, if the principal is not passionate about equity for all kids, is not passionate about practices that ensure equity, and cannot lead the learning and mobilization of the faculty, change will not occur.

14. Leaders must be humble, trust that all teachers want the best for students, take little credit, and assume responsibility.

After 13 years of implementation, continuous rethinking, and tweaking, is this school a perfect place? Of course not. It learns more every day and asks better questions. The changes in structures and practices at Noble described here have not detailed the school's connections with the community, the opportunities for students to explore learning and work beyond the school, or partnerships with other organizations. The journey of change at Noble has positioned the school to do all of these things well for all students. The challenge addressed in 1990 was one of equity. The school did not embark on change by trying to invent clusters of career pathways that may be based on a group of adults' ideas about which kids may be interbred in learning. The conscious decision was to design a school that would provide the greatest social capital to all students: a strong core program of essential skills and knowledge. It is true that one size does not fit all, but the starting point here is that all kids can acquire rigorous academic skills and concepts. How these are applied in objects, exhibitions, and real-world experiences may be personalized to every learner. This is a delicate work of choreography, challenging every day.

Pamela Fisher was the principal of Noble High School from 1990 to 1997. She left the principalship to work on the drafting of Promising Futures, *Maine's guide for improving learning for all Maine students. She cochaired the commission that produced the guide. In her own words, "Noble has broken ranks to ensure a Promising Future for all students." Upon leaving Noble, she was succeeded by a teacher team, though now, a principal again fulfills the role. She currently is director of the Great Maine Schools Project at the Mitchell Institute. Fisher credits CES, state funding, the federal Comprehensive School Reform Demonstration, and SLC programs for supporting the teacher successes at Noble. It is a testament to the sustainability of the changes implemented that a half-dozen years after she left the Noble principalship, the changes remain.*

Addendum: Conversation with the Author

Q: *How did your role as principal evolve in light of the changes you made?*

A: When I first went to Noble, I wanted to learn as much as I could about the faculty, identify who would be eager to take on new challenges, and to understand what they expected from me. My style of leadership is highly collaborative, and so, it was challenging for me, in the first few months, to be a bit more aggressive: sharing my vision, challenging inequitable practices, and setting a "kids come first" tone. I felt that, in the first year, I was working hard to help others learn to lead. Very quickly, a group of highly creative and talented faculty became the leadership team for the school. Once the new strategies and structures were in place, my role gradually shifted to ensuring that the teams were consistent regarding curriculum and the expected state Learning Results. It was like conducting a symphony. I was orchestrating the teams so that everything worked smoothly, and I had much more time to be in classrooms and to make sure team meetings were productive. Each section of the orchestra had diverse talent and experience, and its own ideas of how the "music" should be interpreted. I highly valued the creativity of the teams (and, basically, thrive on chaos!) but had to be sure that all the teams worked well in concert. Over time the teams became more and more independent, and so, I had to be sure parents could be confident that the overall curriculum goals were the same on each different grade-level team.

Overall, I advised, I lobbied, I provided research, etc., to make sure we stayed the course, but the school, after three years, became pretty much teacher-led. I always asked hard questions, asked for evidence, and let teachers know what decisions I felt had to stay with me. For example, I always involved a team in selecting a new teacher, but I told everyone that new hires were my responsibility—and my cross to bear if a mistake were made. I think it is critical to let teachers know what decisions rest with the principal, what decisions involve input, and what decisions are totally up to the faculty. Over time, we grew clear on this.

I used my position of authority to boost expectations for learning and to maintain strong forward motion regarding the grouping practices. I feel that this is where the principal always has to push so that teachers never "teach to the middle."

School Profile 1:
Noble High School

The administration—my two assistants and I—and the guidance director always made sure that each team meeting was attended by one of us. We divided up our work to focus on specific groups. This prevented meetings from focusing on specific problem kids all the time.

Q: *How have you used* **Breaking Ranks***?*

A: I used the recommendation and supporting material in Chapter 5 that discusses tracking and ability grouping on countless occasions for text-based discussion.

Q: *You mentioned that, in order to make parents comfortable with heterogeneous grouping, Noble invited parents into any and all classrooms. What was your experience?*

A: The parents who showed up to observe classes were few—but the ones most opposed to the idea. However, they did come away convinced that we weren't trying to hide anything from them, that we wanted their input, and that they could trust our efforts. It was about trust and fear of change. The students had come from a tracked junior high and the parents of the privileged felt they were losing something.

Q: *Do you have a specific example of how raising the bar was greeted by teachers?*

A: We did an experiment with the AP biology teacher. He agreed to accept a group of would-be "general bio" students into his "college prep" class. He was amazed at how well these kids performed when the bar was set higher. He eventually left the school because he did not want to teach on a team. It was too bad, because, although he didn't like to mix the kids, he was fabulous at getting every kid to learn to a high standard.

Q: *You mention that success often hinged on veteran teachers taking the lead. Can you provide an example?*

A: One excellent example of junior/senior teachers taking the lead is in science. I will never forget the day that a chemistry teacher, at a meeting, said, "We need to do this for all kids. We have to believe that all kids can learn chemistry." She was instrumental in untracking the entire junior class. She had been the former department head and was quite hurt at the loss of the department-head positions early on. But her integrity and her ability to put kids first came through. She was instrumental in convincing other teachers to go along with the change because of her position in the school. She, the former math department head, and the physics teacher were the ones who met with the school board to convince them to change the graduation requirements. A few years ago, the now three full-time physics teachers published an article entitled "Physics for Everybody." These folks are key opinion leaders in the school and very important in helping the community embrace change. I asked the veteran physics teacher to speak at public meetings in all three towns to help convince the public to build a new school that would match the vision we all embraced for teaching and learning. The strategy worked. I am convinced that teachers are the ones who can best convince parents to accept changes in practice. Parents trust teachers—especially ones they had in school.

Q: *How did you use data to open up communication with parents and the community?*

A: It is important to be brutally honest, but to have the teachers with you regarding the data. Share it and discuss it with them first. Have a "data day." I always started the year with data.

Q: *What student support strategies did not work for your school?*

A: The strategy of letting Incompletes go on for eons. If students did not pass a term paper, for example, they would earn an Incomplete because the paper was a course requirement. It was decided not to grant a grade until all the work was done and all standards met. The problem was managing Incompletes going on into summer school.

Q: *How did Noble make teaming effective?*

A: Effective teaming strategies were taught by professionals from Pratt & Whitney Corp., Hussey Seating, and GE, all local businesses. This was the first step to teaming as it relates to the real world. Effective teaming professional development included strategies for using planning time well, designing integrated curricula, and understanding adult development and learning styles. We required teams to have a written agenda and keep a notebook of their meetings. Some teams began sessions with a text-based discussion. It takes about three years for a team to become top-notch. Teams need training in how to deal with personality issues.

Q: *Why did you institute what you call a "unique lunch program"?*

A: Students and teachers got together to figure out a lunch schedule that would allow kids to be with friends on different teams. We settled on a 40-minute lunch, with all the kids eating at the same time. Kids met with the lunch staff, who decided the food would be better if it were not reheated five times! Kids were able to buy lunch in several places set up throughout the building. In the old building there was no carpeting, so kids could eat anywhere except the obvious— library, computer labs., etc.

Teacher teams made up a duty schedule so that teams could eat together. We opened the gym, art studios, etc., for kids to use during the lunch block. It worked really well. In the new building, there are two lunch blocks. The concept was to give kids time to be with friends, see teachers, or work out in the gym.

Q: *What do you mean when you say "putting students at the center" of your changes?*

A: Putting students at the center means one has to focus on the work that students do—their products—rather than on the performance of teachers. That means that we look at student work together at faculty meetings. We use protocols such as the Tuning Protocol or the Collaborative Assessment Protocol to look at student work. This became part of the culture of many teams. Teachers "tuned" their units with each other and students learned to use the protocol for prepping for exhibitions.

Q: *How did you, as principal, create an environment in which teachers and students were willing to take risks, to do things they had never done before?*

A: I made lots of mistakes—and admitted them openly. This builds a safe environment for experimentation. I stood by teachers when they made errors when testing out a new idea or project. I also supported teachers' efforts by making sure they received lots of credit and recognition for their work. I spent a year convincing teachers to try new ideas. In the past, teachers were fearful of making mistakes or taking on new roles before their peers. They learned, over time, that I was not the type of principal who was going to criticize anyone for failure when trying out a new idea. We celebrated failures at faculty meetings! I remember a group of teachers bringing in their "projects from hell" to talk about what went right and where they went wrong. I had to lobby to get folks to do this sort of thing, but it got us into the habit of sharing and looking at student work together. The environment changed—it shifted from teachers worrying about how they performed to worrying about how the students performed!

I also think I helped them gain confidence by having teacher groups regularly speak at board meetings and other community meetings. I really believe that teachers are willing to try out all sorts of innovative practices, to experiment, if they know they are appreciated and supported. The key piece is that the focus is on the students—making the world of school better for kids first. Ultimately, the teachers designed a new school that feels like it belongs to the students— which it should.

Breaking Ranks II Recommendations Related to Collaborative Leadership and Professional Learning Communities

At the end of this chapter and in Chapters 3 and 4, individual Breaking Ranks II *recommendations are listed along with very brief summaries of the benefits, strategies, and challenges of each. For information on schools pursuing some of these recommendations, see the "Strategies and Recommendations in Practice" section at the end of this handbook.*

> Recommendations Related to
> Collaborative Leadership and
> Professional Learning Communities

RECOMMENDATION 1: The principal will provide leadership in the high school community by building and maintaining a vision, direction, and focus for student learning.

BENEFITS

- Ensures a comprehensive approach to reform and pedagogy.

STRATEGIES

- Use surveys, mapping, student questionnaires, parent surveys, and community forums.
- The principal needs to create and work with a site-based leadership team.
- Identify a mentor [principal] who has done this before and learn from him or her.
- Become an active member of professional organizations that will support you and expose you to like-minded people and to resources to accomplish your goals.
- Understand what the district or state (authorizers) require (also parents, students, unions, etc.) so that you can understand what your mandate is. Understand the mandate in order to encourage school support in engaging in the transformation.

CHALLENGES

- Providing leadership, or there won't be a vision, direction, or focus on student learning.
- Finding mentors and connecting with them.
- Acting on what you, the principal, are told by staff and others via surveys, etc.

RECOMMENDATION 2: Each high school will establish a site council and accord other meaningful roles in decision making to students, parents, and members of the staff in order to promote student learning and an atmosphere of participation, responsibility, and ownership.

BENEFITS

- Creates a feeling of shared purpose that will allow for cooperative work.

STRATEGIES

- Ask for volunteers, conduct elections.
- Include students, parents, community members.
- Ensure that the council/team is all-inclusive, diverse, and a place where everyone is comfortable and willing to participate.
- Establish a separate site council for parents or students; each will send representatives to the larger site council.
- Provide a written mandate for the site council with ground rules and power and accountability.
- Provide training on conducting meetings.
- Create mechanisms for establishment of the team(s) and bylaws or other guidelines.
- Give teams the power to make decisions, not just make recommendations, within parameters agreed upon between principal and team.

CHALLENGES

- Creating a school that is supportive of the concept so that it will be accepted and recommendations of the council will be implemented schoolwide (investigate models that allow for this culture change).
- Allocating money and time for training and professional development.
- Without power to make decisions, a team can flounder.
- Requiring clarification and revision of existing authority and accountability structures.
- Finding convenient times to meet with members of the community.

RECOMMENDATION 3: A high school will regard itself as a community in which members of the staff collaborate to develop and implement the school's learning goals.

BENEFITS

- Ensures sustainability and legacy.

STRATEGIES

- Create an action planning team for reform.
- Create and implement interdisciplinary teams of both teachers and students.
- Ensure that everyone has a voice—student surveys, focus groups, morning meetings.
- Be sure everyone understands the need for redesigning the time spent at the school (allow time for meetings and conversations).
- Get teachers together at least one hour a week.
- Use protocols to facilitate discussions.

CHALLENGES

- Defining community: getting true representation from the school and outside community.
- Finding common time to meet.
- Making people understand that they have to give up something in order to create change.
- Establishing common understanding.

RECOMMENDATION 4: Teachers will provide the leadership essential to the success of reform, collaborating with others in the educational community to redefine the role of the teacher and to identify sources of support for that redefined role.

BENEFITS

- Empowers teachers and fosters ownership of the reform effort.

STRATEGIES

- Change expectations of teachers in order to support new leadership roles for teachers in the form of advisers or time spent with students.
- Reduce workload (number of students, number of classes taught, etc.) to allow for the time to do this.
- Relieve duty assignment in order to do this (can be done by students—e.g., giving students hall monitor duties).
- Fund teacher buyout in order to allow time for new leadership roles.
- Provide for professional development and leadership training.
- Counsel out teachers who don't want to work in a new way.
- Allow sufficient common planning time (weekly or more often) in order to set and accomplish goals.
- Move beyond the department-head concept in order to cultivate leadership in teams.

CHALLENGES

- Current contract language might preclude this—possible resistance from the union.
- Allocating resources, time, or schedule.
- Existing accountability and departmental or department-head structures.
- Getting teachers to see themselves in a new way and step up to take on new roles.

Recommendations Related to Collaborative Leadership and Professional Learning Communities

RECOMMENDATION 5: Every school will be a learning community for the entire community. As such, the school will promote the use of Personal Learning Plans for each educator and provide the resources to ensure that the principal, teachers, and other staff members can address their own learning and professional development needs as they relate to improved student learning.

BENEFITS

- Allows for the strategic alignment of professional development with action plan goals. Alignment may free up resources for other development.
- Changes perceptions of the role of educators.
- Facilitates acceptance of change.

STRATEGIES

- Critical Friends Groups.
- Align Personal Learning Plan with school goals.

CHALLENGES

- Resources.
- Time.
- Finding appropriate models.

RECOMMENDATION 6: The school community will promote policies and practices that recognize diversity in accord with the core values of a democratic and civil society and will offer substantive, ongoing professional development to help educators appreciate issues of diversity and expose students to a rich array of viewpoints, perspectives, and experiences.

BENEFITS	STRATEGIES	CHALLENGES
■ Promotes safer schools.	■ Celebrate achievement in multiple realms.	■ Personal racism or cultural norms of members of the school community.
■ Models democracy in action.	■ Differentiate instruction.	■ Inappropriate curriculum (textbooks).
	■ Recruit and hire a diverse staff.	■ Community outside of the school.
	■ Recognize, honor, and celebrate cultural diversity.	■ Uniform testing.
	■ Change to a multicultural curriculum.	■ District mandates.
	■ Allow Personal Learning Plans and student-led conferences to showcase individual strengths.	■ Bullying.
		■ Defining diversity (is it racial, socioeconomic, sexual preferences, religious, etc.?).
	■ Help school community to understand that diversity goes beyond race—the school needs to understand "otherness."	■ Finding resources for appropriate professional development.

RECOMMENDATION 7: High schools will build partnerships with institutions of higher education to provide teachers and administrators at both levels with ideas and opportunities to enhance the education, performance, and evaluation of educators.

BENEFITS	STRATEGIES	CHALLENGES
■ Encourages higher expectations for all.	■ Develop teacher training programs with an institute of higher education on the high school campus.	■ Financial resources required to ensure access for all.
■ Allows opportunities for research.	■ Provide professional development and training opportunities for teachers.	■ Willingness of teachers to participate.
	■ Provide teacher externships.	■ Carnegie unit—the college credit doesn't have the seat time of a Carnegie unit; trouble transferring credits.
	■ Develop school-based masters programs in school improvement.	■ Budgeting for college tuitions—scholarships are needed.
	■ Allow dual enrollment of students in high school and college or community college classes.	■ Reallocation of resources to achieve the goals (time, money, etc.).
	■ Provide school-based summer institutes on school improvement for action planning and design teams.	■ Union negotiation issue.

RECOMMENDATION 8: High schools will develop political and financial relationships with individuals, organizations, and businesses to support and supplement educational programs and policies.

BENEFITS

- Offers additional resources.
- Increases support from the community.
- Supports accountability.
- Allows for possible reallocation of resources.

STRATEGIES

- Principal and leadership team should join the Rotary, Chamber of Commerce, CBNO, VFW, AARP, Seniors, etc., and use connections to support changes being undertaken in school.
- Establish network or form partnerships to provide students with places for internships, funding, etc.
- Establish a community advisory board to focus on school issues.
- Establish a clear public relations strategy and make sure that school leaders are articulating it uniformly.
- Encourage project-based collaboration.
- Develop a volunteer and mentor corps (use connections with retired persons, etc.).

CHALLENGES

- Recognizing that commercialization of the school is a danger.
- Ensuring that the strategy is focused on all students.
- Recognizing that professional development is vital.
- Developing and articulating public relations strategies.

Recommendations Related to Collaborative Leadership and Professional Learning Communities

RECOMMENDATION 9: At least once every five years, each high school will convene a broadly based external panel to offer a public description of the school, a requirement that could be met in conjunction with the evaluations by state, regional, and other accrediting groups.

BENEFITS

- Promotes accountability to the public.
- May increase support from the community.
- Promotes the review of disaggregated data.
- Aligns with accreditation.
- Allows the school to report the results— rather than having them reported for you (i.e., get ahead of the story).

STRATEGIES

- Engage in a "data day" for the community or the staff.
- Align description with accreditation report.
- Encourage automatic reporting of results.

CHALLENGES

- Negative data will require immediate action.

3 Personalizing Your School Environment

On any given day, I think every adolescent is at-risk in some way. How many schools approach such concerns with purposeful, planned and progressive awareness-building, educational, and intervention strategies in place as opposed to trying to deny these realities or being caught in a reactive, crisis-oriented position?

—Marnik (1997) as cited in Promising Futures
(Maine Commission on Secondary Education, 1998, p. 37)

What Do We Mean by Personalization?

If high achievement for all students is the goal of reform, then personalization and a rigorous curriculum are two essential ingredients. Although some students might be able to make it through four years of high school despite the lack of any personal connections, all students require a supportive environment—some more than others. Creating that environment is essential to bringing learning to fruition. In keeping with the sentiment implicit in the word, personalization can mean different things to different people, but most definitions converge on a few common principles associated with providing students with opportunities to develop a sense of belonging to the school, a sense of ownership over the direction of one's learning, the ability to recognize options and to make choices based on one's own experience and understanding of the options. The following provides a working definition linked to the *Breaking Ranks* call for a more student-centered, personalized experience in high schools:

> Personalization: A learning process in which schools help students assess their own talents and aspirations, plan a pathway toward their own purposes, work cooperatively with others on challenging tasks, maintain a record of their explorations, and demonstrate their learning against clear standards in a wide variety of media, all with the close support of adult mentors and guides. (Clarke, 2003, p. 15)

This chapter and its accompanying recommendations will focus on one facet of personalization: Implementing structural and behavioral models to strengthen *relationships among people*—students, teachers, staff members, families, and the larger community. Chapter 4 addresses another facet of personalization: the *relationships between students and ideas*—how the student interacts and directs his or her own learning with the oversight, coaching, and motivational strategies associated with student-centered curriculum, instruction, and assessment. Significant overlap clearly exists between these two facets, providing further evidence of the need to review the *Breaking Ranks* recommendations in their entirety—not as isolated pockets of "good ideas."

Practices Associated with Personalization and People

Many of the practices associated with personalization set the stage for learning. They are practices that address the school environment, climate, and culture, such as:

- Creating structures so that students cannot remain anonymous for four years

- Establishing schedules and priorities that allow teachers to develop an appreciation for each student's abilities

- Creating structures in which the aspirations, strengths, weaknesses, interests, and level of progress of each student are known well by at least one adult

- Providing opportunities for students to learn about the values associated with life in a civil and democratic society, their responsibilities within that society, and the ability to exercise those values within the school

- Offering parents, families, and community members opportunities for involvement in students' education

- Ensuring that the physical and mental health needs of students are addressed

- Providing students with opportunities to demonstrate their academic, athletic, musical, dramatic, and other accomplishments in a variety of ways.

Implementing these structural changes provides the "shell" in which productive interaction—relationships—can occur systematically.

Why Build Relationships?

The presumed need to build relationships rests on the premise that many students require a supportive relationship with the school or with someone at the school who understands them personally. Critics may counter that schools are in the business of conveying knowledge, not catering to the personal needs of students. To help principals, teachers, and families understand why personalization is important and to prepare them for potential discussions surrounding the broader issues of personalization, a Question and Answer forum is presented below.

Q: *Why do we need to go to the trouble of "personalizing" our school? We have one of the best graduation rates in the state and our test scores are consistently high.*

A: Yes, we are very pleased with both our graduation rate and test scores. However, even though in comparison to most schools our graduation rate is almost unheard of, still 3% of our students didn't graduate last year. For our school of 1,000, that means a lost opportunity for 30 students—statistically speaking, those 30 students have to look forward to higher unemployment, lower compensation, and possibly jail time. Could we have reached these students? Maybe. Should we try? I believe we should. Furthermore, we have heard reports that a significant number of our graduates have had to take remedial courses in their first year of college. They should not have to take courses to learn what they should have learned here. As for test scores, our averages are good, but our team believes the scores could be much better if we can get more students excited about learning. Finally, and most wrenching and "personal" of all, I think we all remember the suicide of one of our juniors last year. Could we have referred this young lady for professional help before she became despondent? We'll never know because no one knew her well enough to even see the danger signs.

Q: *It sounds like you want schools to fill the role of social services.*

A: No. Schools cannot be all things to all people; however, we can do better. We have to remember the consequences of indifference to the personal needs and aspirations of students. Remember the effect that suicide had? Not only was her family devastated, but so too were many of the parents and students in our school community. Emotionally and academically, everything was put on hold for more than a week. That's an extreme example, but similar tragedies happen more often than we'd like. Let's not forget the less cataclysmic events, the behavioral and discipline issues associated with students not engaged—those clearly affect all students. Every student will be better off if we can reach each student.

Q: *Will establishing these relationships lead to higher achievement?*

A: Yes. First we have to get all students to school. Research shows that personalized learning initiatives can increase attendance, decrease dropout rates, and decrease disruptive behavior. Next, we must engage them—know their interests and how each student learns. Teens are developing academically, socially, emotionally, and physically while they are here. Students will tune in or tune out based on how we engage them in each of those areas. These are not independent "silos" that can be filled when we see fit. Learning is not the highest of priorities when a student's parent loses a job, has health problems, or there are stresses related to divorce, or when a student is homeless, or a student doesn't get invited to a dance or party, or a student did not make the cut for the band, the play, or the soccer team. While differing in their level of importance to you or me, each of these is, at any given moment, potentially much more important to a student than learning. Our challenge is to ensure that the issue is appropriately confronted so that learning can again become a priority. A quick look at the potential items that interfere with learning leads me to guess that, on any given day, one-quarter of all students are somehow distracted from learning. In our school of 1,000, that's 250 students.

Q: *So you have the students at school and you're attempting to address these issues. What is the tie to learning?*

A: There are many different "developmental assets" that determine the way different students engage learning. Among them are:

- Family support
- Parent involvement in school

- Positive peer influence
- Time at home
- Bonding to school
- Personal power
- Sense of purpose (Scales and Leffert [1999], as cited in Clarke, 2003, p. 9)

Our job is to make sure we find the right entrée to get them personally engaged, and we believe that the *Breaking Ranks* strategies can accomplish that. Once we find that entrée, we are on our way to getting them interested and engaged in learning—and wanting to learn more.

Addressing Student Needs

In an effort to understand the events and interactions that engage students during a typical school day, teams of researchers from the Education Alliance at Brown University shadowed students at seven high schools. They discovered six developmental needs that students have (Clarke & Frazer, 2003):

- **Voice**—the need to express their personal perspective
- **Belonging**—the need to create individual and group identities
- **Choice**—the need to examine options and choose a path
- **Freedom**—the need to take risks and assess effects
- **Imagination**—the need to create a projected view of self
- **Success**—the need to demonstrate mastery

How a school addresses each of these student needs will determine the outcomes of its personalization efforts. In the diagram in Figure 3.1, the students' personal needs are on the left, the school practices are on the right, and in the middle are the resulting benefits—presuming that the school's practices meet the student needs.

Your school's practices may not be meeting student developmental needs if you see no signs of these relationships. In *Changing Systems to Personalize Learning* (Clarke, 2003), these relationships are discussed in detail:

Recognition: Personalized learning allows each student to earn recognition—largely from peers but also from teachers, parents, and school leaders. Earning recognition can happen only if each student has many chances in a school day to voice a personal perspective and assert a unique identity. Schools that personalize learning by expanding opportunities for recognition have to develop equitable processes that let many voices be heard and many kinds of success be celebrated. While most high schools prevent inequity by setting uniform expectations, those same practices prevent the majority of students from being recognized for their unique talents. For example, the honor roll, class rank, football lineup, student government, and arts prize allocate recognition only to the few students ranked as the best in predetermined categories. The rest may receive very little recognition during a school day, often lapsing into passive disengagement that barely disguises their disappointment. In at least one of the shadowing study schools, none of the shadowed students received recognition or became engaged during a six-hour day. *Personalized learning depends on earning recognition under expectations designed to allow all to succeed.*

Figure 3.1 Interactions in Personalized Learning

Personal Needs	Relationships	School Practices
Voice The need to express personal perspective	**RECOGNITION**	**Equity** Democratic processes for deliberation
Belonging The need to create individual and group identities	**ACCEPTANCE**	**Community** Shared commitment to all students
Choice The need to examine options and choose a path	**TRUST**	**Opportunity** Range of options for individual development
Freedom The need to take risks and assess effects	**RESPECT**	**Responsibility** Experimentation with adult roles
Imagination The need to create a projected views of self	**PURPOSE**	**Challenge** Tasks that mirror adult roles
Success The need to demonstrate mastery	**CONFIRMATION**	**Expectations** Clear standards for performance

Developmental Needs, Talents, and Aspirations

Flexible Options for Engaged Learning

Personal Learning: Using information from the school experience to direct one's own life and to improve the life of the community

Source: Clarke & Frazer (2003). Reprinted with permission.

Acceptance: The shadowed students all exhibited delight when their learning became a vehicle for gaining wide acceptance in their school. The need of young adults to belong to a group where they can establish a personal identity has been well described. In the shadowing study, wide acceptance depended on the school's commitment to accepting all students, for whatever talents, ideas, or perspectives they bring to bear on community issues. Comprehensive high schools, however, are often enormous institutions that cannot even fit the whole community into the school gym. For many high school students, gaining acceptance within a group can be achieved only with a small group of four to five friends, who then form a self-protective compact or clique in the halls and cafeteria. Some cliques develop a tentative sense of belonging and earn small-scale acceptance by rebelling against the larger community—through drugs, violence, and habitual truancy. *Personalized learning depends on being able to gain acceptance within the whole school community for productive and distinctive achievements.*

Trust: The shadowed students wanted to be trusted to plan and carry out daily activities and direct their own learning. They wanted to exercise choice, examine their available options, and set their own path on a daily basis. Most high schools limit choice to long-term questions, for example, whether to enroll in physics or not, whether to switch to vocational courses, or whether to write for the newspaper. In highly personalized schools, mutual trust between students and educators was visible hourly—in classes, hallways, and neighborhoods, where individual students were exploring specific tasks from a wide range of options and reporting the results of their inquiry to their teachers and peers. In many comprehensive high schools, the tradition of *in loco parentis,* bolstered by legal requirements for custodial supervision, has replaced trust with specific rules for both faculty and students. Those rules may restrict the growth of trust. *Personalized learning depends on maintaining a wide range of opportunities for students to manage their own learning and direct their own lives.*

Respect: The engaged students in the shadowing study wanted freedom to take some risks on behalf of their aspirations, and the opportunity to earn respect from their peers and from adults in the school. Disrespect in any form incited anger or withdrawal. High school tends to grant at least minimal respect, not for freely designed activities, but for compliance with existing rules and expectations. The student who says little in class but completes homework assignments regularly and prepares well for tests and quizzes earns the gratitude of teachers and administrators—and a modicum of respect. Students who press with questions, push their own perspective, act out in defiance of authority, and ignore rules of behavior earn disrespect. *Personalized learning allows students to earn respect from teachers and peers by asking their own questions and pursuing their own answers, even against the tide of opinion.*

Purpose: The engaged students in the shadowing study were confident that high school offered a clear way for them to fulfill their own purposes by adhering to the school's declared purpose. They could use their daily work in classes, school activities, and community learning experiences to imagine themselves leading successful adult lives. In a subject-based curriculum, knowledge of facts and ideas is often represented without adult applications and without reference to the adult world where knowledge truly makes a difference. Unless it is connected to problems and opportunities in the community at large, high school classes seem irrelevant and boring. *Personalized learning provides students with challenges that mirror the tasks and challenges of adult life.*

Confirmation: The engaged students in the study used their daily work to confirm their sense of progress toward personal goals. They needed to see small instances of success in order to understand that they were moving toward their longer-term goals. Being able to demonstrate mastery of skills or knowledge, particularly when their efforts could support others working on similar challenges, increased their confidence and often opened new avenues for exploration. In the classrooms visited during the study, students could succeed by generating a unique response to a challenge, not by repeating the success of others. High school classes in which students all seek the same "right answer" prevent students from recognizing how they can use knowledge to make a difference in their lives and the lives of others. *Personalized learning celebrates the unique achievements of individuals against broad standards shared by the whole community.*

Addressing the developmental needs of students can be facilitated by schools that create small units through house, school-within-school, or advisory structures; decrease the total number of students for which a teacher has responsibility; implement Personal Plans for Progress for each student; provide a mentor and Personal Adult Advocate for each student; ensure that teachers and staff promote a sense of caring and concern for students; adopt flexible schedules; involve families; promote civic responsibility and core values; and help coordinate social services so that all students are prepared to learn.

How to Assess Your School's Level of Personalization

Defining the preceding relationships was done by shadowing students—perhaps a difficult task for an "insider" or school staff member. Systematic observation of these relationships will provide your school with excellent insight into how well your school is able to personalize the school for students. Another rubric by which to judge your school's progress toward personalization was developed by the Northwest Regional Education Lab (NWREL) in conjunction with its work in small learning circles (SLCs). (If you do not have SLCs, then read "SLC" in the following chart as "school.")

This rubric will not only allow you to gauge your current level of personalization, but can serve as a benchmark to illustrate progress as you strive to personalize your school.

Once you have assessed your school's level of personalization, you can address the weaknesses that your team has found. To help you do so, we offer an extended profile of a school attempting to address its own challenges in the area of personalization. Immediately following this profile, you will find relevant *Breaking Ranks* recommendations designed to build a culture and community dedicated to personalizing your school for the benefit of each student. Benefits, strategies, and challenges are provided for the recommendations.

Personalization

Key Element	Beginning SLC	Making Progress	Achieved
Connectedness	Students are not well known by their peers or their teachers within the SLC.	Students know the majority of their peers within their SLC; teachers know the names and abilities of all of their students.	Teachers and students know each other by name, and teachers are able to identify individual students' strengths and challenges.
Student involvement	No process is in place for students to play an active role within their SLCs.	Students may choose to play active roles within their SLCs and to participate in SLC functions.	Students select specific roles within their SLCs and play an active role in governance.
Student involvement	Students are assigned to SLCs on the basis of individual academic performance and abilities.	SLCs are organized in heterogeneous groupings wherein individual needs are recognized and addressed.	SLCs are organized in heterogeneous groupings; teachers receive professional development to learn how to meet multiple needs of students with multiple abilities.
Student involvement	Students are not involved in activities beyond the classroom.	A majority of students participate in extracurricular activities beyond the classroom.	All students take advantage of opportunities to participate in extracurricular and SLC activities.
Teacher Involvement	Teachers do not follow students for multiple years and possess limited knowledge of students' personal lives.	Teachers follow students for multiple years and have a process in place to know many students on a personal level.	Teachers follow students for multiple years and know students' personal strengths, challenges, and goals.
Teacher Involvement	Teachers' primary contact with students is within the confines of the classroom.	Teachers have regular opportunities to interact with students through other intentional or ad hoc conferencing, e.g., advisories.	Teachers collaborate regularly with their team members and individual students to ensure academic and personal achievement for students.
Parent and Community Involvement	Parents and community members do not participate in academic/instructional support, governance, or activities within the SLC.	Some parents and community members participate in academic/instructional support, governance, or activities within the SLC.	The majority of parents and some community members participate in academic/instructional support, governance, and activities within the SLC.

Source: Cotton (2004). Rubric developed by Northwest Regional Education Lab. To download and customize this rubric for your school, visit www.principals.org/breakingranks.

In Their Own Words...

This is the second of three profiles about school changes consistent with Breaking Ranks–*style reform. Each of the profiles has been written from the personal perspective of a member of the team responsible for implementation. The profiles are designed to show the comprehensive and interdependent nature of the reforms your school is being called upon to undertake. Although not all of the changes each school has instituted will be appropriate for your school, the perspective of your colleagues should nevertheless be valuable and may form the basis of a text-based discussion for your team.*

School Profile 2:
Wyandotte High School

An Urban High School Emerges from Chaos

by Mary Stewart

Wyandotte High School in Kansas City, KS, has a rich history as one of the oldest high schools west of the Mississippi. Its current building was a Works Project Administration project in the mid-1930s and now is on the National Register of Historic Places. In the 1960s and 1970s, the school was the pride of the area. Then, urban flight and changes in demographics sparked a dramatic decline. By the mid-1990s, safety and academic decline had district officials contemplating closing the school's doors.

In 1995, Wyandotte test scores were among the worst in the state of Kansas. Accreditation was in question. Even at their worst, other schools in the district could always guarantee that they were "at least better than Wyandotte." Safety was an issue. Fires were frequently set inside the building, students were often seen more in the halls than in the classrooms, and fights were frequent occurrences. In addition, the staff was beaten down. Teachers worked in isolation. As a survival tactic, good teachers would go into their classrooms, lock the doors, and try to block out the chaos enough to teach the students who showed up. By April and May, the number of students who attended classes was sometimes less than half of those who started the previous fall. The rest had just quit coming to class.

In 1996, instead of closing the school, the district wanted to make one last effort to turn this troubled school around. They began by bringing in a new principal and making a commitment to a framework of reform, "First Things First." The framework identifies seven critical features for school improvement based on developmental and educational

Profile
Wyandotte High School
Kansas City, KS
Urban
1,295 students
http://www.kckps .org/disthistory/ openbuildings/ wyandotte.html

Practices to look for include:
- *Creating small units*
- *Interdisciplinary teaming*
- *Teacher leadership*
- *Flexible scheduling*

research on children and youth, on current research on organizational change, and on current work in public schools:

For Students

1. Lower student/adult ratios by half during core instructional periods through redistribution of professional staff.

2. Provide continuity of care across the school day, across the school years, and between school and home by having the same group of 8–10 professional adults within each school level stay with the same group of no more than 10 students for extended periods of time during the school day for at least two years of high school.

3. Set high, clear, and fair academic and behavior standards that clearly define what all students will know and be able to do within and across key content areas by the time they leave high school and at points along the way in their school career. Standards of conduct should be agreed upon by adults and students, reinforced by adults modeling positive social behaviors and attitudes, and sustained by clear benefits for meeting and consequences for violating those standards.

4. Provide enriched and diverse opportunities: to learn, by making learning more authentic (active, cooperative, integrated, and real-world based); to perform, by using assessment strategies linked directly to standards that use multiple modes of learning and performance; to be recognized, by creating individual and collective incentives for student achievement and positive social behavior and leadership opportunities in academic and nonacademic areas.

For Adults

5. Ensure collective responsibility by providing collective incentives and consequences for teaching teams and schools based on improvement in student performance.

6. Provide instructional autonomy and support to these teams of teachers, such that they can develop instructional strategies that will best meet the individual and collective needs of their students.

7. Allow for flexible allocation of available resources by teams and schools, based on instructional and interpersonal needs of students. Resources include people (students and staff), instructional facilities (on and off campus), instructional planning and professional development time, and discretionary funds.

Though the research was important, making the features part of the reality of the school had to come from the people who worked there. Fortunately for the Wyandotte community, the principal assigned to the job, Walter J. Thompson, had a genuine belief in and respect for teachers. Teachers were given the autonomy and support to "create a school they wanted to send their own children to." Thompson, a former football quarterback and coach, knew how to quarterback his faculty and value his line of teachers enough to get out of their way and let them take the lead. He knew it was going to take a high-functioning team to turn things around.

Getting Everyone Involved

Planning for the implementation of the seven critical features at Wyandotte began with the 1997–1998 school year. A Stakeholder Team comprising 13 staff members began working together in August to build capacity around the seven critical features. The team facilitated a two-day roundtable experience for the entire Wyandotte staff in late October. After the roundtable, *all* staff members at Wyandotte began meeting weekly in small teams (randomly assigned with attention to having diversity in representation of subject areas, personalities, strengths of individuals) to discuss the options available to them. These sessions provided everyone an opportunity to comment on, question, and discuss the alternatives available. Two members of the Stakeholder Team cofacilitated each of the small team sessions after school. The stakeholders were charged with ensuring that all staff members stayed informed about the ideas, research, and alternatives being studied. The small teams provided a structure to promote good communication. Once the communication structure was in place for staff, communication links with the students, parents, and community were established, including significant one-to-one work with parents and interaction with a Student Stakeholder Team.

During the planning year, Wyandotte staff members were actively involved in work focused on reorganizing the way teaching and learning occurred in order to improve student achievement. The seven critical features guided the decision making. Decisions had to align with the philosophy of the critical features. Decisions about SLCs were made after asking a question such as: "What is meant by 'continuity of care' and 'collective responsibility,' and how do we 'get there'?"

Small Learning Communities

School Profile 2:
Wyandotte High School

By December 1997, the staff had decided that, beginning with the 1998–1999 school year, Wyandotte would be organized into self-contained SLCs, which were defined as "schools-within-a-school" taught by interdisciplinary teams of teachers serving approximately 200 students. Each SLC was to be set up around a common theme, and all members of the community would focus teaching and learning around that theme. SLC themes were developed based on the needs and interests of students. It was also decided that each SLC would include students from grades 9, 10, 11, and 12. The structure was set up to provide a close relationship among students, staff, families, and communities for the students' entire high school career. All individuals involved in the SLC (students, teachers, parents, community, etc.) were to be responsible for improved student performance. Teachers would be involved in ongoing staff development opportunities within their communities, focused on their SLC theme and on ways to address the individual needs of students.

By February 1998, the SLCs were staffed on the basis of a staffing survey analyzed by an outside consultant. In addition, the Staffing Committee interviewed and selected a lead teacher to serve as coordinator for each SLC. This was followed by students selecting their SLCs, and the beginning of the SLC staff development and team building.

During the summer of 1998, staff members were afforded the opportunity to be paid for 56 hours of time spent preparing for the implementation of the First Things First plan. Each SLC developed its own agenda around Reading, Problem Solving, Assessment, and Instruction. In addition, SLCs defined and developed their goals, expectations, and parental involvement component, and identified and analyzed their students' academic needs. The summer work by no means completed study in any area. It did, however, provide a foundation on which to build. Most important, it strengthened the development of a culture of studying and learning as a staff.

Excitement, Fear, Reservation

The beginning of the 1998–1999 school year brought with it a mixture of excitement, fear, and reservation about this new approach to high school. There were still many unanswered questions about this idea the staff had created. Many of the excuses with which students were comfortable had been taken away from them. No longer was it easy to skip classes and go unnoticed. Teachers were talking to each other. A student's various classes were held in close proximity to each other, eliminating opportunities for students to be "lost" or late. Teachers had the autonomy to make schedule changes and to handle students' scheduling concerns, thus eliminating both the long lines outside the counselor's office and one more excuse to get out of class. Consequently, this schoolwide change met with some student resistance.

Concerns were also raised by the staff when this new "program" was not in place and fixing things by the end of September. In some cases, there appeared to be even more chaos than before. Now that students were coming to class, many of the previously unknown problems and issues with which students were dealing were becoming apparent to the classroom teacher. Their responsibility was growing from teaching those who chose to come to class to being collectively responsible for all 150 students in their SLC. Furthermore, if one of the students didn't come to class, teachers were working together to figure out why. Some teachers had found a comfortable niche teaching upper-level classes to seniors and were now having to collaborate with other teachers and be collectively responsible for students outside the high-achieving group. As a result, staff members were also being faced with personal changes—and not everyone liked it. Providing staff members with support to manage the multiple transitions they were facing through this change process was an important focus. Continual dialogue, questioning, and collaboration were critical tools in this process.

An End to Chaos?

By December 1998, there was evidence of a shift in the chaos. In fact, on the last day of school before the winter holiday, students and teachers could still be found saying their goodbyes more than an hour after dismissal. No longer were the teachers beating the students out the door. The relationships developing between teachers and students were contagious—so much so that the staff identified relationships as "the one thing" needed as the foundation of their work.

As the 1998–1999 school year ended and the 1999–2000 school year got under way, the changes became deeper than surface level. Staff members became better and better at understanding that this school improvement process looked at change from an inquiry approach rather than from a "one size fits all" program approach. The work became an ongoing approach to changing a school culture for improved student performance. To support the development of staff, the local school board approved the reorganization of Wednesdays to allow for an early release of students. Two hours each Wednesday afternoon are spent in SLC study groups. With the thematic SLC approach, teachers within an SLC work together to connect the SLC theme to their content. The flexibility and empowerment of the SLC are essential to allowing the critical features to become real.

During the 1999–2000 school year, the structural changes were becoming stronger, and so, the staff increased its focus on teaching and learning. Teachers knew that the structural change was not enough to make the impact on student performance that they wanted. Teachers and administrators worked together at the district level to develop a Teaching and Learning Document that articulates a focus for all teachers and students. Through study of professional readings, dialogue, and collaboration, three key topics were chosen: classroom environment; instruction (to include active engagement, connectedness, and reflection); and professional learning community. Since its creation, the document has served as the target for instructional improvement at Wyandotte.

An Eye on Data

Keeping a focus on teaching and learning was coupled with keeping an eye on the data. Test scores, attendance rates, and other performance indicators were no longer presented just as a school report. Teachers began looking at data just for the students in their SLC. Since all teachers within an SLC are collectively responsible for their students, SLC data became very important to everyone. It was no longer somebody else's problem; it was everyone's concern.

One piece of data of particular concern was the reading performance of students. Though teachers knew that students in their classes struggled with reading, the urgency to do something about it hadn't surfaced. By 1999, once relationships among teachers and students had strengthened and data were isolated to the SLC level, the urgency arose. Teachers could no longer keep reading support away from the top of the priority list when it was so necessary for "their kids." By this time, the SLCs were like families.

True to the culture being established, teachers came together to research and explore what could be done for students with poor reading skills. Soon a reading approach caught their interest and teachers were being trained. By January 2000, each SLC was offering a course to support a small group of their students. The course employed a multidimensional approach to address the needs of struggling high school readers.

School Profile 2:
Wyandotte High School

Teacher Study Group

Not only did the students need support, the teachers were new to teaching reading and needed something. That something started as a support group and has grown in sophistication ever since. The group was first established after school for the purpose of open discussion around teaching reading strategies. Teachers exchanged materials, discussed implementation, shared their successes and difficulties with the current classes, and discussed the effectiveness of the strategies used. This dialogue encouraged teachers to explore and improve their delivery systems and established a feeling of confidence in their teaching of reading.

Teachers continue to gather weekly for the study group in order to discuss teaching strategies. It has evolved into a group that has created an environment of trust and respect in which teachers are able to share their failures as well as their successes. Teachers use this opportunity to demonstrate lessons designed for class, discuss the appropriate uses for strategies, and offer suggestions for improvement, all with the hope of achieving student success. The group has allowed for a continuous learning experience during which thinking and reflection on teaching and learning have increased and instructional strategies can be added to each teacher's repertoire. The study group has instilled confidence and knowledge in the members, which in turn has enhanced teaching. Teachers also feel rewarded in the knowledge that students are able to transfer the strategies taught in the reading class to classes in other content areas.

Study group teachers have been planting seeds with other teachers in their communities to incorporate the strategies in their classes. They have branched out to encompass the entire SLC staff in the training and implementation of these strategies across the curriculum. The focused work on reading has paved the way for similar work in all content areas. The flexibility and autonomy of the SLC to identify its area of need for staff development is an essential component of changing the culture of the school.

Peer Coaching

To support the implementation of the reading intervention and other instructional changes being implemented, beginning in January 2001, the staff developed a peer coaching system at Wyandotte. Teachers studied the research on peer coaching and identified a non-evaluative process of collaboration and reflection. Substitutes were brought in two days a week to allow teachers to observe another teacher in the classroom. As the process developed, teachers spent time collaboratively planning lessons, observing lessons, and participating in reflective conferences after lessons. The process further enhanced the development of a collaborative culture at Wyandotte, which now identifies collaboration as a part of the teacher's professional role as opposed to something to be done "on your own time." The peer coaching system continues to evolve to include mentoring new teachers, collaborating with teachers in other schools, and embedding support from outside consultants into the classroom. The development of the study group and peer coaching structures have enhanced the implementation of Wyandotte's instructional improvement efforts.

As the culture of teaching and learning changes at Wyandotte, both teachers and students are impacted. Students know their teachers better and let down the walls of resistance. An eleventh-grade student shared that it took him two years to feel comfortable enough with his peers and teacher to really be able to write the kind of poetry of which he is proud. But it is not just anecdotal data that indicate changes in student behavior and learning.

By the Numbers

In 1997–1998, the student attendance rate at Wyandotte was 73%. During the 2001–2002 school year, it climbed to 86%. This increase is coupled with increasing enrollment in a time when the district secondary enrollment is *decreasing*. This increase is also occurring despite a change in student demographics. Such changes include a 10% increase in students on Free and Reduced-Price Lunch (72% in 1997–1998; 82% in 2001–2002 and 2002–2003) and a growing English-language learner (ELL) and Hispanic population. The ELL enrollment has grown from 50 students in 2000–2001 to 187 students in 2002–2003. The Hispanic population increased from 12% of the student body in 1997–1998 to 26% in 2002–2003.

Dropout data are also improving. Teachers know their students better and work with them to stay in school. A comparison of our dropout rate shows:

- 1996–1997: 28.8%.
- 2001–2002: 5.1%.

The graduation rate, which is determined by following a class for its four years of high school, has improved also. It was at a low in 1998–1999 with 40%, but has improved to a high of 70% in 2000–2001.

Incidents of violence against students declined from 155 in 1997–1998 to 14 in 2001–2002, a 93% decline.

Though these indicators were the first to appear, achievement gains are also beginning to surface. On the Kansas Math and Reading Assessment and the norm-referenced MAT7 Assessment, growth is being seen especially in moving students out of the bottom quartile or performance standard.

On the Kansas Math Assessment, the number of students scoring in the "Unsatisfactory Performance Standard" has decreased by 9% since spring 2000. This decrease is coupled with a 20% increase in the number of students tested. In addition, the overall mean score has continued to increase each of the past two years.

On the Kansas Reading Assessment, the gain is even more dramatic, as evidenced in Figure 3.2. There was a 28% decrease in the number of students scoring in the Unsatisfactory Performance Standard from 2001 to 2003. In addition, there was a *20% increase* in the number of students scoring at or above Proficient. This was coupled with a *31% increase* in the number of students tested.

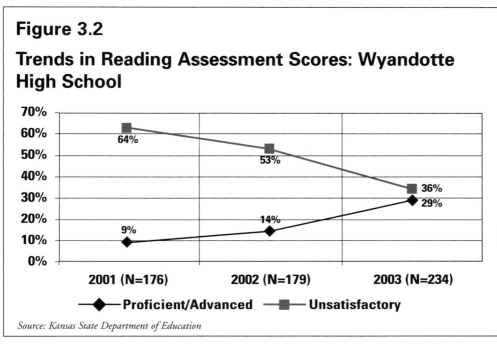

Figure 3.2

Trends in Reading Assessment Scores: Wyandotte High School

Source: Kansas State Department of Education

Against a backdrop of poverty, crime, and unemployment, Wyandotte staff members have committed to work together with their students, parents, and community to change the culture of their school from one of chaos and isolation to one of hope and collaboration. As a large high school in one of the most diverse communities in the state of Kansas and one of the poorest in the nation, Wyandotte has transformed itself into eight caring SLC families that support and value each other and build on the foundation of relationships to impact student achievement. Teachers at Wyandotte by no means believe that they have reached their goal. Their work continues to evolve based on the needs of the students. Yet, it is *their* work. Eight years ago, the district was thinking of closing the school. No one would consider that action today.

Summary of Success

- The change at Wyandotte is both meaningful and substantial. There has been measurable change in attitudes, beliefs, and values that has been a result of people coming together trying to create the best school for their students. Classroom instruction has changed dramatically, framed by the Teaching and Learning target of active engagement, connectedness, and reflection, and supported by the school's peer coaching and study group structure. The change has been bottom-up rather than top-down. The staff has been afforded the opportunity to study, learn, and explore together and have been empowered with the autonomy to create the conditions necessary to improve their students' performance. All of this is based on "the one thing" (relationships) that makes students and staff feel like family. As a result, students' and teachers' work is not governed by a clock, but by a commitment to learning and to each other. (Wyandotte operates under a modified 4X4 block schedule. Each SLC designs its schedule and has the flexibility to adjust the daily schedule as necessary.)

- The culture of the school has changed significantly over the past six years. The culture is one of collaboration and hope, supported by a process of study and inquiry. Professional development is embedded in the work of the school. The school day has been reorganized on Wednesdays to allow for two hours of professional study each week. This emulates the Professional Learning Community component of the Teaching and Learning Document.

- The change at Wyandotte is broad and systemic. Beginning with the 1998–1999 school year, the entire school was restructured into SLCs. Every teacher and every student is a part of an SLC. Every teacher is collectively responsible for the students in his or her SLC. Every aspect of the school, including governance, organization, instruction, and accountability, is affected by this change. Teachers and administrators work collaboratively in all aspects of the work. All stakeholders in the Wyandotte community, as well as educators and politicians from across the country, have recognized the positive change that has occurred over the past five years. Families used to stand in line to have their children transferred *from* Wyandotte. Now families are asking to transfer their children *to* Wyandotte. The work is a collaborative partnership between Wyandotte High School, the Kansas City Kansas School District, the Ewing Marion Kauffman Foundation, and the Institute for Research and Reform in Education. The accountability of each member in the partnership to the others has proved to be a valuable vehicle for continuous support and pressure.

Mary Stewart is the school improvement facilitator and Walter J. Thompson is the principal of Wyandotte High School in Kansas City, KS. The school has been the subject of much attention. Over the past five years, teachers and school officials from Texas, Missouri, California, Washington, Iowa, North Dakota, New Mexico, Mississippi, Minnesota, and North Carolina have visited Wyandotte to learn about and experience the positive changes. Wyandotte has been written about in US News & World Report, NEA Today, The Kansas City Star, *the U.S. Department of Education* Community Update *and the University of Minnesota's* Smaller, Safer, Saner Successful Schools *report. Stanford University has included Wyandotte as a case study in their work on high school reform.*

Addendum: A Question for the Principal (excerpted)

Q: *How has your job at Wyandotte changed since your school has implemented the changes just described?*

A: Being an effective building manager used to be good enough…and principals still need to do all those things, but they must to do more. However, the role of the principal has changed considerably because we are held accountable for more things, such as student achievement, public relations, communication with parents, evaluation, safety in and out of school, technology, implementing best practices, supervision…. You get the picture. I find there is a need to delegate more to staff and trust that they will implement the plan.

Principals today face many issues surrounding personnel, families, social issues in the community, funding challenges, No Child Left Behind (which drastically changes the way we do business and recruit fully certified staff), special education, ESL programs, and political issues. All of these can drain you by the close of a day. These and others have changed the principalship for many years to come.

I tend to say, "We are a work in progress."

Breaking Ranks II Recommendations Related to Personalizing Your School Environment

RECOMMENDATION 10: High schools will create small units in which anonymity is banished.

BENEFITS

- Gives students sense of belonging and the feeling that someone cares whether they are doing well academically, socially, etc.

- Improves student attitudes, attendance, participation, satisfaction.

- Promotes higher achievement, particularly among females and nonwhite students.

- Develops stronger peer and student-teacher relationships.

- Teaches social interaction skills.

- Makes students feel safer.

- Provides opportunities for teachers to team with colleagues and develop closer relationships with students.

STRATEGIES

- Develop advisories.

- Promote opportunities for student voice.

- Involve students in workshops.

- Implement conferences and meetings in which students take the lead.

- Freshman orientation.

- Looping (students keep teachers rather than changing teachers each year).

- Students remain with same group of peers, rather than an entirely different set of classmates for each course.

- Limit enrollment to self-operating units of no more than 600 students (house plans or clusters can accomplish this without the expense of constructing new buildings; i.e., school within a school).

- Change schedules to allow students to spend a longer time with the same students and the same teachers.

- Lengthen school year or day to allow for staggered schedules so that the school accommodates fewer numbers of students at any one time.

- Peer mentors.

- Personal Adult Advocates.

- Freshmen academies.

- Career academies.

- Transition programs to adult life.

CHALLENGES

- Scheduling issues.

- Space constraints.

- Students are not always consistent at team meetings.

- Teachers lack experience with including students in meetings and discussions.

RECOMMENDATION 11: Each high school teacher involved in the instructional program on a full-time basis will be responsible for contact time with no more than 90 students during a given term so that the teacher can give greater attention to the needs of every student.

BENEFITS

- Increases time for the instructional needs of each student and getting to know him or her.

- Increases time for professional development, curriculum writing, and instructional preparation.

- Allows time to implement Personal Adult Advocate and Personal Learning Plan programs.

STRATEGIES

- During a given term, a teacher might meet daily with two large classes of 45 students each; in the next term, the teacher might meet with five smaller classes of 18 each, using instructional strategies appropriate to the varying sizes of their classes.

- Team teaching.

CHALLENGES

- Budget cutbacks.

- Scheduling.

- Shifting enrollment.

- Overcrowded schools and growing enrollment.

RECOMMENDATION 12: Each student will have a Personal Plan for Progress that will be reviewed often to ensure that the high school takes individual needs into consideration and to allow students, within reasonable parameters, to design their own methods for learning in an effort to meet high standards.

BENEFITS

- Recognizes the individuality of student learning styles, histories, interests, and aspirations, and allows the student, in concert with school staff and family, to guide the learning experience. (Vermont High School Task Force, 2002)

STRATEGIES

- Students participate in establishing learning goals.

- "Progress is reviewed every 6–8 weeks: past activity and assessments are used to revisit and, if appropriate, revise learning plans." (Maine Commission on Secondary Education, 1998, p. 22)

- "Parents and staff use the plan as a planning device for the transition from secondary school to a future appropriate for each student; plans and assessments constitute a portfolio that exhibits, for future purposes, the student's talents, challenges, and future potential." (Maine Commission on Secondary Education, 1998, p. 22)

CHALLENGES

- "[D]epends on enlisting a teaching faculty in academic advising, preparing teachers to use authentic tasks in the classroom, reorganizing the school day to include time for [the plans] and authentic tasks, adjusting the schedule so students have time for authentic tasks and teachers have time for advising, reframing the teaching contract to allow advising, finding room for advising meetings and project development, engaging parents in supporting student projects...." (Clarke, 2003)

RECOMMENDATION 13: Every high school student will have a Personal Adult Advocate to help him or her personalize the educational experience.

BENEFITS

- Ensures that at least one adult knows each student well.
- Sets and reviews personal learning goals regularly.
- Allows students to discover their strengths and weaknesses and interests and how to express themselves as learners.
- Exposes students to in-school and community educational resources to support learning goals.
- Encourages students to work to extend their interests to their postsecondary education plans.
- Casts student learning in the form of projects, portfolios, presentations, or public discussions documented in the portfolio. (Vermont High School Task Force, 2002, p. 30)

STRATEGIES

- Advisories.
- Professional development around advocacy.
- Changing the role of the teacher.
- Schools restructure schedules.
- Advocate helps tailor Personal Plan for Progress.
- Advocate facilitates student's dealings with others in the school—identifying problems that should be taken up with guidance counselor, speaking with a teacher or student with whom the student is having difficulty, and perhaps, visiting the student's home.
- Guidance counselors can help train the advocates and coordinate the program.
- Multigrade or single-grade peer group that works 1–4 years together.
- Discussion might include important issues, school work, conflict resolution skills, college plans, planning their work for the week (service learning, internships, and coursework). (Maine Commission on Secondary Education, 1998, p. 13)

CHALLENGES

- Scheduling.
- Adding to duties of already busy teachers and principals.
- Making a clear distinction between the typical "homeroom" and the Adult Advocate program.

Recommendations Related to Personalizing Your School Environment

RECOMMENDATION 14: Teachers will convey a sense of caring so that students feel that their teachers share a stake in student learning.

BENEFITS

- Opens students to learning and trying harder.
- Fosters emotional and intellectual development of students.
- Fills a void for some students.

STRATEGIES

- Teaming provides an opportunity for teachers to collaborate to address student issues and to establish new relationships with students.
- Discipline with dignity.
- Use data to determine what programs students need.

CHALLENGES

- Lack of training and professional development.
- Perhaps a danger of confusing caring with "being a buddy."

RECOMMENDATION 15: High schools will develop flexible scheduling and student grouping patterns that allow better use of time in order to meet the individual needs of students and to ensure academic success.

BENEFITS

- Facilitates enrichment.
- Makes it easier to offer tutoring.
- Provides time for students to work on projects—alone, in groups, and in collaboration with teachers.
- Provides time for students who lag to catch up and for the ablest students to delve deeper into their studies.
- Provides time for staff to pursue professional development, engage in joint planning, conduct research, work together in the classroom.
- Allows teachers to devote more time to actual classroom instruction and less time to classroom management.
- Allows students to concentrate on a smaller number of courses at one time, typically four instead of the usual six or seven.
- Allows teachers to design and implement better project- and work-based learning opportunities.
- "Flexes" the walls of the high school and provides multiple opportunities for learning through work- and community-based learning, community service learning, partnerships with employers in curriculum development and delivery, and independent study and capstone projects that take students into the workplace and community. (Vermont High School Task Force, 2002, p. 35)

STRATEGIES

- Adjust length of class periods: AB Block schedule, etc.; Copernican Plan permits the school day to include either one 4-hour class each day for 30 days or two 2-hour classes that meet for 60 days.
- Adjust length of school day.
- Adjust length of school year: trimesters or year-round school.
- A.M./P.M. structures: mornings for class instruction, afternoons for work- and community-based learning, student activities, professional development, and integrated team planning.

CHALLENGES

- Requires new instructional strategies for teachers.
- Scheduling.
- Different departments' concerns.

RECOMMENDATION 16: The high school will engage students' families as partners in the student's education.

BENEFITS

- Benefits students by reinforcing education in the home.
- Encourages parental confidence and community involvement in education.

STRATEGIES

- Students leading the discussion during parent-teacher-student conferences and other conferences.
- Freshman orientation, which includes families.
- Teams can have parent coffees.
- Computer/home connections—train parents to use computers at school/ from home.
- Send information, hold seminars, involve families in activities.
- Teach parents how to deal with influences outside the classroom as well as how to help with homework assignments, and teach the importance of private, quiet places to study.
- Invite parents to serve as tutors and lecturers.
- Involve families in their student's Personal Plan for Progress.
- Involve families in the site council and action planning teams.
- Involve transfer students and incoming freshmen families.
- Schedule convenient meeting times and vary locations if you cover a wide geographic area.

CHALLENGES

- Getting parents to respond.
- Establishing convenient meeting times.

Recommendations Related to Personalizing Your School Environment

RECOMMENDATION 17: The high school community, which cannot be value-neutral, will advocate and model a set of core values essential in a democratic and civil society.

BENEFITS

- Helps students to understand the responsibilities that accompany democratic values.
- Allows students to take more control.
- Helps solve conflict creatively.
- Increases parent involvement.

STRATEGIES

- Student activities programs, honor societies, student council, etc.
- Make certain that, when appropriate, high schools infuse their studies with lessons that prod students to examine, weigh, and practice the core values of a democratic and civil society.
- Teachers devote specific lessons to the teaching of values, but values are also embedded in the regular curriculum.
- Modeled in the conduct of members of the high school community and accentuated by policies and practices under which that community functions.
- Honor courts.

CHALLENGES

- Skeptics who do not believe schools should teach values.
- Reinforcement of school values at home.

RECOMMENDATION 18: High schools, in conjunction with agencies in the community, will help coordinate the delivery of physical and mental health and social services for youth.

BENEFITS

- Helps get the community involved in the school.

- Promotes student health.

- Encourages support of teachers by "outside" professionals.

STRATEGIES

- Cultivate close working ties with agencies to which to refer students and allow the agencies to deliver some of those services in the school.

CHALLENGES

- Limited resources.

4 Making Learning Personal: Curriculum, Instruction, and Assessment

This dichotomy of thought, that we should improve high school education but not change the basic structure of the educational process, is even more perplexing when you realize that high schools are hard pressed to define what the intended result—the educated student—looks like. Most high school officials are not able to describe in holistic terms what a graduate knows and is able to do, but they can tell you what the student "took," how many credits the student earned, and what student did it best.

—*Gainey and Webb (1998, p. 1)*

Building Relationships Between Students and Ideas

In the preceding chapter, we discussed the critical importance of building relationships to open the door to learning. Here, we will enter the classroom door, the office in which the internship takes place, or the college campus where students take advantage of dual enrollment, and begin to address the *relationships between students and ideas*—how the student interacts and directs his or her own learning with the oversight, coaching, and motivational strategies associated with student-centered curriculum, instruction, and assessment. Teacher-to-student and student-to-student relationships cannot be left outside that door, however. In fact, they become a tool within the classroom to generate excitement about ideas and learning.

What are some of the ideas associated with, or indicators of, personalized learning?

■ Personalized schools promote the achievement of standards for all students

■ Personalized learning begins with individual interests so that each student becomes engaged in learning

■ Teachers get to know each student's strengths, weaknesses, and interests

■ With school support over four years, students become self-directed learners who can use learning to manage their lives

■ As students pursue an increasingly independent pathway, parents can assume new roles as guides and mentors in the learning experience

- As students explore real options for their futures in the community, community members become involved in the schools in a meaningful way

- Adults in the school model and benefit from stronger professional and student relationships

- Students learn to set goals and measure success for themselves against common standards

- Students graduate upon demonstrating high performance in a variety of media, not simply norm-based tests

- Reaching all students depends on reaching each one (DiMartino, 2001, p. 19)

Principals Provide Structure

None of the indicators of personalized learning mentioned above will appear without the principal and the leadership team creating the proper conditions. For example, integrating the curriculum may not happen unless teachers have common planning time. Similarly, working across the disciplines may require scheduling changes or schedule flexibility that the principal, ultimately, must be willing to shepherd into existence. The principal and the leadership team provide a structure and a vision in which interdisciplinary teaching, teaming, and other practices detailed at the end of this chapter can unfold.

Few undertakings require more leadership than the establishment of essential learnings. Politically sensitive, resource-intensive, and emotionally draining, developing and implementing essential learnings is at the heart of education. It is important to make students feel a part of an organization and to support them in emotional and physical development, but those can be done in other settings as well. High school must be about intellectual development and what students learn—the relationship between students and ideas. What ideas? What content? What curriculum? To promote success for each student, each strategy, practice, and recommendation should be aligned with academic rigor or how it affects academic rigor. If your program is not rigorous for each student, then the potential for the success of each student is diminished. Pursuing rigor requires you to devise a process to formulate essential learnings that take into account state standards and the standards set by individual disciplines and the school community.

Although state standards are often beyond your control, the process related to identifying the school community's essential learnings might be similar to the one outlined in *Providing Focus and Direction Through Essential Learnings* (Westerberg & Webb, 1997):

1. Cultivate staff commitment and ownership.

   - Teachers should lead this process and the rationale for the process must be centered in benefits to students.

   - It must be clear how essential learnings development will help teachers do their job more efficiently and effectively.

   - Discussions should focus on how essential learnings will help staff members hold students and one another accountable for learning, how essential learnings can help staff members decide what to teach and what to leave out, how essential learnings can help clarify and demystify the curriculum for students and teachers, how working together toward common targets for student learning will bring synergy to the staff's efforts, and how having a common vision for the school will help guide decision making.

2. Commission a broad-based essential learnings steering committee.

   - A steering committee, composed of students, teachers, parents, and community members, will oversee the process outlined in the following steps.

3. Use community focus groups to identify essential learnings.

   - The steering committee should focus on helping others understand the concept of essential learnings, not prepackaging and selling a set of essential learnings.

   - The community "should identify learnings only as essential if they are fundamental to further learning and absolutely necessary and indispensable to obtaining a diploma." (1997, p. 4).

   - The steering committee should help others understand the difference between the conceptually broader essential learnings and the more specific content and behavioral standards that "flesh out" the essential learnings.

4. Develop content standards, performance standards, and assessments.

   - The steering committee establishes committees of teachers to develop standards for each of the essential learnings defined by the community that tell us what students should know and be able to do (content), how well students must do these things (performance), and which instructional techniques or recommended activities (curriculum) should be used to assist students in accomplishing the "what" and the "how."

5. Implement standards-based education.

    ■   For some, the move from time-based (Carnegie unit) to standards-based education may require a longer transition because of internal or external factors. As the steering committee discusses your school's and community's circumstances, see sidebar on "Options" for alternatives to seat-time requirements.

6. Restructure your school.

    ■   Restructuring your school and its practices will be dictated by the essential learnings and how you propose to help students accomplish them. Implementing the changes (interdisciplinary learning, cooperative learning, block development, etc.) without aligning the practices with the student outcomes may lead to an incoherent overall strategy.

7. Conduct community forums.

    ■   Assess the community's level of support for the drafts of the essential learnings, the content and performance standards, and the restructuring recommendations. One option for the forums is to divide the community into specific interest groups (e.g., the business community, parents, students, or senior citizens) to determine patterns or trends or perceptions about the essential learnings specific to each group (Schlechty, 1990).

Options for Moving from Time-Based to Standard-Based Education

Standards-based model: Eliminate Carnegie units as the basis for earning a diploma and adopt standards-based graduation requirements centered around identified essential learnings.

Combined model: Retain some or all of your Carnegie unit graduation requirements, but supplement them with a limited number of standards-based requirements.

Endorsement model: Disassociate the standards from graduation, but add "endorsements" to the diploma (or transcript for each standard or requirement met).

In-class model: Disassociate the standards from graduation requirements, but build them into required courses as major assignments. Attach significant weight to these assignments when determining course grades. Possibly eliminate "D" grades.

Dual diplomas: Offer students/parents a choice of following either the credit track or the standards-based track to a diploma. Attach incentives to the standards-based track.

Dual diplomas and endorsements: Students who elect to and do accomplish all standards are awarded a standards-based diploma (plus incentives). Students who elect to or are advised to pursue a credit-based diploma are given a regular diploma plus endorsements.

Internal compliance: Disassociate the standards from graduation requirements, but develop a building system for monitoring student and teacher accountability.

School within a school: Students and teachers could elect to be in a special standards-based system, possibly combined with dual diplomas, endorsements, and/or incentives.

Source: Westerberg and Webb (1997).

---

8. Design performance tasks.

   - Teachers design individual tasks for students.

9. Develop a final implementation plan and a time line.

   - The preceding eight steps are part of the implementation plan. At this stage the steering committee should develop a final implementation plan and time line and propose it to the administration and the board of education. Among the questions that should be addressed are: "When will the standards-based graduation requirements become effective?" "What staff development activities will be necessary to effectively carry out the new system, and how much time will be needed to conduct those activities?" and "What are the budget implications of the system of education being proposed?"

Implementing these nine steps is not easy in terms of effort, time, resources, and physical or mental energy. "At a minimum, schools can expect to spend three to five years on the steps," Westerberg and Webb caution. In addition, schools will have to secure funds for released time, for summer stipends, for clerical assistance, and for consultants.

Making Learning Personal: Curriculum, Instruction, and Assessment

What the Research Shows

A rigorous curriculum is the bedrock of learning—personalized or otherwise. Its benefits are clear. When Adelman (1999) followed a cohort of students from 1980 to 1993 to determine what contributes most to a bachelor's degree completion, his findings showed that:

- The completion of a solid academic core was more strongly correlated with a bachelor's degree than high school test scores, grade-point averages, or class rank.

- An intensive academic curriculum had the strongest effect for African American and Latino students.

- Finishing a mathematics course beyond the level of Algebra 2 more than doubled the odds that a student would earn a bachelor's degree.

- At the top of the achievement scale were high school students who took more than one AP course; more than three years of both English and mathematics (including math beyond Algebra 2); a minimum of two years each of laboratory sciences, foreign languages, and history; and no remedial math or remedial English courses.

- Students from the lowest income groups who had high test scores, high grade-point averages, and a strong academic core were more likely to earn a degree than the majority of students from the top income group.

Personalization, high performance, high expectations, essential learnings, and standards are themes that thread their way throughout *Breaking Ranks,* and especially in the context of curriculum, instruction, and assessment. The challenge for schools is to align curriculum, instruction, and assessment so that students know what standards they need to meet and then are given the support to become engaged in achieving those standards.

That support might include taking

> …actions to help students who aren't making the grade, such as enrolling students at risk of failure in a ninth grade academy where they can receive extra support; increasing instruction time in reading and mathematics; offering English language learners sheltered classes; establishing alternative schools-within-schools, academies, and other more personalized learning settings; and providing additional resources to students who are challenged by academically rigorous work, such as after-school tutoring, small classes, Saturday school, and "catch up" classes. (Sullivan, 2004)

As school improvement teams tackle the issue of alignment, one tool to consider is curriculum mapping. The North Central Regional Educational Laboratory (2003, p. 2) provides a rationale for using curriculum mapping in the improvement process.

> The continuous improvement process can be summarized with three critical questions:
>
> 1. **What do you want?**
>   This question refers to the vision or goal for what a student will know at the end of a particular phase of education (be it a single grade level or the whole K–12 span of grades). It can also be represented by scores on standardized assessments.
>
> 2. **What are you doing to get what you want?**
>   The curriculum map roughly answers this question.
>
> 3. **What are you going to change, and how?**
>   When faced with low assessment scores, teachers and administrators must consider a range of options for improving what they do. With the help of an experienced facilitator, the school's personnel can identify practical changes to the curriculum.
>
> In summary, curriculum mapping facilitates conversations about how to change the curriculum to meet particular challenges. It provides answers to critical questions about student performance.

It becomes very difficult to tailor instructional strategies to the needs of individual students without knowing exactly what students need to learn and how they can demonstrate what they have learned. Because many of the recommendations at the end of this chapter rely on new approaches to learning and new instructional strategies, mapping how your curriculum will promote student mastery of the essential learnings becomes critical.

Successfully implementing a rigorous curriculum relies on engaged students willing to be challenged and to challenge themselves. Engaging them is the goal of the recommendations outlined in the preceding chapter on personalization and at the end of this chapter. However, assuming that strategies associated with personalized learning "engage" students in learning, do they really affect student achievement?

Valerie Lee and her colleagues at the University of Wisconsin (1995 as cited in Clarke, 2003, p. 23) found that schools adopting three or more of the following "restructuring" practices scored higher than more conventional schools on the National Assessment of Educational Progress (NAEP):

- Students keep the same homeroom throughout high school
- Emphasis on staff solving school problems
- Parents volunteer in school
- Interdisciplinary teaching teams
- Independent study in English/social studies
- Mixed-ability classes in math/science
- Cooperative learning focus
- Student evaluation of teachers
- Independent study in math/science
- Teacher teams have flexible planning time
- Flexible time for classes.

In the same publication (p. 27), the Education Alliance cites the following in support of personalized learning:

> A recent study by Linda Darling-Hammond, Jacqueline Ancess, and Susanna Ort (2002) testifies both to the difficulty of personalizing high school systems and to the promise of systemic change for improved learning outcomes. Darling-Hammond and her colleagues studied change in student outcomes when a large, urban high school in New York was replaced by six smaller schools designed to personalize learning. The Coalition Campus Schools Project compared measures of success for the original Julia Richmond High School (1992–1993) with the same measures for the six smaller, personalized schools that replaced it (1995–1996).

Student Outcomes

	Julia Richmond High School 1992–1993	CCSP Average 1995–1996
Average daily attendance	72%	86.2%
Incident rates (disciplinary)	3.3	1.2
1-year dropout rates	6.1	1.2
Students with reading gains	52.4%	56.9%
eleventh grade passing RCT or regents		
in reading	79%	80%
in mathematics	57.5%	76.6%
in writing	75.2%	71.4%
LEP students with adequate language gains	53%	91.2%

A similar pattern of outcomes appears when the percentage of CCSP students (general education) passing Regents Examinations is compared to percentages passing in schools demographically similar to CCSP but conventional in structure and size.

Students Passing Regents Examinations 1996–1997		
	Similar School	**CCSP Average**
Passing reading	82.4%	93.6%*
Passing writing	70.4%	85%*
Passing mathematics	81.2%	79.4%
*$p < .001$		

Rather than discuss personalizing curriculum, instruction, and assessment in abstract terms, a principal in Colorado will explain how his school addressed these issues. The following pages profile the practices of Littleton High School, a school that has attempted to align curriculum, instruction, and assessment in an effort to personalize learning. As you will see, establishing essential learnings played a critical role in the school's improvement initiatives. Littleton's profile is followed by *Breaking Ranks* recommendations regarding curriculum, instruction, and assessment, along with the benefits, strategies, and challenges of each.

In Their Own Words...

Below is the final of three profiles about school changes consistent with Breaking Ranks–*style reform. Each of the profiles has been written from the personal perspective of a member of the team responsible for implementation. The profiles are designed to show the comprehensive and interdependent nature of the reforms your school is being called upon to undertake. Although not all of the changes each school has instituted will be appropriate for your school, the perspective of your colleagues should nevertheless be valuable and may form the basis of a text-based discussion for your team.*

Breaking Ranks at Littleton High School: Progress, Challenges, and Promise

by Tim Westerberg

I have had the privilege of serving as principal of Littleton High School for nearly two decades now, and during that time I have worked alongside my colleagues, our students, and members of our community to implement some of the recommendations that coincidently, and not so coincidently, are found today in both the *Breaking Ranks* and the *Breaking Ranks II* NASSP documents. The "not so coincidentally" part of this *Breaking Ranks*-Littleton connection stems from the fact that, from 1994 to 1999, I served on both the NASSP/Carnegie Foundation Commission that produced the original *Breaking Ranks* document and the advisory council that worked to support implementation of the document in the years following its release. Some of what is reported in this profile was developed, or was beginning to be developed, prior to the publication of *Breaking Ranks*. Other initiatives unfolded while *Breaking Ranks* was under development; still others have been implemented within the past year or are still under development. This sequence of events suggests that a school never *becomes* a *Breaking Ranks* school. Instead, schools are always in the process of *becoming* or, in the parlance of the day, in the process of continuous improvement.

Profile
Littleton High School

Littleton, CO

Suburban

1,589 students

*http://littleton
.littletonpublic
schools.net/*

Practices to look for include:
- *Power standards*
- *Advisories*
- *Portfolios*
- *Varied instructional strategies and assessments*
- *Flexible scheduling*
- *Personal learning plans for students and adults*
- *Teacher collaboration*

The thoughts offered below are not offered with the attitude that we have somehow "figured it all out," or that the initiatives undertaken by our school are all functioning in an exemplary manner. Instead, and as the title of this profile suggests, our efforts to implement *Breaking Ranks*–type recommendations at Littleton have resulted in a mixture of progress, challenges, and promise.

It is difficult, at the very least, to understand Littleton's school improvement efforts without first understanding a little about the large-scale school restructuring initiative, Direction 2000, which forms the philosophical and structural foundation for much of what we do.

The Direction 2000 Years: 1988–1994

Progress and Promise

Direction 2000 was a school transformation initiative that began in its design phase in 1988 and was in operation at Littleton from 1991 to 1994. The initiative was based on the beliefs that graduation from high school should be based upon demonstrated performance of clear, specific, publicly stated content standards; that high school education can and should be personalized and individualized; and that both students and schools should be accountable for results. A more complete list of the new system of schooling we sought to design can be found in Figure 4.1. An examination of that list brings to mind many of the recommendations found in *Breaking Ranks*.

Our efforts to base graduation on performance rather than seat time necessitated the development of what, in *Breaking Ranks* language, are called essential learnings. Our efforts to establish essential learnings and corresponding standards for student performance were guided by four questions:

1. What, specifically, is it that we want students to know and be able to do when they leave our school?

2. How well do we want them to know/do these things?

3. How will we know if students know and can do these things?

4. How will we redesign schooling to better ensure that we get the results we want?

Answering the first question required us to identify useful content standards or essential learnings. Under Direction 2000, essential learnings were stated in the form of 19 performance-based graduation requirements and descriptions.

The second guiding question asked our school community to determine how good is good enough for each of our essential learnings or content standards. This question was answered in the form of criteria that a student's work must satisfy in order to meet Littleton's expectations in the knowledge and skill areas represented by a particular essential learning.

The third question involved us in the issue of student assessment. More specifically, what exactly will students be asked to do to demonstrate that they know and can do what is expressed by a content standard, or essential learning, at the level of performance necessary to meet graduation standards? Since we believe that it is important for instruction and assessment to fit together "hand-in-glove," our teachers developed our assessments, or what we called demonstration tasks, during the Direction 2000 years. These demonstration tasks were assessment activities that teachers valued and incorporated into instruction on a regular basis. Like the essential learnings themselves, demonstration tasks represented what teachers considered to be the essence of learning in a particular

---

Figure 4.1

Schooling System for Direction 2000

June 1, 1990

- Students earn graduation by demonstrating mastery of stated goals.

- Students demonstrate the intellectual skills and knowledge necessary to thrive in a changing world.

- Students demonstrate a positive work ethic and behaviors associated with good citizenship.

- Education is individualized and personalized.

- Faculty, staff, parents, students, and other members of the community participate in decision making for the school.

- Learning projects and activities go beyond the traditional lecture and textbook approach, often involve several disciplines, teach students to work cooperatively, and have application to real situations.

- Students take ownership and are actively involved in their own education.

- Students demonstrate the responsible use of technology to solve problems and assist in everyday living.

- The staff will be accountable for the success of the school's objectives.

- The needs of students and staff dictate the use of time.

School Profile 3:
Littleton High School

---

area. We took it as an indication that we had selected the wrong demonstration task, the wrong content standard, or both, if teachers felt a demonstration task under development was not worth spending considerable instructional time on. Today, state content standards would, or should, guide educators in the selection of local essential learnings.

In developing our essential learnings and corresponding performance standards and demonstration tasks, it became obvious that certain elements of our high school would have to be redesigned or restructured so that students could meet the standards we were setting for them. Thus, the fourth and final guiding question, "How will we redesign schooling to better ensure that we get the results we want?" This, the "restructuring question," was considered in light of the standards for student performance we had identified. At this point, the essential learnings development process also became a school improvement process. This was also the point at which we developed the structures necessary to accommodate the remaining foundational values, personalization/individualization and accountability. We developed a student advisement program, individualized programs of study for each student tied to essential learnings, a portfolio system for collecting evidence of student proficiency, remedial opportunities for students, interactive instructional strategies, and, in some cases, new courses. Block scheduling, a system of managing time in service of our constructivist learning theory, came about later in the process.

Challenges

In November 1993 the Littleton community elected a three-member "back-to-basics" slate to our five-member school board. The slate effectively campaigned against what it called a preoccupation with reform in the district. Targets of the newly elected board majority included whole-language instruction, multiage grouping, cooperative learning, some aspects of middle-level education, and performance-based graduation requirements, to name a few. For a variety of reasons, both political and practical, the issue of graduation requirements was identified by the new board as its first order of business. Strong community support for the Direction 2000 system of education at Littleton extended the community discussion about graduation requirements for some months. However, in February 1994, the new board of education voted by a three-to-two margin to return Littleton to credit-based graduation requirements. Our first class of performance-based students was in the second semester of their junior year by that time. The Littleton staff, in particular, was devastated.

We were faced with the leadership challenge at Littleton of reconceptualizing performance-based education based on essential learnings. A breakthrough in thinking came a few months later for several of us when we realized that Direction 2000 was not the goal but rather the means to an end. In fall 1994, the Littleton staff elected to continue to pursue that vision, albeit in a less direct and less powerful way. Our former demonstration tasks were reconceptualized as required major projects, assignments, or tasks administered within the regular course structure. In short, the essential learnings we had identified earlier were no longer stand-alone graduation requirements, but became, instead, significant components of a student's course grade. Students could not earn the grades they needed for admission to college, or in some cases, even the grades they needed to earn credit-based graduation requirements, without meeting the standards we had set.

The essential tasks program (as it is now called), our efforts to personalize and individualize education through a student advisement program and individualized learning plans, and our belief in both student and school accountability continue today, although each of these critical components of a *Breaking Ranks* high school has evolved considerably over the years. It is the current state of affairs at Littleton to which we now turn our attention.

Curriculum, Instruction, and Assessment

Four of the eleven *Breaking Ranks*–related initiatives or characteristics under way at Littleton today fit within the *Breaking Ranks II* core area of Curriculum, Instruction, and Assessment. They are "power" standards and essential tasks, the elimination of remedial classes, the introduction of the IB program, and our constructivist learning theory.

Power Standards and Essential Tasks

Progress and Promise
In fall 2001, Littleton formally launched its power standards project as one of four schoolwide goals. The seeds of the project were sown during the previous school year when Doug Reeves from the Center for Performance Assessment (CPA), in presentations to the Curriculum Council and to the entire faculty, offered a solution to what is one of the most demoralizing problems teachers face in today's schools—the problem of a professional existence dominated by the frantic, and seemingly hopeless, coverage of an ever-expanding curriculum.

In *101 Questions & Answers About Standards, Assessment, and Accountability*, Reeves (2001) offers his perspective on this "problem":

Every school district in the nation has some form of local or state academic content standards. These standards describe what students are expected to know and be able to do. The standards do not, however, give the classroom teacher and school leader clarity about which standards are the most important for future success. Because of the limitations of time and the extraordinary variety in learning backgrounds of students, teachers and leaders need focus and clarity in order to prepare their students for academic success. (p. 167)

How do we get from frantic coverage of the curriculum to focused instruction and the desired end—higher student achievement? *Focus* and *clarity* at the school level are the means to that end. According to Reeves, power standards help to provide that focus and clarity. So, what are power standards?

Power standards are not intended to be exhaustive of all the things students will be "taught" in a course or during a high school career. Instead, they represent the "core of the core"—the essential knowledge and skills that students must have to enter the next level of education. They form the network or *connections* among curricular objectives, and research has shown them to be highly transferable across academic disciplines. In short, they represent the skills and knowledge that, once mastered, equip students to do well in coursework and on standardized tests in high school, as well as to succeed in college and in the world of work later in life. Power standards vary somewhat from school to school, but for the purpose of providing examples, a short list supported by research would include informative writing, measurement, and tables/charts/graphs.

School Profile 3:
Littleton High School

In an October 2001 training session with a representative from the CPA, representatives from the LHS Power Standards Project Team identified the following characteristics of power standards:

- Standards that cross disciplines and make connections between the curricula in various disciplines

- Standards that emerge from course, department, district, state, or national standards

- Standards that are assessable

- Standards that are for all students

Reeves (2001) suggests using three "screens" to identify power standards:

1. **Endurance**—Will this provide students with knowledge and skills that will be of value beyond a single test date?

2. **Leverage**—Will this provide knowledge and skills that will be of value in multiple disciplines?

3. **Essential**—Will this provide students with essential knowledge and skills that are necessary for success in the next level of instruction?

An LHS team of approximately 30 faculty members, administrators, students, and parents used these characteristics and screens to develop four power standards, which were adopted by the faculty in spring 2002. Those power standards are Writing/Speaking, Information Literacy, Critical Thinking/Reasoning, and Citizenship/Work Habits.

The 2002–2003 school year was spent developing the writing part of the Writing/Speaking power standard for implementation in fall 2003. Our expectations for this power standard are captured by the expression, "Every teacher, every class, every trait (of the rubric), every semester." In other words, all students will receive instruction, feedback, and an opportunity to improve their work in every class they take, guided by a department adaptation of the building anchor document to ensure common expectations and language. A system for monitoring performance is under development. Figures 4.2 and 4.3 contain our expectations for Writing/Speaking power standard.

Figure 4.2

Littleton High School Writing Standard

Writing: Students write and speak effectively for a variety of purposes and audiences using proper conventions.

As students in grades 9–12 extend their knowledge, what they know and are able to do includes:

- Convey information in a written form appropriate to the audience.

- Select a clear and focused topic.

- Draft, revise, edit, and proofread a legible final copy.

- Develop a main idea using relevant, accurate supporting details.

- Organize writing so that sequencing is logical and effective and transitions show how ideas are connected.

- Align voice, tone, and style to further purpose and appeal to audience.

- Use specific and accurate words and phrases that are natural, effective, and appropriate.

- Incorporate and cite material from a wide range of sources (e.g., newspapers, magazines, interviews, technical publications, books) in their writing and speaking.

- Use conventional grammar, sentence structure, and mechanics (spelling, capitalization, punctuation).

Figure 4.3
Anchor Document for Writing Power Standard

	Ideas and Content	Organization	Voice	Word Choice	Sentence Fluency	Conventions
5	■ Clear, focused topic. ■ Relevant and accurate supporting details.	■ Clear intro and body and satisfying conclusion. ■ Thoughtful transitions clearly show how ideas are connected. ■ Sequencing is logical and effective.	■ Tone furthers purpose and appeals to audience. ■ Appropriately individual and expressive.	■ Words are specific and accurate. ■ Language and phrasing is natural, effective, and appropriate.	■ Sentence construction produces natural flow and rhythm.	■ Grammar and usage are correct and contribute to clarity and style.
3	■ Broad topic. ■ Support is generalized or insufficient.	■ Recognizable beginning, middle, and end. ■ Transitions often work well; sometimes connections between ideas are fuzzy. ■ Sequencing is functional.	■ Tone is appropriate for purpose and audience. ■ Not fully engaged or involved.	■ Words are adequate and support the meaning. ■ Language is general but functional.	■ Sentences are constructed correctly.	■ Grammar and usage mistakes do not impede meaning.
1	■ Unclear topic. ■ Lacking or irrelevant support.	■ No apparent organization. ■ Lack of transitions. ■ Sequencing is illogical.	■ Not concerned with audience or fails to match purpose. ■ Indifferent or inappropriate.	■ Improper word choice/usage makes writing difficult to understand. ■ Language is vague or redundant.	■ Sentences are choppy, incomplete, or unnatural.	■ Grammar and usage mistakes distract the reader or impede meaning.

The remaining three power standards are scheduled to be introduced over the next three years with Information Literacy scheduled for development in 2003–2004. Figures 4.4 to 4.6 identify our expectations in these areas as they have been developed to this point. Obviously, much more detail needs to be added.

Figure 4.4

Power Standard—Information Literacy

(Find It, Read It, Evaluate It, Use It)

Find It: Information Acquisition

- Formulates questions based on information needs (Colorado State Standard 1, Indicator 3—abbreviated CSS 1:3).
- Develops and uses successful strategies for locating a variety of information sources and information (CSS 1:4,5).
- Recognizes accuracy, currency, and comprehensiveness of available information (CSS 1:1).

Read It: Use of Literacy Skills and Strategies

- Pre-reads: previews, predicts, infers (CSS Literacy 5).
- Reads: identifies author's purpose, recognizes main idea; paraphrases, summarizes, organizes, synthesizes (CSS Literacy 5).
- Understands structure, organization, and use of variety of texts and genres (CSS Literacy 5).
- Determines meanings of words using contextual and structural clues (CSS Literacy 5).

Evaluate It: Critical Evaluation of Information

- Selects appropriate information (CSS 2:4).
- Determines accuracy, relevancy, and comprehensiveness (CSS 2:1).
- Distinguishes among facts, point of view, and opinion (CSS 2:2).
- Evaluates sources (CSS 4:2).

Use It: Applying Information to Make Meaning

- Organizes and integrates new information into one's knowledge (CSS 3:1,2).
- Applies information in critical thinking and problem solving (CSS 3:3).

Figure 4.5

Thinking and Reasoning

The goal of incorporating thinking and reasoning skills into the Littleton curriculum is to develop individuals who value knowledge, learning, and the creative process, and who can and will think for themselves. At Littleton, thinking and reasoning consists of the following skills:

- Evaluating information
  - Assessing the reasonableness and quality of information (ideas)
  - Setting standards for making judgments
  - Confirming the accuracy of claims

- Identifying similarities, dissimilarities and patterns
  - Comparing and contrasting
  - Analyzing relationships
  - Classifying

- Logic
  - Argumentation
  - Making inductions
  - Making deductions

- Investigation
  - Identify what is known or what is commonly accepted about a concept
  - Identify contradictions and points of confusion
  - Offer and defend solutions, or make and test predictions, related to the contradictions and points of confusion

- Problem solving
  - Uses appropriate trouble-shooting strategies
  - Isolates and reframes alternatives
  - Predicts, evaluates, and defends a solution

- Decision making
  - Investigates and defines alternatives
  - Predicts consequences of alternatives
  - Makes personal and relevant decisions based on data and criteria

Figure 4.6
Citizenship/Work Habits

- Consistently meets assignment expectations
- Uses time efficiently and effectively
- Shows sufficient effort in class and on assignments
- Demonstrates a positive attitude
- Willing to share, compromise, and work toward a goal alone or with others
- Engaged, ready to respond, willing to respond
- Attends class regularly
- Accepts responsibility for own performance and actions
- Follows class and school procedures
- Demonstrates integrity in academic and interpersonal affairs
- Uses respectful speech toward others
- Respects cultural and social differences
- Shows a tolerance for other points of view
- Participates or engages in community service

Our essential tasks, which have been operational in courses and departments for approximately 10 years, have in some cases been "set aside" during the development of our building-wide power standards. Our thinking is that essential tasks at the course and department levels should be in service of or advance one or more of the building-wide power standards. It is likely, then, that at least some of our present essential tasks will need to be reworked to fit under the umbrellas of our four power standards. A description of this essential tasks/power standards hierarchy, as it functions within the school setting, is described in the fictional news story contained in Figure 4.7.

Figure 4.7
Power Standards at Littleton High School

2006–2007

This year saw the implementation of the final phase of a project that began seven years earlier with a presentation to the faculty on power standards by educational consultant, Dr. Doug Reeves. The process of identifying, defining, implementing, and assessing power standards at Littleton High School took longer and was more difficult than anyone imagined when the project was launched. However, the common instructional focus that the power standards provide has simplified schooling for both students and members of the faculty and increased student achievement by bringing coherence and organization to what was previously a fragmented and overwhelming curriculum.

A picture of how power standards impact teaching and learning at Littleton High School is best gained by examining what is currently happening with the power standard implemented by the faculty during the 2003–2004 school year, Writing and Speaking.

Early in the 2002–2003 school year, members of the Power Standards Committee, working in conjunction with members of the Literacy Committee, identified the following "descriptors" of the power standard, Writing and Speaking:

1. Select a focused topic; draft, revise, proofread, and edit
2. Convey information in an appropriate genre (Descriptive, Persuasive, Technical, Narrative)
3. Develop main ideas and content with relevant (thorough and effective) support
4. Organize writing/speaking so that it has logical and effective development of ideas (Introduction, Body, Conclusion, Transitions)
5. Use vivid and precise words
6. Align voice and style to purpose and audience
7. Use conventional grammar, sentence structure, and mechanics (punctuation, capitalization and spelling)
8. Credit others for ideas, images, and information (according to Writers Inc. format or school-accepted format).

Bringing definition to this power standard through these descriptive statements, which were the subjects of rather intense faculty training in October of that year, shifted the level at which the work to operationalize this power standard was being conducted from the Power Standards and Literacy committees to individual academic departments.

Each department began its work by determining which Writing and Speaking descriptors (1–8 above) legitimately fit the fundamental nature, organizing concepts and principles, and essential skills of its discipline. For example, members of the science department agreed that all of the descriptors except #6 are critical to understanding science and the work of scientists, and to communicating that understanding, and that with some modification of existing assignments, these descriptors not only could, but should, be taught (instruction, practice, feedback) and assessed in specific department courses. Much of the department's work for the remainder of the year, at course-level meetings, at department meetings, and on staff development days, focused on reorganizing curricula around selected descriptors, identifying instructional strategies to teach the descriptors, modifying or developing formative and summative descriptor assessments, and identifying the level of performance necessary for mastery. The department's Essential Tasks were also carefully analyzed throughout this process, with modifications being made to ensure that the ETs both facilitated and supported the department's commitment to the Writing and Speaking power standard. Each of the other departments engaged in a similar effort that year.

Meanwhile, the Littleton Power Standards Committee provided coordination and quality control for the project. As individual departments reported on which Writing and Speaking descriptors they were accepting ownership of, the Power Standards Committee constructed a composite coverage matrix to make sure *all* students had *multiple* opportunities to receive instruction on *each* descriptor. Where gaps were found, members of the committee worked with the Curriculum Council to either fill those gaps or reassess the importance of the descriptor(s). The Power Standards Committee also examined the assessments developed by each department to ensure fidelity to the intended meaning of each descriptor. Where confusion and inconsistency existed, staff training was suggested.

The final service provided by the Power Standards Committee, one that is provided on an annual basis, is to collect student success-rate data, by descriptor, from departments and to present that data to the faculty and administration for analysis. In cases where performance has not met expectations, department and/or schoolwide adjustments were made to curriculum, instruction, or assessment.

Each year since 2003–2004 has seen the successive development and implementation of the Information Literacy, Thinking and Reasoning, and Citizenship/Work Habits power standards using the process first developed for Writing and Speaking. The process is somewhat recursive in that each new standard has necessitated some rethinking of previous standards. It is also the faculty's intention that the power standards be dynamic in nature, revised from time to time as dictated by student performance data and changing student needs.

Challenges

The challenges that we are presently facing with our power standards and essential tasks project are threefold. First, although staff buy-in is strong, some members of the faculty are, understandably, overwhelmed by the magnitude of the commitment. What are the implications of the "every teacher, every class" expectation for a vocal music instructor who has 225 students? If that is not frightening enough, play those implications out imagining that power standards Two, Three, and Four are added.

The Power Standards Committee has to attack this problem on two fronts. We have to help members of the faculty find ways to incorporate power standards into their content-specific instruction rather than add them on to an already crowded curriculum. In addition, we need to design an appeal process to the general expectation that allows teachers with special circumstances (e.g., high student caseloads or content less amenable to integration) to phase into or modify the expectation. Failure to demonstrate flexibility in this regard will result in the power standard initiative collapsing under its own weight.

The second challenge with which we must deal stems from the fact that not all of our teachers feel equally equipped to provide instruction, coaching, and feedback on every one of our power standards. For example, members of our faculty vary widely in their readiness to teach writing and speaking. In a couple of cases, entire departments have been granted permission to phase in some of the traits on the writing/speaking rubric over a period of two to three years as members of these departments gain confidence in their abilities to teach those traits. Our staff development program must provide differentiated training for members of the faculty in order for many of our teachers to be able to accomplish what we are asking them to do. Finally, we need to design a system for monitoring student performance on each of the power standards that allows us to engage in data-informed decision making, but that does not overwhelm members of the faculty with burdensome recordkeeping. This too is a task with which the Power Standards Committee must grapple.

Elimination of Remedial Classes

Progress and Promise

One of the original *Breaking Ranks* recommendations asks schools to develop alternatives to ability grouping and tracking. Littleton has been successful in eliminating tracking and in minimizing the negative effects of ability grouping by encouraging more students to take AP and IB courses and by virtually eliminating all remedial courses.

By the mid-1980s, Littleton was experiencing difficulties with remedial courses ("basic skills") and tracks in its offerings in math, science, language arts, and social studies. Two particular problems are worth noting here. First, placing all low-performing and poorly motivated students together resulted in behavior problems and a lack of the intellectual stimulation one normally associates with heterogeneously grouped classes. In addition, students who were in, for example, ninth-grade "basic skills" language arts classes ended up in tenth-grade basic skills language arts classes, eleventh-grade basic skills language arts classes, and twelfth-grade basic skills language arts classes. In other words, they never really improved their "basic skills," but instead continued to fall further and further behind their classmates placed in regular college-prep and honors sections.

Today, we have eliminated all remedial courses except for one section of ninth-grade language arts, and we are working on that. All ninth-grade students begin their mathematics experiences at Littleton enrolled in either geometry or honors geometry.

Social studies classes are heterogeneously grouped in ninth grade and then split into regular and honors courses in tenth grade. Our language arts department offers only regular college prep and honors coursework beginning in tenth grade, and the science department utilizes heterogeneous grouping in ninth and tenth grades, and then allows students to choose electives in grades 11 and 12. Geometry and language arts labs offer additional time and assistance for two periods each week for students who need extra time and support to master those disciplines.

An analysis of course grades reveals a slight decline in the percentage of students failing core coursework over the past few years, although we have no evidence to support the conclusion that this slight decline is the result of a reduction in tracking and remedial coursework at Littleton. What we can say is that the move toward more heterogeneous grouping in grades 9 and 10, the elimination of tracking, and the elimination of most remedial courses certainly has not resulted in more student failures.

Challenges
The challenges we have experienced with heterogeneous grouping in the lower grades, with the elimination of tracking, and with the reduction in remedial courses have been few. With regard to heterogeneous grouping, we had difficulty challenging our high-end students in heterogeneously grouped ninth-grade language arts class, so we have allowed language arts to join the mathematics department in offering an honors ninth-grade option. Of course, not all regular education teachers are equally adept at differentiating instruction to accommodate learners with special needs, and so, counselors and special education teachers sometimes exercise "selective scheduling" to increase at-risk students' chances of success. This latter point is not a big problem at our school, however, because the vast majority of our teachers are willing to work with students of all skill and motivation levels.

School Profile 3:
Littleton High School

IB Program

Progress and Promise
A parallel initiative to the elimination of tracking and the reduction in remedial courses at Littleton is the increase in the number of students pursuing rigorous, college-level coursework. Littleton has had a strong AP program since Advanced Placement began. However, we want to challenge our students with not only the highest standards available in this country, but also the highest academic standards available in the world.

In March 1995, the Littleton Public Schools Board of Education approved Littleton High School's proposal and budget recommendations for an IB program. Littleton was accepted as an IB affiliate in 1996 and became a full participating member in 1997. In May 1999, Littleton's first group of IB students graduated. Today, we have approximately 50 IB students in each senior class (out of a total of approximately 325 seniors), and our five-year record for students receiving the IB diploma is 98%. This latter point is particularly gratifying in view of the fact that Littleton maintains an open enrollment policy for students enrolling in the IB program, consistent with our philosophy of encouraging students to take on the challenges offered by rigorous academic coursework.

Challenges
Again, problems with our IB program have been few. Funding is always an issue and particularly so during times when the economy is down. The district is supportive, but resources are limited.

The other issue that surfaces from time to time, particularly among some members of the faculty, is a concern over "elitism," or the perception of elitism. Our faculty is committed to serving the needs of all students, and so, any sense that more fortunate students are getting special privileges cuts across the grain of our culture.

In addition to maintaining a consistent awareness of the possibility of favoritism, our open admissions policy and our insistence upon involving as many teachers as possible teaching in the program mitigate this problem. Jealousies are reduced when no one, student or teacher, is prohibited from participating in the "privileges."

Standards-Based Constructivism

Progress and Promise

In response to much of what we had learned from cognitive psychology, and from the emerging applications of brain research to education, about how people learn, Littleton moved formally in the mid-1990s to the adoption of standards-based constructivism as a guiding learning theory. If all that education consists of is repeating what the teacher or the textbook says the meaning of something is, then education becomes a hollow experience that, for students, usually produces little more than a "data dump" after each unit exam. At Littleton, we believe that teachers must design work for students that engages them in constructing personal meaning out of knowledge and information. That means, of course, that, in addition to reading textbooks and listening to lectures, students must be given opportunities to manipulate, create, apply, evaluate, and demonstrate the meaning of content and skills identified in relevant content standards. This last point is important in that there is a significant difference between activity-based and standards-based constructivism.

Assessment takes on a different nature, too, in a constructivist school. For example, final exams are no longer collections of questions from previous unit exams but are instead opportunities for students to "pull it all together" and communicate in unique and creative ways the personal meanings they have brought to key course content standards. With final exams of a constructivist nature, students and teachers need rubrics, not scoring keys. The memo in Figure 4.8 represents the nature of our constructivist approach to teaching as reflected in our final exams.

Figure 4.8

MEMORANDUM

DATE: January 21, 2003

TO: All Members of the Faculty

FROM: T.W.

SUBJECT: Final Exams

If you have not already done so, now is the time to think about your final exams for this semester. Introducing the semester by describing for students the kind of performance that will be expected of them at the end provides a destination for the arduous learning journey they are being asked to begin. Focus, direction, and context are essential to motivation, meaning, and purpose.

With that in mind, I would like to share a few of my thoughts with you regarding final exams.

It is important that you think about your philosophy and the purpose of final exams in your courses. For example, do you believe that the primary purpose of a final exam is to serve as a review of the content and skills uncovered throughout the semester in the hopes that one more "run through" of class notes and textbook materials will ensure long-term retention? Do you believe that the purpose of final exams is to give students a chance to boost their grades? In either case, do research and your own experiences support these beliefs?

My own view is that the final exam should be a *culminating* experience that asks each student to bring *personal meaning* to *essential* course learnings. The final exam is not a recapitulation of the "parts" of a course. It is, instead, an opportunity for the student to put the parts together in a personally meaningful "whole." The whole is, indeed, more than a sum of the parts!

If you subscribe to this philosophy, a final exam that consists mostly of test questions from previous unit tests is probably inappropriate. If you subscribe to this philosophy, your exams focus on student answers to course essential questions rather than student regurgitations of predetermined "expert" answers. If you subscribe to this philosophy, you have a scoring rubric, but no answer key, because bringing personal meaning to knowledge means that each student's response will be unique. If you subscribe to this philosophy, you view the final exam as more of a learning than an evaluative tool.

The research is pretty clear—learning is not retained sans personal meaning. What are you telling students about the performances that will be expected of them in May? Whose "answers" will be on the final exams you give, yours or your students'? Whose final exams are they? Will students be given an opportunity to demonstrate "the whole thing," or are the words of the commercial slogan from the 1980s words to live by in the case of final exams—"parts is parts?"

Think about it.

Challenges

The challenges associated with the constructivist approach to teaching and learning have mostly to do with training, coverage, and time.

As you can well imagine, not every teacher is equipped with the repertoire of skills necessary to engage students in a constructivist approach to learning. Staff development then becomes critical, new teachers must have effective mentors, and all teachers need to be supplied with examples of lessons and assessments exemplifying the constructivist approach to teaching and learning. Building administrators can do a lot to promote risk-taking in this regard by recognizing teachers who take the time to develop and implement effective constructivist instructional units.

Embracing a constructivist approach to teaching and learning means embracing the notion that it is important to cover a few key topics, concepts, and skills in depth rather than engage in a cursory approach to dozens, or even hundreds, of objectives. That can appear to run afoul of district- and state-level high-stakes standards-based assessments. One response to this perceived conflict between constructivism and high-stakes testing is to recognize how little students are learning in the "shotgun" approach to curriculum coverage. Another response is to identify course, department, and building essential tasks and power standards in accordance with research by Reeves and others, which indicates that a thorough mastery of certain high-leverage content and skills (reading, writing, and thinking, for example) produces better standardized test results than does an attempt to frantically cram every minute content objective that could possibly be included on an exam into students' heads. As discussed previously in this profile, Littleton is basing its reputation on this latter approach.

The issue of time to engage in constructivist learning activities brings us to the issue of the master schedule. Littleton's solution to this problem is the subject of the next section of this profile.

Personalization and the School Environment

Block Scheduling

Progress and Promise

After an extensive, two-year study of various ways to organize time, Littleton moved to a modified block schedule in the mid- to late-1990s. The "modification" is that all eight periods (students typically take six or seven classes) meet on Mondays, and then the odd periods (1, 3, 5, 7) block for 90 minutes on Tuesdays and Thursdays and the even periods (2, 4, 6, 8) block for 90 minutes on Wednesdays and Fridays. This move to block scheduling was made specifically to accommodate our standards-based constructivist approach to learning. Teachers operating in 46-minute periods under our previous schedule found that they were simply not able to get into the depth necessary to allow students to construct personal meaning out of knowledge and information. The instructional day was fragmented and frenetic for both teachers and students. When the decision to move to the block schedule was finally made following a collaborative decision-making process under the direction of our School Accountability Committee, both students and faculty were fairly equally divided on whether or not such a move should be made. Today, an overwhelming number (over 90%) of faculty and students support the block schedule.

Challenges

The biggest challenge in moving to a block schedule, or to any other non-traditional approach to the use of time, is getting high school teachers to actually make the move. My approach was to announce that we would not be continuing with our present schedule, but that the decision as to what schedule would replace it would be left to the faculty. That meant that some kind of change had to occur, but that the faculty would have ownership in the new schedule.

Once the decision to move to a more flexible use of time was made, the challenge became one of staff development. As you can imagine, teachers need a much deeper reservoir of instructional strategies when teaching in the block than is typically true of the 45- or 50-minute class period. Simply employing traditional instructional strategies for twice as long is deadly and will sabotage the new schedule. At Littleton we devoted all of our staff development time for a full year prior to implementing the new schedule to training teachers on the use of effective instructional strategies for both the block schedule and constructivist learning. In addition, considerable attention is devoted to training teachers new to our school in the effective use of the block.

The Freshman Academy

Progress and Promise

"High schools will create small units in which anonymity is banished."

In spring 2003, the Littleton faculty and administration took a bold step toward addressing a long-standing problem in our school, the problem of failing freshmen. The solution, approved by department chairpersons upon recommendation from the building At-Risk Committee and the building administration, was to establish a "school within a school," beginning in fall 2003, to provide intensive intervention in literacy (reading and writing) and mathematics to no more than 80 high-risk freshmen. This is a bold move for Littleton because of the academy's programmatic implications and because of what it says about our mission, a move not unlike the decision several years earlier to add the IB program to our offerings to meet the unique needs of a particular population of students. First, some details.

The "traditional" comprehensive high school model works well for most students at Littleton and at other high-performing high schools across the country. But one of the dirty little secrets in America's *best* high schools, including Littleton, is that about 20% of our students, and particularly our younger students, are not succeeding academically. This failure to meet the needs of all students is often masked in good high schools by high *average* test scores and by an impressive list of academic accomplishments on the part of hundreds of students who are thriving. Lift the mask and you see an underserved population, a population with unique needs, whose members receive multiple "Ds" and "Fs" every grading period. What's more, we can predict with a high degree of accuracy just who these students will be when they are in eighth grade.

Can we, in good conscience, allow a system to remain unaltered that we know will not meet the needs of one in every five students? We would not tolerate such a situation for our high-performing students (witness the expectations of AP, IB, and Gifted and Talented programs). The decision to devote resources to what is called the Freshman Academy at Littleton signals our resolve to do everything within our means so that, in the parlance of recent federal legislation, no child is left behind. The faculty is to be commended and supported for this resolve.

Having said all that, I must now add that there is no guarantee that the Freshman Academy will solve our problem. Turning failing high school students around is far from an exact science. In fact, Littleton has tried a couple of other models on a smaller scale over the past five years with only limited success. What we do have are examples of programs and schools from within our district and from across the country that have been successful in improving the academic achievement of high-risk high school students. From our own Littleton Public Schools Options program, we have learned that a small, highly supportive, and family-like environment is critical to the success of these students. From the research of the Center for Performance Assessment and elsewhere, we have learned that an intensive focus on reading, writing, mathematics, and thinking produces results. Equipping at-risk students to be successful in the mainstream program is not an exact science, but neither is it a total mystery. We do know some things, and we must act accordingly.

And so, we move boldly forward, creating the future of our choice—4 teachers and 60-plus ninth-grade students spending five periods each day focusing primarily on literacy, mathematics, work habits, and attitudes, with no guarantees, but with some promise for success.

Challenges

The challenges we encountered in deciding to move to a Freshman Academy concept included issues of staffing because staff had to be shifted out of other departments and into the Freshman Academy, facility needs because the proposal called for designating a dedicated site for this school within a school, and concerns about segregation and the return of tracking. The first two issues, those of staffing and facilities, were handled fairly easily because normal attrition in our larger departments enabled us to shift staff without costing anyone his or her job and because we were able to move regular classes out of the north wing of our building without much disruption to create a space for the program. We did need to take steps to ensure that those teachers and classes "displaced" by the Freshman Academy had equal or superior facilities and equipment in their new locations.

The concern surrounding segregation of these high-risk freshmen and the potential for tracking were addressed by distinguishing between tracking and what Reeves (2001) refers to as "intensive assistance." The students in the Freshman Academy are not tracked. There is no sophomore academy. The goal to return Freshman Academy graduates to regular-track sophomore classes equipped with the knowledge and skills necessary to be successful prevents tracking from occurring.

The major problem we have yet to completely address is the issue of follow-up support service in tenth, eleventh, and twelfth grades for graduates of the Freshman Academy. Literature is replete with examples of schools within a school or alternative schools in which students have been successful in that context but have returned to their habits of poor performance when returned to the mainstream setting. At least a partial solution to that concern at Littleton is to schedule graduates of the Freshman Academy with teachers active on the At-Risk Committee that created the academy for student advisement and, when possible, for regular academic classes. Obviously, the jury is still out on this one for us.

Student Advisement

Progress and Promise

Breaking Ranks recommends that "every high school student have a Personal Adult Advocate to help him or her personalize the educational experience." At Littleton, that program is now called PRIDE. Students are grouped by grade level and by gender, and they remain with their PRIDE advisers and their PRIDE groups for all four years of their high school experience. PRIDE groups at Littleton meet for 35 minutes every Monday. A brief history of the PRIDE program is provided below but, in short, the purpose of the program is to provide instruction and support for students to be successful in connecting with the community, in academics, in relationships with peers and teachers, and in transitions beyond high school.

The belief that students need connection to their classmates, to significant adults, and to their community is not a new one at Littleton. In 1988, during a North Central Evaluation process, administrative and counseling personnel saw the need for a curriculum that would assist students in being successful in life—a curriculum that would connect each student to at least one significant adult at Littleton and one that would create a sense of worth for each student.

In fall 1991, the Educational Advisement Program (EAP) began at Littleton. Each staff member worked with four freshmen students; in subsequent years, the groups added four freshmen while maintaining their current students. Thus, after four years, each EAP group would have four students from each grade level. In 1994, the EAP was replaced by PEP, the Personalized Education Program. This program was designed to meet similar goals, but met with freshmen only on a weekly, and then biweekly, basis. Upperclassmen attended PEP for registration and grade distribution/grade counseling purposes only. As PEP continued, interest on the part of both students and staff advisers declined. It was this breakdown of PEP that prompted the School Accountability Committee (SAC) to form an ad-hoc committee in fall 1999 to study the future of student advisement programs at Littleton. This committee recommended, and SAC adopted, a proposal to create a program that would "support the Littleton Public Schools' Mission Statement and the Littleton High School Vision Statement by providing instruction and support for students to be successful in academics, interpersonal interactions, and transitions into, and within, the Littleton High School community." (PEP Ad-Hoc Committee, fall 1999)

After studying many successful programs from throughout the country, a team of eight staff members identified two focus areas for each grade level and proposed the PRIDE program as it currently exists. The PRIDE program mirrors the goals and objectives of the EAP and the PEP that preceded it. The desire to connect all students to a significant adult, to themselves and their classmates, and to the Littleton High School community and beyond is reflected in the individual and community components of the curriculum as well as in the random groupings. Students with differing academic abilities, varied interests and talents, and diversified backgrounds and experiences are able to work together to learn, grow, and contribute to their community.

The purpose of PRIDE is to provide a transition from high school to the real world by creating a connection to the community. Students connect to their community through increased understanding, volunteerism, and enhancement of relations with peers and significant adults. Academic transitions assist students in meeting postgraduate challenges.

As Littleton's student population increasingly becomes more racially, ethnically, and experientially diverse, the commitment to creating a sense of belonging for all students and a school atmosphere in which every student can be comfortable becomes even more important.

Challenges

Two challenges have plagued our advisement program since the demise of the Direction 2000 program in 1994. First, the very direct and important link between advisement and the academic program at Littleton that was present in the Direction 2000 program is not as clear with PRIDE. That causes problems with both students and faculty advisers sometimes asking, "What is the purpose of this program?" or "Why are we doing this?" The other problem we face is that some high school teachers are simply not comfortable serving in the capacity of adviser, especially when the curriculum is largely affective in nature. The fact that I list these challenges as perennial in nature suggests that we have not found a way to totally ameliorate them. The PRIDE Standing Committee, which consists of teachers and students, is continuously surveying teachers and students in an effort to find out how the program might be strengthened. Staff development is provided on a regular basis, and our PRIDE coordinator and Standing Committee produce and distribute instructional activities designed to better enable teachers to accomplish the PRIDE curriculum.

We are at the point where the new PRIDE program has been fully implemented and where we now need to "call for the question" to determine whether or not sufficient student and faculty support exists to continue the PRIDE program. In my opinion, the program serves a worthwhile purpose in helping to personalize education and in helping students make key connections. However, consistent with the culture at Littleton, students and members of the faculty must see the program as a valuable part of what we do in order for us to continue to devote time and resources to the effort. The next couple of years will be critical for the advisement program at Littleton.

The Senior Year Plan

Progress and Promise

The Senior Year Plan is our most concrete example of developing a Personal Plan for Progress for students at Littleton. The Senior Year Plan actually constitutes the senior year of our student advisement program (PRIDE), and was first implemented in the 2002–2003 school year.

The purpose of the Senior Year Plan is to counteract the dreaded senior slump, the uniquely American phenomenon that has become so much a part of the high school culture in this country that most students, many parents, and even some high school faculty and administrators view the last year of high school, and particularly the second semester of the senior year, as an opportunity to relax and take time off before entering adulthood. This rather cavalier attitude toward the final months of the K–12 experience may in fact be a rational response to a system that provides few incentives to work hard and finish strong. The focus on admission to college rather than on preparation for success in doing college-level work, the admissions calendar, and the lack of alignment between high school and college-testing programs and coursework all contribute to "checking out early" and the feeling on the part of many students that the second semester of the senior year is boring, repetitious, and pointless. Figure 4.9 presents a time line for the activities of the Senior Year Plan at Littleton.

Figure 4.9
Senior Year Pride Time Line

January–May

- Eleventh grade PRIDE meets as a group to communicate time line.
- Juniors conduct credit checks to ensure that graduation requirements are met.
- Juniors begin reflection piece of senior plan.
- Reflection pieces due to PRIDE adviser by the last PRIDE session of the school year.
- Postsecondary Options Act applications turned in by May 1.

August–November

- Twelfth grade PRIDE meets as a group to begin organizing second-semester plans.
- Twelfth grade PRIDE advisers meet with individuals during PRIDE to check on progress of second-semester senior plan.
- Twelfth grade PRIDE advisers distribute six-week grades.
- Seniors with plans containing experiential activities turn in draft of plan to PRIDE adviser by November 1.
- Seniors with plans containing traditional coursework and activities turn in complete and signed plans to PRIDE adviser by November 1.

Senior Plan Approval Committee
- **Parent/guardian**
- **PRIDE adviser**
- **Community member (if applicable)**

December

- Seniors with plans containing experiential activities present plans to committee for approval by December 1.
- ALL senior plans complete and signed by finals week.

January–April

- Seniors implement second-semester plans. PRIDE advisers monitor and advise individual seniors.

May

- PRIDE meets as a group over several weeks to share experiences and conclude Final Thoughts.
- GRADUATION!!

School Profile 3:
Littleton High School

A look at the Littleton High School Class of 2002 revealed that 53% of the students in that class already had enough credits to graduate by the end of the first semester. AP and IB programs keep some students working until May, but even at Littleton, a school in which approximately 90% of graduating seniors express an intent to go on to college, only about 25% of the students in each senior class are enrolled in the IB program or are taking multiple AP classes. Like their counterparts across the country, for too many seniors at Littleton, second-semester registration is a game of finding courses to fill a schedule that won't be too demanding.

The Senior Year Plan at Littleton hopes to make the senior year, and particularly the second semester of the senior year, more of a transition to life after high school by broadening the field of experiences in which students can be engaged. In addition to coursework at Littleton, options in student-developed transition plans can include community service work, coursework at area colleges and universities, distance learning, internships, travel, independent study, and/or a capstone or research projects. The intent is to make the second semester of the senior year meaningful and important to students and to reduce the incidence of students with "attitude problems" in classes they do not want to be in. Students work with their PRIDE advisers during the second semester of their junior year to write a reflection piece that focuses on the question, "What knowledge/ experiences have brought me to this point in my life?" In many cases, this reflection piece doubles as a college essay or as a resume, greatly increasing the assignment's importance to students. During the first semester of the senior year, students develop a Senior Year Plan for the second semester of the senior year that, with parent, adviser, and, in some cases, administrator approval, is then put into effect for the last semester of their high school experience. At the end of the senior year, students meet with their PRIDE groups to share experiences in the form of an oral presentation entitled, "Final Thoughts."

During the second semester of the 2002–2003 school year, 66 seniors—20% of the senior class—took 150 courses totaling 450 credits at a local community college. All except a dozen of those students were concurrently enrolled in coursework at Littleton. To give you some idea of the impact of the Senior Year Plan initiative at Littleton, in previous years we typically have had between 12 and 15 students take advantage of this opportunity. Getting a little taste of college life while still in high school is a good transition for many of our students.

At some point in life, everyone, or at least almost everyone, has to go to work. Our career interests should be important determinants of the programs of study we pursue in whatever form of postsecondary education we choose. Exploration of potential careers through work experiences is also a legitimate transition activity for the senior year of high school. During the second semester of the 2002–2003 school year, 53 Littleton students included an internship or some other form of work experience in their Senior Year Plans. Again, most of these students were enrolled in courses at Littleton, and some of these students were among those taking courses at the local community college. Students learned what it is like to be dancers, photographers, coroners, automotive technicians, certified public accountants, interior designers, firefighters, culinary artists, physical therapists, public defenders, and real estate agents. Both private businesses and public agencies stepped forward to accommodate these positions, and some students received offers for full-time employment following graduation.

With Littleton's Senior Year Plan, the second semester of the senior year, to borrow from a recent national report, is "more like a launching pad than a rest stop." Students at Littleton have one foot planted firmly in the coursework and environment of our school while with the other foot they step out into the future.

Challenges

The program is so new that, to date, we have had few problems. In a few cases, students have failed to take their college enrollments seriously and now have failing grades on their college transcripts. More will have to be done in the future to make sure that students understand the consequences of "blowing off" these experiences. Students receive credit and grades at Littleton for these off-campus experiences, and so, failure to complete their obligations carries consequences on their high school transcript and negatively impacts their GPAs.

It was also difficult for some of the advisers to monitor the off-campus work experiences, although in the vast majority of cases, employers were quite willing to fill out the forms designed for the purpose of helping advisers evaluate student work.

Collaborative Leadership and Professional Development

Leadership and professional development are of obvious importance to any high school in the process of becoming a *Breaking Ranks* school. At Littleton, we have experience with Personal Learning Plans, with mentoring programs for new teachers, and with tying staff development to school goals, all in the service of moving Littleton in the direction of becoming a true learning community.

Personal Learning Plans

Progress and Promise

For about six years, Littleton has had the practice of allowing nonprobationary teachers the option of developing a three-year Personal Learning Plan in lieu of participating in the traditional observations/conferences evaluative process. This option was developed in direct response to one of the recommendations in *Breaking Ranks*. Today, most of our nonprobationary teachers choose this option because it places them in control of their professional growth.

In the first year of this three-year process, teachers prepare a philosophy of teaching and learning, develop a collaborative professional reflection worksheet with a colleague, and write a goal statement rationale and expected outcomes for their learning plan. Learning opportunities that support a stated goal can include anecdotal records, authentic teacher-made materials, individual or group action research, data collection and analysis, log entries, reflective journals, videotaped lessons, peer coaching, cognitive coaching, school visits, team teaching, and various forms of self-assessment. During the second year the teacher actually implements the learning plan. Documentation must be kept regarding results. In the third year, the teacher prepares a one- to two-page summary of his or her progress toward the goals in a reflective piece entitled, "My Final Thoughts." That reflective piece addresses such questions as, "What did you do?" "How do you feel about what you did?" "What did you learn that was significant to you?" "How will this affect your teaching?" and "What future studies would you consider doing to help your students learn?" The teacher's evaluator must sign off on the professional growth goal or goals, must approve the learning plan, and must sign a learning-plan report at the end of the process documenting successful completion of the plan. In addition and in accordance with Colorado law, the evaluator conducts one classroom observation and conference with the teacher during each of the three years the plan is in place. Professional Learning Plans work quite well at Littleton because they allow teachers to be in charge of their own professional growth, because they allow for creativity, and because they save tremendous amounts of administrative time.

School Profile 3:
Littleton High School

Challenges

Few problems have been associated with this initiative. The most important thing we have done to assist teachers in completing the Personal Learning Plan in a meaningful way is to provide them with models of exemplary plans.

New-Teacher Mentoring

Progress and Promise

During the 2002–2003 school year, Littleton implemented an orientation program designed to equip teachers new to our building to meet our expectations regarding many of the initiatives described earlier in this profile, and in particular regarding our standards-based, constructivist learning theory. Under the direction of an assistant principal, new teachers meet each month to discuss a chapter from the book, *Classroom Instruction That Works,* by Marzano, Marzano, and Pickering. We have found that the text provides an effective vehicle for communicating the "Littleton way of doing things" to new teachers. In addition, the book helps provide teachers with the skills necessary to meet our expectations. Finally, the monthly meetings serve to help new faculty members form an identity as a group.

In addition to these monthly meetings, the same assistant principal works intensively with new teachers one-on-one. By the end of the first semester, each teacher new to Littleton has had at least six full-period classroom observations and follow-up conferences with that assistant principal. The focus of these conferences is on providing support, not on "checking up on" our new teachers. Our goal is to ensure that every new teacher feels fully supported by the administration.

The final component of our new-teacher mentoring program is the mentoring itself. Each teacher is assigned a mentor in the building, usually from the department in which he or she serves. Professional literature makes it clear that almost half of the teachers new to our profession leave within the first three years because of unclear expectations, lack of administrative support, and feelings of isolation. Our teacher-mentoring program holds promise in that during the first year of implementation, Littleton did not lose any of its 15 new teachers.

Challenges
The only challenge we have encountered is that new teachers are often tired and overwhelmed by the demands of the job and are not always looking forward to "another meeting." However, once people get to the meetings and begin to interact with other colleagues, feelings of fatigue dissipate because the content addresses challenges that teachers are facing and the relationship-building is essential to their survival.

Connecting Staff Development to the Building of Goals

Progress and Promise
Too often, staff development programs consist of a collection of disjointed one-shot affairs that produce little lasting effect on teaching or learning. For the past three years, Littleton has sought to alter this pattern by ensuring that every minute of staff development time is tied directly to one of our four building goals. The four building goal areas for the past several years have been power standards, at-risk (Freshman Academy), literacy, and PRIDE.

To facilitate the coordination of professional development time and accomplish the objectives of our building goals, the faculty chairs of each of those building goals committees and members of the school administrative team meet monthly to develop long-term professional development plans for approval by our Curriculum Council (department chairpersons). Intensive planning ensures that the outcomes of each session are clear, that each year our staff development program presents a coherent "whole," and that every minute is used wisely. Figure 4.10 provides a sample of the planning that goes into staff development days and of how staff development is tied to building goals.

Challenges
The challenges we have incurred in connecting staff development to building goals are that we do not have enough time to accomplish everything we would like to accomplish with regard to our building goals and that no time is provided on staff development days

for the treatment of other important topics (school safety or prevention of sexual harassment training, for example). Our solution has been to use monthly faculty meetings to address these latter topics, leaving staff development time for the sole purpose of advancing building goals.

Figure 4.10

Wednesday, May 28, 2003
LHS Staff Development

Outcomes	Agenda	Assignments
■ Staff knows which Power Standard is chosen for development in 2003–2004 and has opportunity to provide feedback to Power Standards Committee ■ Departmental progress in specified areas of reading, writing, and speaking is determined and goals for the following year (2003–2004) are identified ■ Writing/speaking rubric is complete and is aligned with anchor rubric. Grade-level targets on writing/speaking rubric are identified. Writing/speaking rubric is incorporated into tasks, assignments, and assessments. ■ Staff is aware of progress in reading, writing, and speaking made by other departments as well as departmental goals for 2003–2004 ■ Staff understands expectations for meeting writing/speaking standard and using the rubric in 2003–2004	■ **7:45–8:30** Power Standard is presented in forum and staff meets in interdepartmental groups to provide feedback on form distributed ■ **8:30–11:45** Departments use form provided to assess level of progress in specified areas of reading, writing, and speaking standard and identify goals for 2003–2004 ■ Departments work on completing writing/speaking rubric **and/or** work to identify grade-level targets on writing/speaking standard and rubric **and/or** discuss/work to incorporate writing/speaking standard and rubric into tasks, assignments, and assessments ■ **12:45–2:00** Staff gathers in forum and departments identify level of progress in reading, writing, and speaking on large grid. A member from each department summarizes progress and goals chosen for next year ■ **2:00–2:30** Member(s) of Power Standards and Literacy committees describe(s) expectations for next year to staff in forum	■ Individuals have sample assignments and student work that demonstrate levels of progress in literacy areas (reading, writing, and speaking) ■ Departments have completed writing/speaking rubric or have work in progress

continued on next page

Final Thoughts

Well, the final thought is that nothing is final. The process of becoming a *Breaking Ranks* high school at Littleton has been, and will continue to be, a long, strange ride. It has, for the most part, been rewarding. It has, in all parts, been challenging. It is a process that will never be completed. It is a journey of progress, challenges, and promise.

Figure 4.10 (continued)

Thursday, May 29, 2003
LHS Staff Development

Outcomes	Agenda	Assignments
■ Teachers will have used and shared their "Adopt-A-Kid" strategies; they will have shared their successes and failures and what they have learned about their "kid"	**7:30–8:15** Break out into interdepartmental groups ■ Strategies used ■ What learned ■ Successes ■ Failures—what to do differently	■ Continue working with your "Adopt-A-Kid" ■ Complete Yellow "Adopt-A-Kid" Certificate and bring to Inservice on May 2ninth ■ PRIDE Standing Committee will use results to report back to staff and to direct PRIDE 2003–2004
■ Teachers will have increased knowledge of Freshman Academy and will know process for referring to Freshman Academy	**8:15–8:30** Forum ■ Empowerment stats ■ This year's tenth ■ Next year's tenth	

■ Teachers will know process for referring other at-risk students grades 9–12 to counseling	**8:30–9:00** Forum
	■ Information about Freshman Academy
	■ Next steps for teachers:
	  • How to ID ninth for F.A.
	  • How to ID 9–12 At Risk
	■ To counseling
	■ Questions?	

■ Advisers will have completed a program evaluation of the 2002–2003 PRIDE year	**9:00–9:30** BREAK	
■ Each adviser will have a clear understanding of grade level expectations and strategies for meeting grade level objectives	**9:30–11:15** ■ Complete individual evaluations at April 23rd staff meeting ■ Meet by grade level (gender, ninth & tenth) to brainstorm areas for improvement and determine activities/ideas to keep ■ Prioritize lists and voting procedure	
■ Each adviser will have a clear understanding of the PRIDE calendar for 2003–2004	■ Meet by grade level (gender, ninth & tenth) and distribute curriculum time lines ■ Include goals/expectations for each six-week segment ■ Include suggested activities to meet goals/expectations within each segment ■ Allow for Q&A; ask for successful additions ■ Distribute calendar specific to each grade level ■ Include grade distribution, registration, holidays, block Mondays, deadlines for required curriculum, and recommended activities (when applicable) ■ Review calendars; allow for Q&A **11:15–11:45** Tim: School goals review & preview!	

Breaking Ranks II Recommendations Related to Curriculum, Instruction, and Assessment

RECOMMENDATION 19: Each high school will identify a set of essential learnings—above all, in literature and language, writing, mathematics, social studies, science, and the arts—in which students must demonstrate achievement in order to graduate.

BENEFITS
- Promotes higher achievement for all students.
- Increases probability of success in college.
- Provides freedom for students to meet standards in various ways.

STRATEGIES
- Increase the level and rigor of all courses.
- AP program.
- Equity 2000 (a College Board initiative).
- Involve the community.
- IB program.
- Portfolios, senior projects, exhibitions, etc.
- Teach literacy across the curriculum.

CHALLENGES
- Too many watered-down courses.
- Standards are set by others.

RECOMMENDATION 20: Each high school will present alternatives to tracking and to ability grouping.

BENEFITS
- Creates a culture of high expectations for all.
- Improves student achievement.
- Leaves no student behind.

STRATEGIES
- Open enrollment for IB, AP, and honors classes (provide tutoring and other instructional support to enhance chances for success; teachers should adapt instructional strategies to meet the needs of the students, which is no less than they should do for all students and all high school courses).
- Organize students in learning groups; diversity can be a criterion and students can learn from each other when those of varying backgrounds work together in the same learning group.
- Multi-age and multi-grade grouping.
- Heterogeneous classes.

CHALLENGES
- Parents of gifted students.
- Teachers object because they can't teach differentiated classes.
- Need for extensive professional development for teachers.

RECOMMENDATION 21: The high school will reorganize the traditional department structure in order to integrate the school's curriculum to the extent possible and emphasize depth over breadth of coverage.

BENEFITS

- Encourages collaboration.
- Prepares students for college.
- Fosters higher-order thinking.
- Prompts teachers to orient themselves according to organizational missions rather than age grouping, etc.
- Encourages each team that presents an interdisciplinary curriculum to function as a kind of mini department.

STRATEGIES

- Interdisciplinary teaming.
- Integration within a subject (present algebra and geometry, for instance, or biology, chemistry, and physics in integrated courses).
- Explore ways in which new academic standards cut across subject areas.
- Curriculum units constructed around themes or directed at answering fundamental questions.
- Let students cover less material while expecting them to learn what they study more thoroughly.

CHALLENGES

- High-stakes testing and the focus on learning discrete information.
- Tradition of departments and department chairs may be difficult to overcome.
- Ensuring that the roles traditionally served by the department chairs are met in the reorganization of responsibility.

RECOMMENDATION 22: The content of the curriculum, where practical, should connect to real-life applications of knowledge and skills to help students link their education to their future.

BENEFITS

- Underscores the practicality of knowledge by showing students how to apply what they know.
- Encourages students to express more interest in material.

STRATEGIES

- Project-based learning and curriculum.
- Internships.
- Service learning.
- Career academies.
- Career exploration in school.

CHALLENGES

- Scheduling.
- Accountability and ensuring that "external" programs are rigorous and aligned with essential learnings.
- Critics may dismiss this recommendation as a plea for relevance.

RECOMMENDATION 23: The high school will promote service programs and student activities as integral to an education, providing opportunities for all students that support and extend academic learning.

BENEFITS
- Participants in student activities have more consistent attendance, better academic achievement, and higher aspirations than nonparticipants.
- One study shows that students who devote 5 to 19 hours a week to co-curricular pursuits are less likely to use drugs or drop out of school (though athletes were more likely than nonathletes to engage in binge drinking).
- Promotes responsibility, character development, critical thinking, and sociability.
- Promotes connection to the community.

STRATEGIES
- Ensure that activities and service programs are tied to the courses and goals of the school, define the educational objectives and establish criteria for assessing the experience or activity.
- Evaluate activities, including sports (the single largest area of participation), in terms of the support they provide for the school's broader objective.
- Nurture a sense of caring about the common good and each other.

CHALLENGES
- Resources.
- Overcoming the perception that service programs must happen outside of school.
- Transportation.
- Busing schedules.
- Opening activities to all students.

Recommendations Related to Curriculum, Instruction, and Assessment

RECOMMENDATION 24: The academic program will extend beyond the high school campus to take advantage of learning opportunities outside the four walls of the building.

BENEFITS
- "[M]entoring relationship between a youth and an older person reduces absenteeism, inspires students to achieve and set high goals, builds confidence and self-esteem and leads to better social and academic performance… allows students to see the direct relationship between academic performance and life achievement." (Vermont High School Task Force, 2002, p. 37)
- "Adults learn more about the high school atmosphere." (Vermont High School Task Force, 2002, p. 37)
- "Partnerships provide employers early identification of qualified, experienced, potential employees." (Vermont High School Task Force, 2002, p. 37)

STRATEGIES
- Work study.
- Independent learning.
- Distance learning.
- Apprenticeships.
- Mentorships.
- Internships.
- Job shadowing.
- Independent study.
- Field trips.
- Travel.
- Courses in colleges, dual enrollment, etc.
- Student-conducted research.
- Collaborative efforts among and between high schools and technical education centers onsite, online, or via distance learning. (Vermont High School Task Force, 2002)
- Break free of Carnegie unit.

CHALLENGES
- Ensuring learning opportunities align with essential learning and the curriculum.
- High-stakes testing and No Child Left Behind.
- Schools in rural areas may lack opportunities.
- Distance/transportation.

RECOMMENDATION 25: Teachers will design high-quality work and teach in ways that engage students, encourage them to persist, and, when the work is successfully completed, result in student satisfaction and their acquisition of knowledge, critical thinking, and problem-solving skills, and other abilities valued by society.

BENEFITS

- Students learn how to reason and solve problems when teachers embed problem solving in the curriculum.

- Students evolve into critical thinkers when teachers challenge them to analyze and judge material.

STRATEGIES

- Insofar as possible, students should have a choice of the types of assignments they do, understanding that specified learning is the objective and that standards will not be compromised or diluted.

- Five "Habits of the Mind":

  - Weighing evidence—How credible is the evidence for what we think we know?

  - Awareness of varying viewpoints—Whose viewpoint is this and what other viewpoints might there be?

  - Seeing connections and relationships—How are things connected and what is here that we have seen before?

  - Speculating on possibilities—Can we imagine alternatives?

  - Assessing value both socially and personally—What difference does it make and who cares?

- Common planning time.

CHALLENGES

- Often, teachers let the acquisition of facts and basic skills become the end product of instruction, depriving students of an education of richer nuances and deeper meanings.

- Teacher qualifications not up to par.

- Some teachers may not be willing to change their ways.

RECOMMENDATION 26: Teachers will know and be able to use a variety of strategies and settings that identify and accommodate individual learning styles and engage students.

BENEFITS

- Involving students in their learning makes things more memorable.

- Levels of engagement increase and academic achievement rises in schools that use these various restructuring practices: seminars, cooperative learning, debates, field experiences, independent study, and laboratories.

- Fewer students drop out.

- Class attendance rates increase.

- Discipline referral decreases.

- Teacher attendance increases.

- Test scores improve.

STRATEGIES

- Seminars.

- Cooperative learning.

- Debates.

- Field experiences.

- Independent study.

- Laboratories.

- Students construct knowledge—teachers offer students a list of key questions to guide inquiry, or provide students with the titles of books and articles that are pertinent to uncovering the knowledge. It is the student's responsibility to unlock the knowledge, analyzing it, synthesizing it, and presenting it as a body of material for which he or she has taken possession.

CHALLENGES

- Requires an understanding of cognitive development and findings from brain research.

- High-stakes testing.

- Teacher training on learning styles and successful teaching to meet students' learning styles.

RECOMMENDATION 27: Each high school teacher will have a broad base of academic knowledge with depth in at least one subject area.

BENEFITS

- Teachers can teach to various learning styles and teach flexibly.
- Teachers can work with other colleagues to integrate the curriculum.
- Teachers can connect learning to real-life applications.

STRATEGIES

- Professional development.
- Thorough hiring practices.
- Active participation in professional discipline's association.

CHALLENGES

- Responsibility of teachers to keep up to date with changes in the disciplines and to remain active in the professional disciplinary associations.

Recommendations Related to Curriculum, Instruction, and Assessment

RECOMMENDATION 28: Teachers will be adept at acting as coaches and facilitators to promote more active involvement of students in their own learning.

BENEFITS

- Students become more responsible for their learning.
- Students become more involved learners.
- More time is devoted to teaching than administrative tasks.

STRATEGIES

- The student investigates multiple approaches to solving a math problem or expounds on the meaning of the novel or conducts the physics experiments. The teacher coach remains nearby—observing, asking questions, and prodding the student to reflect on the product of his or her efforts. The student's response or performance—the learning experience—becomes the subject of the coaching.
- A teacher who turns a student's question back on the student and requests clarification, all the while providing information for the student to ponder, provokes the student to discover his or her own answer, pushing the student to the limits of his or her knowledge.

CHALLENGES

- Teachers' lack of training.
- Teachers' belief systems may not support constructivist approach to learning.

RECOMMENDATION 29: Teachers will integrate assessment into instruction so that assessment is accomplished using a variety of methods and not only measures students, but becomes part of the learning process.

BENEFITS

- Multiple measures of assessment are more likely to capture the full landscape of student achievement.

- Captures the dynamic and varied ways in which a student's academic growth occurs—this assessment, in other words, more closely resembles a videotape than a single snapshot.

- Allows teachers to immediately address students' challenges, rather than waiting until the final or standardized tests that may help address the challenges of the next class.

STRATEGIES

- If, for example, a teacher wants to assess the students' understanding of the scientific method in conducting a particular physics experiment involving electromagnetic fields, the assessment can be the assignment itself. Let the student carry out the experiment until he or she demonstrates the desired competency and understanding.

- Multiple drafts for writing projects.

- Portfolios, performance tasks, and other examples of a student's accomplishments.

- Standardized tests, particularly those that are criterion-referenced.

- Present assessment results in ways that are useful to parents, college admissions officers, personnel managers, and the student.

- Comprehensive Personal Learning Plans; graduation challenge, capstone or senior projects; standardized state assessments; ACT, PSAT, SAT; reporting of student achievement in standards-based transcripts. (Vermont High School Task Force, 2002)

- Clarify essential learnings, specific content goals, course goals, and practices for teachers, students, and families.

CHALLENGES

- Tendency to rely on high-stakes testing alone will not promote the development and use of a variety of assessments.

- Lack of integration of curriculum, instruction, and assessment.

RECOMMENDATION 30: Recognizing that education is a continuum, high schools will reach out to elementary and middle level schools as well as institutions of higher education to better serve the articulation of student learning and to ensure that at each stage of the continuum, stakeholders understand what will be required of students at the succeeding stage.

BENEFITS

- Students are prepared for their classes.

- Increased academic rigor.

- People in the district begin to talk together.

- Ability to work more closely with colleges to end need for them to provide so much remedial education.

STRATEGIES

- Establish transition programs.

- Establish liaison with elementary and middle level schools to make students and teachers in the schools better aware of expectations to come.

- Strengthen the relationships through tutoring of younger children by high school students and faculty-to-faculty programs.

- Reach out to parents when their children are still in the lower grade levels.

- Encourage colleges to encourage their faculties to pursue collaboration with high schools.

- Adjust programs to take into consideration reforms occurring in earlier grades (e.g., Turning Points).

- Form connections with other schools within the same district as well as with nearby nonpublic high schools.

- With colleges: exchanges of personnel, joint efforts in curriculum development, workshops on instructional strategies, exploration of technological applications, research that can be pursued and examined together, dual enrollment, helping them understand the value of portfolios and adjust admissions requirements for that purpose.

- The following are excerpted from *High Schools on the Move* (Vermont High School Task Force, 2002):

  • Align high school standards-based transcripts and postsecondary admission requirements.

  • Ask colleges how graduates are doing—not only in admission but in completion of college.

  • Position the high school as a hub of a comprehensive, community learning network that includes other schools, internships, work-based learning, home schooling, and enrollment in college classes.

  • Survey students after graduation to inform yourself about adequacy of student preparation for postsecondary education; adequacy of student preparation for career choice and career success; relevance and effectiveness of curricula and learning opportunities; the relationship between particular pathways to learning and postsecondary success, whether in career or higher education settings.

CHALLENGES

- District coordination.

- Communication at different levels.

- Moving from blame to taking responsibility for learning.

Recommendations Related to Curriculum, Instruction, and Assessment

RECOMMENDATION 31: Schools will develop a strategic plan to make technology integral to curriculum, instruction, and assessment, accommodating different learning styles and helping teachers to individualize and improve the learning process.

BENEFITS

- Technology helps to individualize learning.
- Technology is uniquely suited to promote school reform; technology can play roles in authentic and multidisciplinary tasks, performance-based assessment, interactive modes of instruction, heterogeneous grouping, collaborative work, student exploration, and teachers functioning as facilitators.

STRATEGIES

- A course about technology—not the mechanics, but to serve as a platform on which students can explore the best writings and ideas about technology itself, where they can ponder the implications of technology for the future, technology's impact on assessment and the classroom and throughout the school.
- In planning a curriculum unit, the teacher should consider how to strengthen a lesson at each point of the way by employing technology.

CHALLENGES

- Student access to computers, lack of infrastructure.
- Teachers' technology skills.

Final Reflections

With great eloquence and inspirational flourish, thousands of authors, politicians, and school reformers have written or spoken about the need for many of the changes outlined in this handbook. Yet the need for dramatic change still exists.

Researchers, regulators, professors, theorists, and practitioners have compiled an impressive array of information and statistics to support the need for these changes. *Yet the need for dramatic change still exists.*

Local newspapers and newscasters pepper their coverage with emotionally wrenching personal interest stories about schools' failure to reach a student or group of students. *Yet the need for dramatic change still exists.*

So why aren't more high schools actively engaged in reform? The problem is that calls for change most often come from external forces—sometimes well intentioned, often not—attempting to trigger inspiration through a poetic turn of phrase, "just the facts" data, or an appeal to empathy or sense of guilt tied to tragedy or the plight of a student or a group of students. Although any and all of these can trigger passion at any given moment, true motivation must come from within and must be *sustained* by more than a catchy sentiment or statement destined for Bartlett's book of quotations. Our hope for *Breaking Ranks II* is that it motivates not only through the words or activities contained herein, but through the questions that it prompts principals and leadership teams to ask of themselves and others. For example, if your leadership team and your school cannot answer the school assessment questions in Chapter 1 including perseverance and success in college, minority and low-income participation in your own rigorous classes, and structural ways in which student aspirations are supported, how can you really know whether or not you are serving all students? If you can answer them, and are not pleased with your answers, then you know for certain you are not serving each student well.

Theories are mere abstractions if they do not cause you to reflect upon how your situation and your interaction with others must change. The questions highlighted in Chapter 1 are a step in the direction of assessing your school culture and how well you serve each student—and perhaps uncovering challenges your team has never discussed.

Once your team performs that initial assessment, then the strategies detailed throughout this handbook become possible. Reflection promotes action over reaction and sustainability of action over implementing "ideas that sound good." Making the reforms discussed take root in your school will be difficult if your leadership team ignores this critical assessment. Furthermore, if this reflection is done only by the leadership team, reforms will receive the same attention you may now give to national, state, or district statistics, and the shortcomings of "other schools"—of interest, but will not be immediately actionable. *Others on your staff will only take ownership of reforms when they are able to ask themselves how it will affect their lives, their teaching, their classrooms, their students.*

Breaking Ranks II illustrates how school principals and their leadership teams hold the key to initiating essential conversations about relationships among people and relationships between students and ideas. These two relationships, elements of personalization, are at the heart of creating an inspirational, personal-interest story for each student, a story with which at least one adult within your school has personal familiarity. These personal-interest stories have the power to inspire far more than the ones in the local paper inspire—because there will be hundreds of inspirational stories that you see walking around every day and because your faculty and leadership team had a hand in making them come to life. Questions of success will not be based on averages, abstractions, or models, but rather on individuals and each student's personal-interest story.

- The question will not be: What program mentioned in the literature or the research will help the most students?

  Instead: What strategy is best to help Melissa and how, as principal, can I support it?

- The question will not be: How can we improve our average graduation rate statistic?

  Instead: How can I help Tom, Claudio, and Cynthia build the desire to learn so they want to graduate and have the tools to do so?

- The question will not be: How do I react to the local reporter's story about gang activity and the insinuation that the school is responsible?

  Instead: How can I help Chandra, James, John, or Roberto so that they feel a sense of belonging within the school and form healthy relationships that satisfy their need to express themselves?

You have the power to ensure that each student within your school hears the message that he or she can tell a personal-interest story, that it will be heard by a faculty member, that the story will be used to help the student direct his or her own story of success, and that the success will be profiled. The need for dramatic change still exists, and you have the ability to make it happen, one student, one story, at a time.

Strategies and Recommendations in Practice

The following are just a few of the schools attempting to implement practices consistent with the Breaking Ranks *recommendations. Each of these schools is at a different stage of implementing practices consistent with the recommendations. As noted earlier—and repeated here for readers who might jump directly to this section— many schools other than those mentioned below have taken significant steps to change how they approach improving the performance of all students.*

These are only examples of schools that have made an effort to reach all students, some with greater success than others. The danger of naming schools is that rather than reviewing a specific practice a school may be implementing, and contacting the school to learn from their lessons—a reader may instead look at the type of school or compare "reputations." We encourage you to look beyond your notions of an individual school or type of school to see whether a strategy they are trying might work well for your school. While most of these schools have been visited by a member of the team working on *Breaking Ranks II*, the information provided is, for the most part, "self-reported" and therefore subjective. The specific *Breaking Ranks* recommendation or strategy aligned with a school practice is highlighted in the margin for easy reference.

Baltimore (MD) City College High School, urban, magnet, 1,350 students, http://knight.city.ba.k12.md.us/.... Class sizes average in the low 20s, the vast majority of teachers teach three classes per semester, the number of students with whom they interact in a given semester averages 69.... Teachers are required to send a "class expectations" letter to each student's family every semester. Teachers are also encouraged to call families of assigned students to introduce themselves at the beginning of each semester. To ensure that families are kept abreast of their student's progress, teachers are expected to call family/parent of any student earning a failing grade at the end of 3, 6, 9, 12, 15, and 18 weeks.... Pre-high school meetings are held with sixth-, seventh-, and eighth-grade students and their parents. In addition, a "Summer Bridge" program is provided for those entering ninth grade. The program is designed to familiarize incoming students with the school routine and building, expectations, approach to teaching in the classroom, as well as form a bond through Outward Bound–style team building day and field day/picnic. Counselors and most administrators teach during the program so that all incoming students encounter them in a program with less pressure.... Counselors meet with students and share a recommended schedule. Students indicate preferences, and the schedule is sent home to parents for confirmation. This process aligns with the Personal Plans for Progress, created by each student, maintained by the counselor, and shared with parents annually.... The IB's initial start as an "all-diploma" program of about 40 students just four years ago has evolved into a combination diploma and elective program and expanded to include complementary AP courses. Approximately 430, or one-third, of its 1,350 students enrolled during 2002–2003 took one or more IB or AP courses. In addition, more than half of teachers are trained in the IB methodology. The teachers say it is the best training they have experienced. The methods and philosophy of the IB "infect" other courses because most of the IB teachers also teach college preparatory courses as well. The IB program is now a "draw" that is bringing students out of the excellent private and parochial schools of Baltimore and to public, City College high school. After seven years of accepting students into its ninth grade who did not meet all of its entrance criteria, the school has had two years of waiting lists.

Small units, family involvement, ninth-grade transition, Personal Plans for Progress, academic rigor

Boston (MA) Arts Academy, urban, pilot Boston Public School, 382 students, http://boston.k12.ma.us/BAA/... has an audition process for attendance that focuses on passion for a specific art form rather than proficiency.... Teachers, the primary resource in the evolution of the school, have autonomy to create their working conditions, schedule, and curriculum. Consistent with the philosophy that teachers should be generalists as well as specialists with a commitment to the whole school, teachers observe each other's classrooms to determine if the schoolwide goals are being met and that democratic and equitable practices are modeled. Furthermore, all teachers provide intensive writing instruction in the advisory/writing class that meets for 45 minutes each day.... Student schedules include a full college preparatory course load (humanities, mathematics, science, and a foreign language) in addition to the 12+ hours per week spent in arts classes.... Students earn diplomas based on demonstrated proficiency through portfolios, exhibitions, and performances, not on the number of Carnegie units.... All ninth- and tenth-grade students take part in an after-school support initiative for 90 minutes two days per week to participate in guided study or other student support activities.... Many seniors participate in dual enrollment programs.

Academic rigor, variety of assessments, dual enrollment with college

Brighton (MA) High School, urban, 1,168 students, http://boston.k12.ma.us/ brighton/ ... in 1997, transformed a large high school into one with career pathways, and in 2002 into SLCs. The ninth-grade academy is separate from the rest of the high school, and in the upper grades, students choose their pathway. Within each SLC, teachers get to know students and have three opportunities per week for common planning time, during which they review student work, develop promising practices, and discuss instructional strategies, curriculum issues, rubrics, alternative forms of assessment, and student concerns.... The curriculum has a school-to-career focus and involves project-based learning.... In its transformation to SLCs, scheduling, communication, and teacher buy-in have been the biggest challenges.

SLC/small units; variety of assessments/ project-based learning; teacher teaming and lesson planning

Brockton (MA) High School, urban, 4,200 students, http://www .brocktonpublicschools.com/schools/high/... has implemented SLCs for all ninth- and tenth-grade students. These students have almost all of their classes assigned to a "house." The school's restructuring committee is currently planning for the next phase—the implementation of "Theme Houses" for juniors and seniors. Each house would adopt a theme, or interest area: School of Business and Finance, School of Human Services and the Law, School of Health and the Sciences, and School of Communication and the Arts. Students will select their theme house, and the curriculum and programs offered in that particular theme house will capitalize on the interest of the student, and offer an important link to possible careers.

SLC/small units

Champion Charter School, Brockton, MA, 107 students, http://www .brocktonpublicschools.com/schools/charter/... is a high school specifically designed for out-of-school youth. It offers project-based curriculum and competency-based assessments, and so, students do not receive traditional grades, rather evaluations of their progress in developing specific skills and competencies tied to the Massachusetts Curriculum Frameworks.... Classes are small; there is a low student-to-teacher ratio, and an ability to accommodate various learning styles.... It features career exploration, college coursework, and an action project that benefits the whole school or the Brockton community.... Students typically attend classes in the morning and internships or college classes in the afternoon.

Small units, variety of assessment, community involvement, higher education continuum

Chapin (SC) High School, rural (20 miles from Columbia), 920 students, http://www.lex5.k12.sc.us/chs/ ... implemented the "Humanities" program because teachers saw a need for a coordinated effort by the social studies and English departments to integrate the two disciplines by grade and subject matter. The teachers share the same students and coordinate strategies that enhance the educational process for the classes. Both departments have worked to enhance writing across their curriculum offerings. Teachers plan together at least once a week and two teachers have developed a comprehensive grading system for the students they "share" and course maps have been completed.... Each of the high schools in Chapin's district has created curriculum maps using state standards. From these maps, essential learnings curriculum maps were developed. Criterion-referenced tests are administered at the end of core academic courses to measure achievement in meeting state and national standards.

Integrated curriculum, essential learnings

Eastern Technical High School, Baltimore, MD, urban, magnet, 1,325 students, http://www.easttech.org/ ... began its reforms in 1991 when the new principal invited members of the business community to visit the school and give their opinion of instruction. The verdict was not good; in fact, one CEO said the school may as well close up shop because it was preparing students for jobs that would not exist. This direct and candid community feedback provided the impetus for change. Now the school issues an annual report card to all stakeholders in the community and each student has an individual action plan designed specifically around one of the 10 career majors offered in the school.... Community involvement goes well beyond the report card and inviting feedback from businesses. The school has more than 100 business/community partnerships. Project-based collaboration between Verizon Communications, Lockheed Martin Corporation, Comcast Cable Communications, the Maryland Business Roundtable for Education, and others resulted in the school being recognized by the U.S. Department of Education as a national demonstration site for business/community partnerships. Visitors from 45 states and 25 countries have visited the school to witness the partnerships in action.... In addition to the business/community partnerships, the school has two major partnerships with higher education institutions. Through partnerships with the Community College of Baltimore County and Towson University several opportunities have evolved: collaborative professional development activities, teacher externships, dual enrollment, action research, portfolio exchange, school-based summer institutes, and, in 1996, the establishment of a Professional Development School (PDS) between Eastern Technical and Towson University. The PDS has brought 138 highly qualified teachers into the profession. In 2002, the U.S. Department of Education recognized this PDS as a national model. Signs of success: Over the past decade the scores on state functional tests have gone from unsatisfactory to excellent (100%), attendance has improved dramatically (97.2%), percentage of SAT takers has grown from 5% to 44%, the number of AP courses taken has increased from 0 to 32%, National Honor Society membership has increased from 3 to 142.

Community partnerships, report card to the community, Personal Plans for Progress, partnerships with higher education

Fenway High School, Boston, MA, pilot school within Boston Public Schools, 269 students, http://fenway.boston.k12.ma.us/... was founded in 1983 as an alternative academic program for disadvantaged and/or disaffected students who were failing in the large public school setting.... Students are grouped into "houses," each with its own faculty and support staff. Students typically remain in the same house throughout their four years at the school, so that they are well known by their teachers and form strong bonds with classmates.... Teachers meet twice a week to discuss the needs of students and make decisions regarding curriculum, assessment, classroom practice, and advisory activities.... The school changed its core curriculum and trimmed down its classes to create cohesion and to concentrate on the three subject areas of Humanities, Science, and Mathematics.... It promotes assessment of student performance in a variety of ways: classroom-based diagnostics, portfolios, exhibitions, standardized tests, work internships, and integrated projects.

Small units, essential learnings, variety of assessments, teachers' common planning time

Foshay Learning Center, Los Angeles, CA, urban, 3,725 students, K–12, http://www.foshay.k12.ca.us/.... All of its high school students have access to and enroll in AP courses.... A significant percentage of juniors and seniors are either concurrently enrolled in community colleges or have paid internships in the financial, technological, or health career–related fields.... The school uses a variety of methods to help make education real and relevant for urban children, such as making connections across grade levels and among different fields of knowledge; offering opportunities for students to test and apply new knowledge to real-life situations while working on projects and internships in the community.... Of note: For the Class of 2004, although statewide a disproportionate number of black and Latino students have yet to pass the California High School Exit Exam, at Foshay over 92% have passed the literacy and 80% have passed the math.

Academic rigor, partnerships with higher education/ community, real-world learning

Fuquay-Varina (NC) High School, rural, 1,400 students, http://fvhs.wcpss.net/ ... promotes the academic achievement of ninth graders. The Freshmen Achieving Successful Transitions (FAST) Program implemented the following strategies: relocated most predominantly ninth-grade classes/teachers to the same building and in close proximity to the FAST Center; linked ninth-grade social studies and English teachers into Freshmen Houses (English and World Civilization teachers are paired, teach the same 90 students/semester, and are encouraged to implement interdisciplinary teaching); scheduled students to have the same math teacher for both Algebra 1A & 1B in order to promote strong relationships; offered FAST tutorials on Tuesdays, Wednesdays, and Thursdays (2:30–3:30) specifically for ninth graders throughout the school year; assigned volunteer staff members to be informal mentors to one repeating ninth grader (during the past three years, the number of freshmen repeaters has been reduced by 68%); and counselors have held individual conferences and developed contracts with struggling ninth graders at the end of each nine weeks. The school originally intended to provide additional counseling services to promote positive behaviors and greater acceptance of diversity; however, they found that ninth graders attach very negative connotations to "being counseled." Therefore, they sought and received permission to use SLC grant money to purchase $25,000 worth of low-ropes course equipment and training in order to promote positive behaviors in a more indirect manner. Numerous teachers have received the training, and the equipment is used in all types of classes, frequently for activities that foster leadership, team building, and acceptance.... Strong relationships have also been promoted through an extensive summer orientation camp (over 75% of FVHS ninth graders attended one of the six days in 2003) that emphasized ice-breaking, fun, and anxiety reduction with activities such as a scavenger hunt and the ropes course, Freshmen Week inspirational assemblies, and a student-initiated Adopt-a-Freshman program.... In addition to other forms of professional development, the school has capitalized on homegrown talent and resident experts. Eight teachers from representative departments serve as members of the FAST Advisory Board, which has been our in-house "think tank."

Middle school transition

Gateway Regional High School, Huntington, MA, rural, 435 students, http://www.grsd.org/hs/index.html ... in 1997 was placed by the accrediting organization on "warning status" in 3 of 10 standards areas, including curriculum/instruction, facilities, and relations among administration, faculty, and staff. Staff morale was low and standardized test scores were languishing below state and national norms and the school scored significantly below the state average in the new state testing program (MCAS). The school used *Breaking Ranks* as a guide to survey different stakeholders and to change the school culture and personalize learning for students. Among the changes made were creation of an advisory program with an adult advisor for groups of 10–12 students that meets 25 minutes daily plus an additional 25 minutes each week; the creation of a career-based advisory curriculum that encourages students to discuss their plans for high school and beyond; the inclusion of Personal Learning Plans that allow students, advisers, and parents to periodically review students' progress toward reaching their goals. In addition to an annual formal review of the Personal Learning Plan with parents, advisers call each of their advisee's parents at least once per month to provide feedback on student progress. And the school hopes to schedule periodic exhibitions of student work structured around the advisory group.... A student advisory committee meets regularly (weekly at the time of writing) with the principal to suggest changes to personalize the school and has implemented changes in the bell schedule, restructured the way student government meetings are conducted (open-mike format), expanded community service activities, created a student lounge, and lengthened the lunch period.... The new community service requirement encourages students to work in small groups on projects.... Professional development is provided for recognizing diverse learning styles and for developing effective teaching strategies for the extended block format.... The school attributes its improvement in several areas to these and other changes. Among its achievements: the dropout rate is declining; the number of students leaving to attend area vocational schools has declined; student performance on standardized tests has improved, in some cases dramatically—MCAS scores have shown such an immediate improvement that for the past two years, the school has shown the second highest percentage of improvement in scores in the entire state; the state department of education released a report indicating that the Class of 2004 improved their own scores 25% from the previous year and 100% of this class has passed the state tests required for graduation.

J. E. B. Stuart High School, Falls Church, VA, suburban, 1,450 students, http://www.fcps.k12.va.us/StuartHS/... implemented a modified school-year calendar in which students who need additional instruction are able to attend school year round. These students attend the traditional fall and spring semesters and two summer sessions. The school day has also been extended, adding an extra block for students who need additional instruction.... It accords meaningful roles to various decision makers. In addition to the PTSA Academic Council's regular meetings to discuss academic topics and future initiatives, the Leadership Council, comprised of leaders from every department, and led by a teacher leader, makes all decisions important to the classroom teacher. Furthermore, the Principal's Executive Council, a group of 15–20 student leaders, meets monthly with the principal to discuss and decide upon key issues regarding student life.... The school promotes a learning community for all by requiring the principal and each teacher to have a written Personal Learning Plan and by endorsing professional development as a continuous, connected, and ongoing process. For the past five years, the comprehensive development program has focused on:

Advisory, personal plans for progress, real-world learning, community learning, student involvement in decisions

Flexible schedule, involvement of stakeholders in decision making; Personal Learning Plans for teachers and the principal

- **Year 1**—Literacy/Reading Across the Curriculum—"Every teacher is a teacher of reading." The school has a reading teacher, who teaches literacy to students, and a reading coach who teaches the teachers how to teach reading to all students in every classroom. The school has identified 15 key reading strategies, which have been published in a manual. The reading coach is charged with ensuring that all teachers know, and are able to use, each strategy.

- **Year 2**—Teaching in the Standards-Based Classroom—Every teacher participated in a 15-session college-level course that dealt with teaching in a standards-based classroom.

- **Year 3**—Instructional Delivery Model—Designed and implemented a model for instructional delivery tied directly to the observation and evaluation process. The model, based on the works of Madeline Hunter and Barak Rosenshine, provides each teacher with an easy-to-understand and useful framework for preparing and presenting each lesson. Stages of the model include Preparation/Planning, Essential Question, Activating Strategy, Teaching Activity, Distributed-Guided Practice, and Closure.

- **Year 4**—Organizing for Instruction—Significant emphasis was placed on implementing the work on standards-based classroom and the instructional model from the very beginning of the school year and each lesson.

- **Year 5**—Tools for Teaching—Focused on managing the classroom, maximizing teacher effectiveness, and increasing student productivity.

Other efforts to build a professional learning community include:

- The formation of "Teacher Research Teams"—the teams choose projects to study the effectiveness of instructional strategies on student achievement.

- A weekly newsletter published by the principal, focusing specifically on instruction.

- A weekly copy of Master Teacher that focuses on one specific aspect of classroom instruction.

- Each new teacher is assigned a mentor and receives monthly training.

- To make professional development convenient and accessible, the school has begun to place many of its materials online.

Kingwood (TX) High School, 3,800+ students (10–12), http://khs.humble.k12.tx.us/... implementing SLCs.... The schedule consists of two 7-period days, two block days, and one day that starts at 9:30 to allow teachers common planning time and professional development opportunities at least once per week.... Success has been aided by low teacher turnover rate; the principal has been in the district for 28 years and the school has been provided with long-term consistent leadership.... Difficulties in the transformation: Assumed teachers knew how to work collaboratively (helping others to realize the difference between cooperating and collaborating); not all teachers bought into the program. To address the difficulties, the school focused on advancing the "cause" rather than on those who were reluctant to join; legitimized dissent and always asked to learn what lay behind it; focused on behavior rather than attitude—believing that positive experiences will change attitudes.... Advisories, designed to support students academically, emotionally, and socially, consist of approximately 18–22 students. Students are divided alphabetically by grade level and remain in the same group for four years, with the same adviser. Activities vary from developing portfolios to pursuing service learning opportunities. An additional benefit has been the development of relationships with the students' families.

SLC/small units, flexible scheduling, advisories, teachers' common planning time

Lincoln (NE) Southwest High School, suburban, 1,500 students, http://lsw.lps.org/... opened in August 2002, and had unique opportunities to implement *Breaking Ranks* recommendations from the beginning. They implemented a 4×4 block schedule and spent considerable time developing the curriculum appropriate for the block schedule and helping teachers to learn best practices and strategies for teaching in the block schedule. The principal attributes the schedule to helping students learn at their own pace—accelerating through the curriculum if they are proficient in a specific area or being able to repeat courses without putting graduation at risk. Other benefits: students are more relaxed because of the block schedule, the average daily attendance is 97%, the reduction in transition periods helps provide a safer school environment and enables the focus of the school to be the activity of the classroom—because the majority of time is spent on academic instruction.

Flexible scheduling

Metropolitan Regional Career and Technical Center, Providence, RI, alternative high school, 600 students, www.metcenter.org... creates unique education programs for each student and blends school-based learning with outside experiences to heighten the student's interest. Advisers are responsible for facilitating and assessing each student's learning. All students are placed in an advisory team that they will remain a part of for four years. Each student creates an individual learning plan during student-led conferences with their adviser, parent, and mentor, specifically outlining the long- and short-term goals for each project. A learning-plan team designs the curriculum of each student in response to his or her interests. Far from a traditional school—there are no classes, tests, or grades—learning at the school is based on student interests and authentic assessment. Every student is responsible for public exhibitions, and the world is used as a classroom.

Advisory, Personal Plans for Progress, real-world learning

Mount Abraham Union High School, Bristol, VT, rural, 7–12, 860 students, http://www.mtabe.k12.vt.us/.... Personal Learning Plan program teaches all students to incorporate and demonstrate their strengths, interests, and aspirations in their learning. Through the plans, students are encouraged to engage in socially diverse learning communities so that they understand other's views and the school's expectations as they develop their own perspectives; build strong relationships between home and school by engaging in a dialogue about strengths, interests, and aspirations with a supportive team composed of parents and at least one teacher; set goals to achieve academic competence and personal excellence as reflected in the school's mission and expectations for student learning; take advantage of productive and engaging educational experiences to reach their goals; take active roles in designing and personalizing their education; and pursue personal independence.... Students have the opportunity to connect school with "real-life experiences" by participating in service learning, career academies, or work-based learning.

Personal Plans for Progress for students, service learning/ real-world experiences

Needham B. Broughton High School, Raleigh, NC, urban, magnet, 2,140 students, http://broughton.wcpss.net/... has two programs to help students of all academic levels learn more about career choices. Juniors and seniors supplement their formal classroom instruction by taking on responsible year-long roles as interns/workers in organizations and businesses. Student interns are given an internship manual with all necessary forms and due dates for the year. Observation and reflection are key components of the internship. All work is completed online and interns send in work electronically every two weeks. Each grading period, the internship sponsor completes an evaluation. At the

Learning extending beyond the campus

end of the year, student interns complete an evaluation and internship project, which is presented and can then be used as a resource for future interns.... To promote a successful transition from school to career and promote career awareness, students have an opportunity to meet with local business representatives and professionals. This is followed by a full day in which a student, matched with a mentor in the student's area of interest, is able to learn about the skills needed for the career. Students are evaluated by the mentors, and interested students can then pursue a year-long internship.

Newcomers High School, New York, NY, urban, 1,200 students, http://schools.nycenet.edu/queenshs/newcomers/... faces unique challenges and opportunities because all of its students are English language learners. Regents exam results convinced the school of the importance of emphasizing—across the curriculum and regardless of English language ability—the critical thinking and vocabulary-building skills required to pass the Regents examinations and pursue higher education. Staff workshops were developed to explore interdisciplinary approaches and a variety of teaching strategies, including providing more ESL methodology in each content-area class and using technology to explain difficult concepts and motivate students. The use of visuals is essential. Pictures, charts, graphs, overhead projectors, computer simulations, lab experiments, video, and role-playing skits are staples in both ESL and content-area classes.... All courses, special classes, and programs were created to help English language learners, what they refer to as "our new Americans," discover themselves as successful participants in the life of their new country with a sense of self-respect and appreciation for their native countries. The school acknowledges the acculturation process as open ended and participates in the process with students across the curriculum. In bilingual projects, they acquire and share data and insights into the history and reality of immigration law, the American market economy, the roles of the police and courts, and the workings and importance of the electoral process. Respect, freedom, and responsibility are three unifying elements within and beyond the classrooms. Popular topics include rites of passage, identity, the world of work, cultural diffusion, human rights, immigration, the environment, and family. Working with Facing History and Ourselves, students broaden their awareness of ethical issues that recur in the lives of individuals, cultures, and nations. Outcome-based, theme-oriented interdisciplinary efforts incorporate evaluation of primary sources including diaries, newspapers and photos, and analysis of literature and films, as a means of approaching basic themes in our evolving American democracy, including diversity, the frontier, change, and the expansion of rights.

Recognition of diversity; integrated curriculum

North Reading High School, Reading, MA, suburban, 600 students, http://www.northreadingmass.com/ NRHigh/NRHS/NRHighsmall.htm... has redesigned itself with *Breaking Ranks* recommendations in mind. The school went to a semester block schedule (AB model) in which all students take eight courses—eight blocks, four each day, a byproduct of which has been the increased opportunities for electives.... To support this and other changes, a new leadership structure was created, incorporating two academic division leaders: one for the humanities and the other for math/science/technology. Teacher Methodology professional development offerings have also increased, including in the areas of teaching in the block schedule, writing across the curriculum, learning styles, and multiple intelligences. Much emphasis has been placed on improving teacher methodology.... Every new teacher is required to take a six-week course (two hours/week) taught by the principal and academic division leader, thereby fostering the use of hands-on practice, learning from each other, and

Flexible scheduling, transformed department structure, variety of learning styles and assessments, Personal Learning Plans for teachers and the principal

camaraderie. An emphasis is placed on student-centered versus teacher-centered learning models and the teacher is the coach, facilitator, and mentor. These changes resulted in a new curriculum, new instructional techniques, varied assessment, and a more positive climate.... In addition, Personal Learning Plans for each teacher as well as for the principal have been instituted; professional development is taken into account during the teacher appraisal process; all new teachers must take a six-week learning style and differentiated instruction course taught by the principal and the Academic Division Leader of Math; a policy exists to ensure that teachers share with other teachers what they learn during workshops or training; time is dedicated to teacher sharing during faculty meetings and divisional meetings; and the Academic Division Leaders and curriculum chair perform observations.... All students' learning styles are assessed as well as teachers' styles, differentiated instruction has been initiated, and writing across all disciplines has been implemented.

Poland (ME) Regional High School, Poland, ME, 583 students, www.poland-hs.u29.k12.me.us... reopened its doors in 1999 centered around recommendations articulated in various reform initiatives including *Breaking Ranks*.... Students are looped in ninth- and tenth-grade teams to reinforce the importance of student-teacher relationships. There are multiple pathways and opportunities, and students are given a choice in terms of what they pursue. In addition, students stay with the same adviser and group of advisees for four years. They meet daily for 30 minutes, which has not only allowed the groups to discuss issues of concern but has connected parents and advisers in the effort to monitor student progress.... Although students are encouraged to forge their own particular path, all of the graduates must meet competency requirements. Meeting those requirements are supported by the following: teachers taking advantage of common planning time, advisory groups, portfolio work, public exhibitions, service learning, student activities, the honor code, heterogeneous classes, and Honors Challenges.... Challenges on the way have included maintaining consistency in grading, developing a system of common assessments, and challenging all students.

Small units, adviser, varied assessment

Rex Putnam High School, Milwaukie, OR, suburban, 1,358 students, http://putnam.nclack.k12.or.us/... was restructured in 1997 into SLCs for the ninth and tenth grades in order to help each student feel like "my teachers know me.... I belong to a group...and I can't let my team down".... Teachers and students are teamed, and students spend 50% or more time each day in their team.... Students are looped—90 students stay with the same three teachers for two years.... The school has implemented a block schedule.... Indicators of success include improved attendance, academic performance, and behavior.

SLC/small units

Roosevelt High School, Yonkers, NY, magnet, bilingual, 1,509 students, http://roosevelt.ypschools.org/... is the only bilingual high school in the district. Therefore, all English language learners are sent here. The school believes that it is organized with the "caring of an elementary school, the schedule of a middle school, and the curriculum of a high school".... It has implemented a number of practices to build a sense of community within the school and with families: students and teachers are organized into teams and remain with these teams for four years, welcoming signs and greetings are provided in several languages, meetings are held in places and at times that are convenient for families.... It created a schoolwide data team in 2001. The current membership of 15 draws heavily from the mathematics and science faculty. Recruitment

Family involvement, using data for assessment and improvement

is planned for more diverse membership, with at least one team member from each department in the building. The goals of the team include: act as the RHS "data conscience"; collect and archive complete and accurate data; analyze data from all sources; use data to monitor reform initiatives; develop implications for curricular, instructional, and professional development decisions; publish user-friendly reports; and create a data plan to guide both annual and ad hoc data-related activities. Data team activities have precipitated several instructional initiatives. Based on an analysis of prior years' student outcomes, the ninth-grade program now provides an extra period daily that cycles among the core subjects. Similarly, the retained ninth-grade program begins period 2 (students come to school late) and ends with lunch (students don't return after lunch). A ninth-grade team uses weekly compiled attendance data to quickly identify student behavior patterns and, with all stakeholders, develop and monitor a situation improvement plan…. Another initiative, the ABC program, offering after-school diagonal-slice (i.e., across multiple teams) Regents mathematics exam support classes, was created to address a correlation between earlier students' math Regents performance and their prior TerraNova math score that suggested gaps in fundamentals. The objective of the ABC program is to reinforce fundamentals…. Indicators of success are an increase in test scores, an increase in attendance rates, and a decrease in suspensions.

Sierra Vista (CA) High School, urban, 1,881 students, http://www.sierravista .wuhsd.k12.ca.us/… has used a variety of methods to assess student progress and has used that assessment to inform curriculum and instructional strategies choices. For example, a senior project is required for all students, including English language learners and special education students. The project has four components: an 8- to 12-page research paper; a physical project that involves a minimum of 15 hours outside of school time under the supervision of an adult mentor (job shadowing, learning a new skill, etc.); a portfolio logging the phases of the senior project; and an oral presentation to a panel of judges from the school and community. As a direct result of the weakness demonstrated on the writing portion of the senior project the first year, the English department modified its curriculum and instruction, placing more emphasis on writing. In addition, this weakness prompted the school to require research papers at all grade levels, rather than simply the senior year. Other changes prompted by the senior project include:

Variety of assessments, assessments integrated into learning

- The English and social science departments have created benchmark projects consisting of research papers, projects, and media-supported oral presentations.

- Other departments modified their curriculum. For example, the Social Science Department changed its curriculum to include oral presentations when the need for students to give more oral presentations became apparent.

- The Language Department has changed one of its assessments—creating an oral final exam and requiring visuals.

- In the Language Department, students complete self-, group-, and individual evaluation forms on presentations.

Other ways in which assessment has guided instruction and learning include:

- The Math Department uses alternative assessments, including projects and portfolios as semester final exams. For example, in algebra classes, students create a Math Game Project, using questions and answers from various classroom assignments; in geometry, teachers assign projects requiring students to design and build models of structures based on geometric theorems and principles. Students must explain the math used for the design and construction of the models.

- Various assessment pieces revealed that many students couldn't successfully read and comprehend textbooks and other required reading material. To help students improve their reading skills, a full-time Reading Specialist/Literacy Coach has been added to the staff. In addition to English classes, students who need to improve reading, reading comprehension, and writing skills may enroll in a five-unit elective reading course. The Reading Specialist and a consultant hired by Sierra Vista have provided in-service development for many staff members on Reciprocal Teaching, a method that trains teachers in instructional strategies that help students improve their reading, as well as writing, study, and test-taking skills. The strategies enable students to become active, engaged readers by predicting what they will read, visualizing as they read, and summarizing what they have read.

Sir Francis Drake High School, San Anselmo, CA, suburban, 1,030 students, http://drake.marin.k12.ca.us/ .... Students choose whether or not they want to be part of the SLC (academies) or if they wish to pursue the traditional route. One of the academies, begun in 1996, was designed by students to be compatible with the needs of juniors and seniors preparing for college and the work force. This academy uses projects directly applicable to the working world, and students participate in projects or internships in their area of interest. Another is the communication academy, whose mission is to build a community of self-directed learners who specialize in communication, collaboration, and creative problem solving and demonstrate learning through integrated media performance-based exhibitions. It is a two-year program for juniors and seniors that provides an opportunity for motivated students to combine academic and artistic interests in an integrated, project-based setting. Peer teaching is a key element of the program. Seniors are expected to pass their knowledge and skills to incoming juniors. One of the mottoes: "Everybody Teaches, Everybody Learns".... The school has been operating with SLC ideas for the past 14 years. For other schools interested in adopting similar forms of SLCs centered on student's interests, the school highlights the importance of a flexible schedule, movement from teacher-centered to student-centered classrooms, inquiry-based learning from projects and internships, teachers who are committed to the belief that serious learning can happen in and out of the classroom, trust, administration buy-in to allow students off campus, and ability for academies to raise money to support such programs. The challenges during their reform have been scheduling and teacher buy-in—even though all the changes at Drake have been teacher initiated.... The school embraces an interdisciplinary approach to education, and links instruction with the student's passion. During sophomore year, students submit a Core Literacy Portfolio (CLP) that indicates completion of communication and reading skills. The CLP is made up of work from across all school curriculum and is graded by a team of staff. Quarterly exhibitions of work for Grades 11 and 12 integrate social studies, English, advanced drama, and advanced video to demonstrate the students' understanding of the academic content. Eleventh and twelfth graders can also participate in a project-based program called the Engineering Academy, which integrates physics, sculpture, and principles of engineering.... Drake has a ninth-grade orientation program that pairs upperclassmen with freshmen to help with the transition... has a "homeroom" program that involves students, teach-

SLC/small units, variety of assessments, real-world learning, interdisciplinary/ ntegrated curriculum

ers, and staff members. Groups of 15–18 students have an adviser for their whole experience at Drake and they receive credit for this attendance.

Souhegan High School, Amherst NH, 982 students, http://www.sprise.com/shs/ default.htm... was founded in 1992 based on the idea of creating a democratic school. Personalization in the school is a democratic system in both philosophy and structure whereby students are encouraged to express their views and participate in school governance with formal power in the Community Council. The Council consists of 45 elected members—25 students and 20 adults (teachers, staff, administrators, board members, and community members) and is responsible for "governing all school affairs." Students have always had a majority voice in key policy decisions. Whole-school conversations about issues of concern to students and adults offer a catalyst for reflection, debate, and action. The school believes that leadership and consistent affirmation of the tenets of democracy are essential components in producing an active citizenry. The development of a democratic approach to school decision making was a process that required a major investment of time and personnel. Finding a balance of power and getting the involvement and participation from all facets of the school took time. Such an undertaking requires the leaders to be empowered in order to empower students and staff. The school hopes that by creating and sustaining a democratic culture at the school, students will continue to have lifelong interest and take action in local and national issues. Schools considering a similar democratic model will need to ask questions of stakeholders such as: "If decisions in your school were to be made more democratically than they are now (parents, students, teachers, staff), what would the benefits and drawbacks be? What would be your fears about that type of system?" This school found that responses centered around ownership, leadership, collaboration, and concerns about a system that could become chaotic, that decisions or priorities addressed may not be supported by the administration, and the critical need to keep everyone informed.

Democratic values, community/stakeholder involvement

South Boston (MA) High School, three schools of approximately 380 each—more than 1,000 total students... reforms included development of three small schools, dividing the building to facilitate a small-school atmosphere, professional development for staff, assigning teachers to new classrooms and learning communities (based on preferences), and reorganizing the leadership structure. The structure of having three small schools within the umbrella of the high school is the school's greatest strength, according to school officials. As a result of creating three autonomous high schools, each with its own budget, faculty, leadership, and pathway program, they have been able to create a caring atmosphere for the students. Each high school, which serves about 380 students, is further broken down into SLCs in order to meet the academic, social, and emotional needs of the students. The results of the reform have been positive for the students: They are given more support as a result of the SLCs; they have developed an identity within one of the small-school cultures, and yet maintain the traditions of the large school because students share sports, arts, and other activities. Early results have shown an increase in MCAS scores and attendance rates, a decrease in the dropout rate, and, overall, there is a feeling of being safer, better organized, and more focused.... Challenges include: The district still sees the school as one building, and hence, one big school versus three autonomous schools; various issues with the teachers' union; integrating bilingual students.

SLC/small units

Southeast Raleigh High School, Raleigh, NC, urban, 2,086 students, http://www.srhs.net/... developed an "Academic Coaching" (AC) model in which every student belongs to an AC team headed by a staff "coach." The team and its coach stay together throughout high school, meeting daily. Monday, Thursday, and Friday are "team times" in which students watch the in-school news channel, talk with their coach, and build a peer support system. Tuesdays are devoted to a teacher-developed, four-year curriculum that focuses on three goals: personal mentoring, academic counseling, and career coaching. An AC manual and annual curriculum plan are supplemented with weekly e-mails on curriculum and school news. Every three weeks, interim reports are distributed and coaches conference individually with students to set goals for student achievement. Students elected from each AC team have opportunities to deliver curriculum and provide input on school issues.

Small units/advisories

Southside High School, Rockville Center, NY, suburban, 1,200 students, http://www.rvcschools.org/... Southside has increased its support of high expectations for all students over the past decade by accelerating students in mathematics, opening enrollment to AP and IB, and using inclusion for virtually all students. Since 2000, approximately 60–70% of students study at the IB or AP level.

Essential learnings/ academic rigor

Stranahan High School, Fort Lauderdale, FL, urban, 2,050 students, http://www.broward.k12.fl.us/stranahanhigh/... has attempted to banish anonymity through the ninth-grade academy, the Urban Teacher Academy, two magnet programs, and by using learning-style inventories for students. The ninth-grade academy students are organized into common teams comprised of academic and elective teachers.... Teachers are provided common planning time and professional development opportunities related to the integration of curriculum, alternative assessment, the Habits of the Mind, and work-based learning.... Incoming ninth-grade students are enrolled in a Seminar of Success course, which assists them with study skill development, career assessment, and investigations using computer-assisted programs and gives them the opportunity to work with business and community mentors. Ninth graders also participate in the "Summer Environmental Seminar" in which students study targeted aspects of environmental issues related to Fort Lauderdale.

Small units, integrated curriculum, middle school transition, community learning

Urban Academy, New York, NY, urban, tenth grade, transfer school, 108 students, www.urbanacademy.org... As a transfer school, many students apply after having been unchallenged in their previous schools, according to school officials. It serves a diverse population of students, and 95% of graduates go onto four-year colleges.... Questioning is the basis of an inquiry approach to teaching and learning at this school. Teachers and students respond to questions together by exploring ideas, conducting research, evaluating information, debating points of view respectfully, developing new sources of fact and opinion, and presenting and defending their findings. Students are able to use the city as their classroom, attend seminar-style classes, and participate in a community service program. Student work is assessed twice each semester.

Real-world learning, small units

Wahluke High School, Mattawa, WA, rural, 370 students.... The community in which the school resides is struggling with the challenges of poverty and transiency. Their efforts to know every student have contributed to a significant increase in the number of college aspirants in the past three years for the mostly poor and Hispanic population—from 21% to 54%. All college-prep classes are open to all students, including honors, AP classes in English and History, calculus, and physics. In addition, the school has increased the graduation requirements from 25 to 29 credits.... Advisories have been implemented and students begin senior year with a "post-12" plan in place.... In an effort to promote parental involvement, the school has put emphasis on hiring bilingual staff.

Supporting academic rigor

Waukesha North High School, Waukesha, WI, suburban, 1,350 students, http://www.waukesha.k12.wi.us/North/WaukeshaNorth2.html... has sought to personalize learning for each student through several programs: a freshman learning community, the Take Responsibility for Yourself (TRY) program for tenth and eleventh graders, and personal student advocates. Student achievement as well as progress on individual projects or assignments is monitored consistently. Teachers communicate regularly with each other and with parents and counselors. Under the personal student advocate program, a core of teachers makes an effort to get better acquainted with individual students and develop relationships that serve to improve student confidence and acceptance. Successes: The principal attributes the drop in the freshman percentage scoring Ds and Fs (from more than 32% to 27%) to the freshman learning community. TRY students have a 92% graduation rate after participating for two or more years in the program.

Small units, Personal Adult Advocates

Woodburn (OR) High School, suburban/rural, 1,215, students, http://www .woodburn.k12.or.us/WHS_web/index.htm.... Communication at the school is trilingual—English, Spanish, and Russian; consequently, every teacher receives training in the English language development needs of new students.... Individual goal setting and educational plans for students are encouraged—including a five-year plan that outlines student plans for life after high school.... The IB has been implemented with teachers being the primary contributors to the application process. Furthermore, the process of applying for the IB program provides a tangible way for the school to identify its strengths and weaknesses and to put into place a plan that will allow every student the opportunity to participate in a challenging academic program. In addition, the implementation of IB caused the district as a whole to look closely at each student in elementary and middle school to ensure that the programs offered there enable students to access the highest levels of curriculum available at the high school.... All teachers participate in IB-related professional development; in that way, IB instructional strategies are embedded in the curriculum for all classes—not just the IB classes.... Students have the opportunity to take college classes through a dual enrollment program with the local community college.... While ninth- and tenth-grade students have the option of accelerated coursework, all juniors enroll in college preparatory courses.... A summer academy helps ninth graders make a successful transition to high school academic work. (Adapted from Camblin, Gullatt & Klopott, 2003.)

Personal Plans for Progress, academic rigor, variety of instructional strategies, P–16 continuum; extends learning beyond the school's four walls, ninth-grade transition

Resources

General Resources on School Restructuring

Boyer, E. L. (1983). *High school: A report on secondary education in America.* Carnegie Foundation for the Advancement of Teaching. New York: Harper & Row.

Carnegie Council on Adolescent Development. (1989). *Turning points: Preparing American youth for the 21st century.* Washington, DC: Author.

Collins, J. (2001). *Good to great: Why some companies make the leap…and others don't.* New York, NY. HarperCollins.

Cotton, K. (2004). *New small learning communities: Findings from recent literature.* Reston, VA: National Association of Secondary School Principals.

Education Week. (2001, April 11–May 16). High school: The shifting mission. Retrieved December 23, 2003, from http://www.edweek.org/sreports/special_reports_article .cfm?slug=highschool.htm.

Gainey, D. D., & Webb, L. D. (1998). *The education leader's role in change: How to proceed.* Reston, VA: National Association of Secondary School Principals.

George, P. (2000). *Breaking Ranks in action. Principal Leadership, 1*(4), 56–61.

George, P. (2001). *Breaking Ranks in action. Principal Leadership, 1*(5), 60–65.

Lee, V., & Smith, J. (1994). *Effects of high school restructuring and size on gains in achievement and engagement for early secondary school students.* Madison, WI: Center on the Organization and Restructuring of Schools.

Maine Commission on Secondary Education. (1998). *Promising futures: A call to improve learning for Maine's secondary students.* Augusta, ME: Department of Education.

Marzano, R. J., Marzano, J. S., & Pickering, D. J. (2003). *Classroom management that works: Research-based strategies for every teacher.* Alexandria, VA: Association of Supervision and Curriculum.

National Association of Secondary School Principals. (1996). *An executive summary of Breaking Ranks: Changing an American institution.* Reston, VA: Author.

National Association of Secondary School Principals. (1996). *Breaking Ranks: Changing an American institution.* Reston, VA: Author.

National Association of Secondary School Principals. (2002). *What the research shows: Breaking Ranks in action.* Reston, VA: Author.

National Commission on Excellence in Education. (1983). *A nation at risk: The imperative for educational reform.* Washington, DC: U.S. Government Printing Office.

North Central Regional Educational Laboratory. (2003, Spring). *Curriculum mapping: A process for continuous quality improvement. Notes & Reflections.*

Painter, B., & Valentine, J. (1998). *The Instructional Practices Inventory.* Columbia, MO: Middle Level Leadership Center.

Reeves, D. B. (2001). *101 Questions & answers about standards, assessment, and accountability* (p. 135). Denver, CO: Advanced Learning Press.

Rose, L. C., & Gallup, A. M. (2003). The 35th Annual Phi Delta Kappa/Gallup Poll of the Public's Attitudes Toward the Public Schools. *Phi Delta Kappan, 85*(1), 41–52.

Sizer, T. R. (1984). *Horace's compromise: The dilemma of the American high school.* Boston: Houghton Mifflin.

Sparks, D. (2002). *Designing powerful professional development for teachers and principals.* Oxford, OH: National Staff Development Council.

Sparks, D. (2003). Transformational learning. *Journal of Staff Development, 24*(1), 29.

Vermont High School Task Force. (2002). *High schools on the move: Renewing Vermont's commitment to quality secondary education* (p. 34). Montpelier, VT: Vermont Department of Education.

Strategic Use of Data

Johnson, J. H. (1997). Data-driven school improvement. (ERIC Document Reproduction Service No. ED401595).

Killion, J., & Bellamy, T. (2000, Winter). On the job: Data analysts focus on school improvement efforts. *Journal of Staff Development, 21*(1).

Kinder, A. (2000, Summer). D^{3}M: Helping schools distill data. *NCREL's Learning Point, 2*(2).

Lachat, M. A. (2001). *Data-driven high school reform: The Breakings Ranks model.* Providence, RI: Brown University.

Lashway, L. (2001). Educational indicators. (ERIC Document Reproduction Service No. ED457536).

Popham, W. J. (2001). *Building tests to support instruction and accountability: A guide for policymakers.* Washington, DC: Commission on Instructionally Supportive Assessment.

Popham, W. J. (2002). *Implementing ESEA's testing provisions: Guidance from an independent commission's requirements,* Washington, DC: Commission on Instructionally Supportive Assessment.

Quinn, D., Greunert, S., & Valentine, J. (1999). *Using data for school improvement.* Reston, VA: National Association of Secondary School Principals.

Recommendations

1. ***The principal will provide leadership in the high school community by building and maintaining a vision, direction, and focus for student learning.***

   Barkley, S., Bottoms, G., Feagin, C., & Clark. S. (2001). *Leadership matters: Building leadership capacity.* Atlanta, GA: Southern Regional Education Board.

   Cotton, K. (2004). *Principals of high achieving schools. What the research says.* Reston, VA: National Association of Secondary School Principals.

   Dalziel, M. M., & Schoonover, S. C. (1988). *Changing ways: A practical tool for implementing change within organizations.* New York: Amacom.

   Goldberg, M. F. (2001). Leadership in education: Five commonalities. *Phi Delta Kappan, 82*(10), 757–761.

   Usdan, M., McCloud, B., & Podomostko, M. (2000). *Leadership for student learning: reinventing the principalship.* Washington, DC: Institute for Educational Leadership.

2. ***Each high school will establish a site council and accord other meaningful roles in decision making to students, parents, and members of the staff to promote student learning and an atmosphere of participation, responsibility, and ownership.***

   Alvoid, K. L. (1999). Leadership: A function of teamwork. *High School Magazine, 7*(3), 16–21.

   Hirsh., S. (1997). *Building effective teams.* Reston, VA: National Association of Secondary School Principals.

   Painter, B., Lucas, S., Wooderson, M., & Valentine, J. (2000). *The use of teams in school improvement processes.* Reston, VA: National Association of Secondary School Principals.

   Painter, B., & Valentine, J. (1999). *Engaging teachers in the school improvement process.* Reston, VA: National Association of Secondary School Principals.

   Turk, R. L., Wolff, K., Waterbury, C., & Zumalt, J. (2002). What principals should know about building and maintaining teams. *NASSP Bulletin, 86*(630), 15–23.

3. ***A high school will regard itself as a community in which members of the staff collaborate to develop and implement the school's learning goals.***

   Bierema, L. L. (1999). The process of the learning organization: Making sense of change. *NASSP Bulletin, 83*(604), 46–56.

   DuFour, R. P. (1999). Help wanted: Principals who can lead professional learning communities. *NASSP Bulletin, 83*(604), 12–17.

   Hord, S. M. (1997). Professional learning communities: What are they and why are they important? *SEDL issues…about change, 6*(1).

   Lashway, L. (1998). Creating a learning organization. (ERIC Document Reproduction Service No. ED420897).

4. **Teachers will provide the leadership essential to the success of reform, collaborating with others in the educational community to redefine the role of the teacher and to identify sources of support for that redefined role.**

Buckner, K., & McDowelle, J. O. (2000). Developing teacher leaders: Providing encouragement, opportunities, and support. *NASSP Bulletin, 84*(616), 35–41.

Childs-Bowen, D., Moller, G.. & Scrivner, J. (2000). Principals: Leaders of leaders. *NASSP Bulletin, 84*(616), 27–34.

Usdan, M., McCloud, B., & Podomostko, M. (2001). Leadership for student learning: Redefining the teacher as leader. Washington, DC: Institute for Educational Leadership.

Wanzare, Z., & da Costa, J. L. (2000). Supervision and staff development: Overview of the literature. *NASSP Bulletin, 84*(618), 47–54.

5. **Every school will be a learning community for the entire community. As such, the school will promote the use of Personal Learning Plans for each educator and provide the resources to ensure that the principal, teachers, and other staff members can address their own learning and professional development needs as they relate to improved student learning.**

Collins, D. (1998). *Achieving your vision of professional development: How to assess your needs and get what you want.* Greensboro, NC: SERVE.

Little, J. W. (1999). Organizing schools for teacher learning. In L. Darling-Hammond & G. Sykes (Eds.), *Teaching as the learning profession* (pp. 233–262). San Francisco: Jossey-Bass.

National Staff Development Council. (2001). *Standards for staff development.* Oxford, OH: Author.

SERVE (1998). *Achieving your vision of professional development.* Greensboro, NC: Author.

Sparks, D., & Richardson, J. *What is staff development anyway? Everything you need to know about professional learning.* Oxford, OH: National Staff Development Council.

Webb, L. D., & Berkbeugler, R. (1998). *Personal Learning Plans for educators.* Reston, VA: National Association of Secondary School Principals.

6. **The school community will promote policies and practices that recognize diversity in accord with the core values of a democratic and civil society and will offer substantive ongoing professional development to help educators appreciate issues of diversity and expose students to a rich array of viewpoints, perspectives, and experiences.**

Calderon, M. (1997). Staff development in multilingual multicultural schools. (ERIC Document Reproduction Service No. ED410368).

Gallavan, N. P., Jordan, T. S., Tanaka, W. N., & Steen, K. M. (n.d.). *Breaking ranks: Making it happen; Affirming diversity in the high school.* Reston, VA: National Association of Secondary School Principals.

Middleton, J. A. (1999). Why administrators need diversity training. *School Administrators*, *56*(6), 1–4.

Sparks, D. (2000). High-powered professional development for high poverty schools. *Principal Leadership*, *1*(4), 26–29.

7. *High schools will build partnerships with institutions of higher education to provide teachers and administrators at both levels with ideas and opportunities to enhance the education, performance, and evaluation of educators.*

Lauder, A. (2000). The new look in principal preparation programs. *NASSP Bulletin*, *84*(617), 23–28.

Zellner, L. J.; & Erlandson, D. A. (1997). Leadership laboratories: Professional development for the 21st century. *NASSP Bulletin*; *81*(585), 45–50.

8. *High schools will develop political and financial relationships with individuals, organizations, and businesses to support and supplement educational programs and policies.*

Clearinghouse on Educational Management. (2002). *Corporate involvement in school reform*. Eugene, OR: Author.

Council for Corporate and School Partnerships. (2002). *Guiding principles for business and school partnership*. Atlanta, GA: Author.

Cunningham, C. (2002). Engaging the community to support student achievement. (ERIC Document Reproduction Service No. ED464395).

Decker, L. E. (2001). Allies in education. *Principal Leadership*, *2*(1), 42–46.

Kuo, E. W. (1999). Creating beneficial institutional collaborations. (ERIC Document Reproduction Service No. ED427818).

9. *At least once every five years, each high school will convene a broadly based external panel to offer a public description of the school, a requirement that could be met in conjunction with the evaluations by state, regional, and other accrediting groups.*

Clinard, J., & Foster, L. (1998). Leadership in a fishbowl: A new accreditation process. *Educational Leadership*, *55*(7), 53–56.

10. *High schools will create small units in which anonymity is banished.*

Dewees, S. (1999). The school-within-a-school model. (ERIC Document Reproduction Service No. ED438147).

George, P. S., & McEwin, C. K. (1999). High schools for a new century: Why is the high school changing? *NASSP Bulletin*, *83*(606), 10–24.

Gregory, T. (2001). Breaking up large high schools: Five common (and understandable) errors of execution. (ERIC Document Reproduction Service No. ED459049).

Vander Ark, T. (2002). Personalization: Making every school a small school. *Principal Leadership*, *2*(6), 10–14.

11. Each high school teacher involved in the instructional program on a full-time basis will be responsible for contact time with no more than 90 students during a given term so that the teacher can give greater attention to the needs of every student.

Callahan, C. M. (1999). Classrooms for learners, not winners and losers. *High School Magazine, 7*(1), 22–26.

Hoffman, D., & Levak, B. A. (2003). Personalizing Schools. *Educational Leadership, 61*(1), 30–34.

Jenkins, J. M., & Keefe, J. W. (2001). Strategies for personalizing instruction: A typology for improving teaching and learning. *NASSP Bulletin, 85*(629), 72–82.

Jenkins, J. M., & Keefe, J. W. (2002). Two schools: Two approaches to personalized learning. *Phi Delta Kappan, 83*, 449–456.

Nagel, J. E., & Smith, P. (2001). The art of personalizing learning. *Principal Leadership, 2*(3), 36–39.

12. Each student will have a Personal Plan for Progress that will be reviewed often to ensure that the high school takes individual needs into consideration and to allow students, within reasonable parameters, to design their own methods for learning in an effort to meet high standards.

DiMartino, J., Clarke, J., & Lachat, M. A. (2002). Creating student-centered high schools. *Principal Leadership, 2*(5), 44–49.

DiMartino, J., Clarke, J., & Wolk, D. (Eds.) (2003). *Personalized learning: Preparing high school students to create their futures.* Lanham, MD: Scarecrow Education Press.

Education Alliance at Brown University. (2003). *Changing systems to personalize learning: The power of advisories.* Providence, RI: Author.

Faas, L., Lindsay, D., Webb, L. D. (1997). *Personal Plans for Progress for secondary school students.* Reston, VA: National Association of Secondary School Principals.

13. Every high school student will have a Personal Adult Advocate to help him or her personalize the educational experience.

Pope, N., Metha, A., & Webb, L. D. (1997). *The Personal Adult Advocate Program.* Reston, VA: National Association of Secondary School Principals.

14. Teachers will convey a sense of caring to their students so that their students feel that their teachers share a stake in their learning.

Flinders, D. J., & Noddings, N. (2001). *Multiyear teaching: The case for continuity. From inquiry to practice.* Bloomington, IN: Phi Delta Kappa.

Hatton, S. D., & Noddings, N. (2002). Interview with Nel Noddings: Reflections on becoming an educator. *Active Learner: A Foxfire Journal for Teachers, 7*(1), 11–13.

Noddings, N. (2002). *Educating moral people: A caring alternative to character education.* New York: Teachers College Press.

Osterman, K. F. (2000). Students' need for belonging in the school community. *Review of Educational Research, 70*(3), 323–367.

15. High schools will develop flexible scheduling and student grouping patterns that allow better use of time in order to meet the individual needs of students to ensure academic success.

Ballinger, C. (2000). Changing time: Improving learning. *High School Magazine, 7*(9), 5–8.

Chaika, G. (1999, August 30). Alternative school calendars: Smart idea or senseless experiment? *Education World.* Retrieved December 23, 2003, from http://www.education-world.com/a_admin/admin126.shtml.

Kneese, C. (2000). Teaching in year-round schools. (ERIC Document Reproduction Service No. ED449123).

Kruse, C. A., & Kruse, G. D. (1995). The master schedule and learning: Improving the quality of education. *NASSP Bulletin, 79*(571), 1–8.

Metzker, B. (2002). School calendars. (ERIC Document Reproduction Service No. ED466007).

National Education Commission on Time and Learning. (1994). *Prisoners of time.* Washington, DC: Author.

Northeast and Islands Regional Educational Laboratory. (1998). *Block scheduling: Innovations with time.* Providence, RI: Author.

16. The high school will engage students' families as partners in the students' education.

Constantino, S. M. (2002). *Making your school family friendly.* Reston, VA: National Association of Secondary School Principals.

Cooper, C. (1999). Beyond the bake sale: How parent involvement makes a difference. *NCREL's Learning Point, 1*(3), 1–6.

Henderson, A. T., & Raimondo, B. N. (2001). Unlocking parent potential. *Principal Leadership, 2*(1), 26–32.

Manning, M. L., & Lee, G. (2001). Working with parents—Cultural and linguistic considerations. *Kappa Delta Pi Record, 37*, 160–163.

National Association of Secondary School Principals. (2003). *Bridge builders: Establishing effective school-community relationships.* Reston, VA: Author.

Sanders, M. G. (1998). *Schools, families, and communities—Partnership for student success.* Reston, VA: National Association of Secondary School Principals.

Simon, B. S. (2001). Family involvement in high school: Predictors and effects. *NASSP Bulletin, 85*(627), 8–19.

17. The high school community, which cannot be value neutral, will advocate and model a set of core values essential in a democratic and civil society.

Association for Supervision and Curriculum Development. (2002). *Building learning communities with character: How to integrate academic, social, and emotional learning.* Alexandria, VA: Author.

Fertman, C. I., & van Linden, J. A. (1999). Character education: An essential ingredient for youth leadership development. *NASSP Bulletin, 83*(609), 9–15.

Harned, P. J. (1999). Leading the effort to teach character in schools. *NASSP Bulletin, 83*(609), 25–32.

Lickona, T. (1996). Teaching respect and responsibility: Reclaiming children and youth. *Journal of Emotional and Behavioral Problems, 5*(3), 143–151.

18. High schools, in conjunction with agencies in the community, will help coordinate the delivery of physical and mental health and social services for youth.

Blank, M., Melaville, A., & Shah, B. (2003). *Making the difference: Research and practice in community schools.* Washington, DC: Coalition for Community Schools, Institute for Educational Leadership.

Dryfoos, J. & Maguire, S. (2002). *Inside full-service community schools.* Thousand Oaks, CA: Corwin Press.

Elias, M. J., Zins, J. E., Weissberg, R. P., Frey, K. S., Greenberg, M. T., Haynes, N. M., Kessler, R., Schwab-Stone, M. E., & Shriver, T. P. (1997). *Promoting social and emotional learning: guidelines for educators.* Alexandria, VA: Association for Supervision and Curriculum Development.

19. Each high school will identify a set of essential learnings—above all, in literature and language, writing, mathematics, social studies, science, and the arts—in which students must demonstrate achievement in order to graduate.

Berger, J. (2000). Does top-down, standards-based reform work? A review of the status of statewide standards-based reform. *NASSP Bulletin, 84*(612), 57–65.

Hadderman, M. (2000). Standards: The policy environment. (ERIC Document Reproduction Service No. ED444239).

Joftus, S. (2002). *Every child a graduate: A framework for excellent education for all middle and high school students.* Washington, DC: Alliance for Excellent Education.

Learning First Alliance. (n.d.). *Standards and accountability: A call by the Learning First Alliance for mid-course corrections.* Washington, DC: Author.

Schmoker, M. (2000). Standards versus sentimentality: Reckoning successfully with the most promising movement in modern education. *NASSP Bulletin, 84*(620), 49–60.

Thompson, S. (2001). The authentic standards movement and its evil twin. *Phi Delta Kappan, 82,* 358–362.

Urquhart, V., Gonder, P., & Stapleman, J. (2000). *Noteworthy perspectives on implementing standards-based education.* Aurora, CO: Mid-Continent Research for Education and Learning.

Westerberg, T., & Webb, L. D. (1997). *Providing focus and direction through essential learnings.* Reston, VA: National Association of Secondary School Principals.

20. Each high school will present alternatives to tracking and to ability grouping.

Burnett, G. (1995). Alternatives to ability grouping: Still unanswered questions. (ERIC Document Reproduction Service No. ED390947).

Cohen, E. (1994). *Designing groupwork: Strategies for the heterogeneous classroom.* New York: Teachers College Press.

Cohen, E., & Lotan, R. A. (Eds.). (1997). *Working for equity in heterogeneous classrooms: Sociological theory in practice.* New York: Teachers College Press.

Harlen, W. (1997). *Making sense of research on ability grouping.* Edinburgh: The Scottish Council for Research in Education.

Rogers, K. B. (1998). Using current research to make "good" decisions about grouping. *NASSP Bulletin, 82*(595), 38–46.

21. The high school will reorganize the traditional department structure in order to integrate the school's curriculum to the extent possible and emphasize depth over breadth of coverage.

Arnold, D. E. (1998). Action research in action: Curricular articulation and integrated instruction. *NASSP Bulletin, 82*(596), 74–78.

Jacobs, H. H. (1999). *Breaking new ground in high school integrated curriculum.* Reston, VA: National Association of Secondary School Principals.

Weber, E. (1999). Uniting to introduce multiple intelligences teaching approaches. *NASSP Bulletin, 83*(604), 57–68.

22. The content of the curriculum, where practical, should connect to real-life applications of knowledge and skills to help students link their education to the future.

Bottoms, G., & Webb, L. D. (1998). *Connecting the curriculum to "real life."* Reston, VA: National Association of Secondary School Principals.

Custer, R. L. (1999). Design and problem solving in technology education. *NASSP Bulletin, 83*(608), 24–33.

Kinder, A. (2002, Spring). Schools on the rise: Connecting classroom lessons to real-life learning. *NCREL's Learning Point, 4*(2), pages 12–14.

Porter, J. R., Cheney, G. R., & Kraemer, J. (2001). Meaningful credentials for career academies. *Principal Leadership, 2*(1), 36–40.

Stripling, B. (2001). Expectations for achievement and performance: Assessing student skills. *NASSP Bulletin, 85*(623), 44–52.

Thomas, J. (2000). *A review of research on project-based learning.* San Rafael, CA: Autodesk Foundation.

23. The high school will promote service programs and student activities as integral to an education, providing opportunities for all students that support and extend academic learning.

Baker, K., Jacoby, J., & Gugliuzza, P. (2000). The fourth R. *Principal Leadership, 1*(2), 42–43.

Coats, S., Payne, D., Van Graafeil, J., & Webb, L. (1999). *Mandatory community service in the high school.* Reston, VA: National Association of Secondary School Principals.

DeWitt, D. M., & Joyce, K. (2001). Merging the community & curriculum. *Principal Leadership, 2*(1), 33–35.

Kinsley, C. W. (1997). Service learning: A process to connect learning and living. *NASSP Bulletin, 81*(591), 1–7.

24. The academic program will extend beyond the high school campus to take advantage of learning opportunities outside the four walls of the building.

Bentley, T. (1998). *Learning beyond the classroom: Education for a changing world.* London: Routledge/Demos.

25. Teachers will design high-quality work and teach in ways that engage students, cause them to persist, and, when the work is successfully completed, result in their satisfaction and their acquisition of knowledge, critical thinking and problem-solving skills, and other abilities valued by society.

Darling-Hammond, L., Snyder, J., Ancess, J., Einbender, L., Goodwin, A. L., & Macdonald, M. B. (1993). *Creating learner-centered accountability.* New York: National Center for Restructuring Education, Schools, and Teaching.

26. Teachers will know and be able to use a variety of strategies and settings that identify and accommodate individual learning styles and engage students.

Jenkins, J. M., & Keefe, J. W. (2001). Strategies for personalizing instruction: A typology for improving teaching and learning. *NASSP Bulletin, 85*(629), 72–82.

Jenkins, J. M., & Keefe, J. W. (2002). Two schools: Two approaches to personalized learning. *Phi Delta Kappan, 83*(6), 449–456.

Nagel, J. E., & Smith, P. (2001). The art of personalizing learning. *Principal Leadership, 2*(3), 36–39.

Newmann, F. M., Marks, H. M., & Gamoran, A. (1995, Spring). Authentic pedagogy: Standards that boost student performance. *Issues in restructuring schools, 8*, (pp. 1–10). Madison, WI: Center on Organization and Restructuring of Schools.

27. Each high school teacher will have a broad base of academic knowledge with depth in at least one subject area.

Darling-Hammond, L. (1998). Teacher learning that supports student learning. *Educational Leadership, 55*(5), 6–11.

Darling-Hammond, L. (1999). *Teacher quality and student achievement*. Seattle, WA: Center for the Study of Teaching and Policy, University of Washington.

Education Trust. (1998). Good teaching matters: How well-qualified teachers can close the gap. *Thinking K–16, 3*(2), 1–14.

Kaplan, L. S., & Owings, W. A. (2002). The politics of teacher quality: Implications for principals. *NASSP Bulletin, 86*(633), 22–41.

Rotherham, A. J., & Mead, S. (2003). Teacher quality: Beyond No Child Left Behind. A response to Kaplan and Owings. *NASSP Bulletin, 87*(635), 65–76.

28. *Teachers will be adept at acting as coaches and facilitators to promote more active involvement of students in their own learning.*

Hackmann, D. G., & Valentine, J. W. (1998). *Promoting student involvement in the learning process: Three successful strategies*. Reston, VA: National Association of Secondary School Principals.

29. *Teachers will integrate assessment into instruction so that assessment is accomplished using a variety of methods and does not merely measure students, but becomes part of the learning process.*

Bradshaw, L. K., Craft-Tripp, M., & Glatthorn, A. (2003). Taking the offensive. *Principal Leadership, 4*(1), 55–59.

Custer, T. J. (2003). Assessment: Changing the focus. *Principal Leadership, 4*(1), 24–29.

Cromey, A. (2000). *Using student assessment data: What can we learn from schools?* Oak Brook, IL: North Central Regional Educational Laboratory.

Dusseau, D. J., Hurst, D. S., & Bitter, D. (2003). The number game. *Principal Leadership, 4*(1), 49–54.

Farrace, B. (2003). The nature of the test: W. James Popham on assessment. *Principal Leadership, 4*(1), 30–33.

Fisher, D., & Frey, N. (2003). Finger pointing. *Principal Leadership, 4*(1), 40–46.

Newmann, F. M., Secada, W. G., & Wehlage, G. G. (1995*). A guide to authentic instruction and assessment: Vision standards and scoring*. Madison, WI: Center on Organization and Restructuring of Schools.

Popham, W. J. (2001). Uses and misuses of standardized tests. *NASSP Bulletin, 85*(622), 24–31.

Ross, S. M. (2003). How to get off the reform roller coaster. *Principal Leadership, 4*(1), 16–21.

Stiggins, R. J., Webb, L. D., Lange, J., McGregor, S., & Cotton, S. (1997). *Multiple assessment of student progress*. Reston, VA: National Association of Secondary School Principals.

Trimble, S. (2003). Between reform and improvement: In the classroom. *Principal Leadership, 4*(1), 35–39.

Westra, K. E. (2003). Measuring more than right answers. *Principal Leadership, 4*(1), 60–63.

30. Recognizing that education is a continuum, high schools will reach out to elementary and middle level schools as well as institutions of higher education to better serve the articulation of student learning and to ensure that each stage of the continuum understands what will be required of students at the succeeding stage.

Fenske, R. H., Geranios, C. A., Keller, J. E., & Moore, D. E. (1997). Early intervention programs: Opening the door to higher education. (ERIC Document Reproduction Service No. ED412862).

Jones, C. (2001). Operation jumpstart. *Principal Leadership, 1*(7), 41–43.

Lucas, T. (1996). Promoting secondary school transitions for immigrant adolescents. (ERIC Document Reproduction Service No. ED402786).

Milton, T., Schmidtlein, F., Mintrop, H., MacLellan, A. M., & Pitre, P. (2000). *The high school to college transition: A case study of policies, practices, and K–16 reforms in Maryland* (Pts. I &II). Stanford, CA: The Bridge Project, Stanford University.

Mizelle, N. B. (1999). Helping middle school students make the transition into high school. (ERIC Document Reproduction Service No. ED432411).

Morgan, P. L., & Herzog, C. J. (2001). Designing comprehensive transitions. *Principal Leadership, 1*(7), 10–16.

Schumacher, D. (1998). The transition to middle school. (ERIC Document Reproduction Service No. ED422119).

31. Schools will develop a strategic plan to make technology integral to curriculum, instruction, and assessment, accommodating different learning styles and helping teachers to individualize and improve the learning process.

Webb, L. D. (1999). *Integrating technology in the high school.* Reston, VA: National Association of Secondary School Principals.

Websites

Achieve, Inc.
http://www.achieve.org/

American Youth Policy Forum
http://www.aypf.org/

Association for Supervision and Curriculum Development
http://www.ascd.org/

Baltimore City College High School, Baltimore, MD
http://knight.city.ba.k12.md.us/

The Big Picture Company
http://www.bigpicture.org/

Bill & Melinda Gates Foundation
http://www.gatesfoundation.org/default.htm

The Boston (MA) Arts Academy, Boston, MA
http://boston.k12.ma.us/BAA/

Brockton (MA) High School
http://www.brocktonpublicschools.com/schools/high/

Chapin (SC) High School
http://www.lex5.k12.sc.us/chs/welcome1.htm

Coalition of Essential Schools
http://www.essentialschools.org/

The Education Alliance
at Brown University
http://www.lab.brown.edu/

Educational Testing Service
http://www.ets.org/

Fenway High School, Boston, MA
http://fenway.boston.k12.ma.us/

Foshay Learning Center, Los Angeles, CA
http://www.foshay.k12.ca.us/

Hanover (NH) High School
http://www.hanoverhigh.org/

High Schools That Work
http://www.sreb.org/programs/hstw/
hstwindex.asp

Institute for Educational Leadership
http://www.iel.org/

J.E.B. Stuart High School,
Falls Church, VA
http://www.fcps.k12.va.us/StuartHS/

The Knowledge Loom
http://www.knowledgeloom.org/index.jsp

Lincoln Southwest High School,
Lincoln, NE
http://lsw.lps.org/

Littleton (CO) High School
http://littleton.littletonpublicschools.net/

The Metropolitan Regional Career
and Technical Center, Providence, RI
http://www.metcenter.org/

NASSP
http://www.principals.org

NASSP's Center for Principal
Development
http://www.principals.org/CPD/

National School Boards Association
http://www.nsba.org/site/index.asp

National Staff Development Council
http://www.nsdc.org/

Newcomers High School, New York, NY
http://schools.nycenet.edu/queenshs/
newcomers/

Noble High School, North Berwick, ME
http://knight.noble-hs.sad60.k12.me.us/

North Reading High School, Reading, MA
http://www.northreadingmass.com/
NRHigh/NRHS/NRHighsmall.htm

Rex Putnam High School, Milwaukie, OR
http://putnam.nclack.k12.or.us/

Roosevelt High School, Yonkers, NY
http://roosevelt.ypschools.org/

School Redesign Network
at Stanford University
http://www.schoolredesign.com/

Serving Smaller Learning Communities
http://nwrel.org/scpd/sslc/resources.shtml

Sierra Vista (CA) High School
http://www.sierravista.wuhsd.k12.ca.us/

Souhegan High School, Amherst, NH
http://www.sprise.com/shs/default.htm

Stranahan High School,
Fort Lauderdale, FL
http://www.broward.k12.fl.us/
stranahanhigh/

The Urban Academy, New York, NY
http://www.urbanacademy.org/default.htm

Waukesha North High School,
Waukesha, WI
http://www.waukesha.k12.wi.us/
North/WaukeshaNorth2.html

Wyandotte High School, Kansas City, KS
http://www.kckps.org/disthistory/
openbuildings/wyandotte.html

Appendix 1:
School Academic Rigor
& Support Self-Assessment Tool

The following tool, from Pathways to College Network, *will help you assess the perceived level of academic rigor within your school and address the results. To download and customize this rubric for your school, visit www.principals.org/ breakingranks.*

School Academic Rigor and Support Self-Assessment Tool

Schools should rank "Important to Our School" from 1 to 3, where 1 is *somewhat important*, 2 is *important*, and 3 is *very important*. They should rank "Exists at Our School" from 1 to 3, where 1 indicates this *barely exists*, 2 indicates it *somewhat exists*, and 3 indicates it *fully exists*. The difference is calculated by subtracting the figure in Exists at Our School from Important to Our School. Where the difference is 0 or negative, the school has no need to act. Where the difference is 1 or more, a school needs to work on closing the gap.

	Important to Our School	Exists at Our School	Difference
Characteristics of Schools with Academic Rigor and Support			
School has a challenging curriculum that engages students.			
There is a rigorous core curriculum that reflects college readiness standards.			
Students cannot get by with taking low-level, unchallenging courses.			
Graduation requirements reflect school expectations that all students complete a rigorous academic program.			
There are a substantial number of advanced placement (AP) courses.			
There are a substantial number of honors courses.			
All students are encouraged to enroll in AP courses.			

	Important to Our School	Exists at Our School	Difference
All students are encouraged to enroll in honors courses.			
Students who ordinarily would not be directed to such courses take high-level courses.			
The school has a strong mathematics program.			
The school no longer offers lower level math courses.			
The school has a strong science program.			
The school has eliminated low-level or remedial-type sections of core courses.			
The school has put in place mechanisms to ensure that students can meet more stringent core course requirements.			
Students have opportunities to take college classes through dual-enrollment program with local (community) college.			
The school has an International Baccalaureate (IB) program.			
The school has established new learning opportunities through internships, community service, and individual research projects.			
The school offers numerous career tracks enabling students to connect academic and work-related skills.			
The school has high-quality instruction.			
The school recruits teachers who are able to deliver the "challenging curriculum.			
The school has initiatives to strengthen existing teacher content knowledge where needed.			
The school's teachers are prepared to teach advanced courses.			
The schools teachers are prepared to teach the IB program.			
Teachers are oriented/trained/prepared to use project-based learning.			
Teachers have been trained in English language development.			
Teachers are oriented/trained/prepared to meet needs of college prep as contrasted with vocational or general education students.			
Teachers are oriented/trained/prepared to meet needs of a diverse group of students.			
Teachers are oriented/trained/prepared to make real-world connections.			
Teachers are oriented/trained/prepared to make the curriculum engaging.			
Teachers are oriented/trained/prepared to work with families of students.			
Teachers are oriented/trained/prepared to work with volunteers and other external sources of support.			
The school has opportunities for teachers to interact and collaborate with one another.			

	Important to Our School	Exists at Our School	Difference
The school has teacher support mechanisms.			
The school has structured opportunities for smaller, more personalized learning environments.			
Large schools create schools within the school to enable teachers to know their students better and operate in a more collegial manner.			
Counselors are oriented/trained/prepared to understand and advise students on test results to help them plan for further education and careers.			
The school has supports in place to ensure student academic success.			
The school provides a welcoming, caring, and hopeful atmosphere.			
The school identifies students who are having difficulty making the grade in order to offer them extra academic support.			
Teachers are available before and after school or during lunch hours to coach and support students.			
The school has established linkages with outside groups to provide students with academic support.			
The school develops individual student learning plans.			
The school has established student advisories.			
The school offers counseling linked to personalized learning plans.			
The school encourages students to become resources to other students.			
The school helps students who are having difficulty making the grade.			
The school enrolls students at risk of failure in a ninth-grade academy or other setting where they can receive extra support.			
The school offers English language learners sheltered classes.			
The school has established alternative schools-within-schools, academies, or other more personalized learning settings.			
The school provides additional resources to students who are challenged by academically rigorous work.			
The school offers Saturday school.			
The school offers catch-up classes.			
The school assigns students in need of extra support to small classes.			
The school has other mechanisms to ensure that students succeed.			
The school provides college application guidance and support.			
The school treats all students as if they were college bound.			

	Important to Our School	Exists at Our School	Difference
The school requires seniors to apply to college.			
Prior to or at the beginning of high school, all students undergo point of entry testing to facilitate four-year planning that includes both academic and interest assessments.			
The school requires all students to take the PSAT or PLAN.			
The school administers the SAT/ACT at the school.			
The school offers onsite SAT/ACT preparation courses.			
The school ensures that testing fees are not a barrier to any student's ability to take a test.			
The school offers career and college counselors and has identified counselors to do this.			
The school frees up class time for counselors to talk and work with students on career and education goals.			
The school encourages student participation in precollegiate academic development programs offered by local colleges and universities such as Upward Bound, Talent Search, GEAR UP, and Smile.			
The school invites representatives of postsecondary institutions to meet with students on site.			
The school connects students with college role models.			
The school helps students research colleges and complete college applications.			
The school meets with families regarding college expectations for students and how families can help.			
The school helps families identify sources of financial support.			
Counselors promote students to local postsecondary institutions.			

Academic Rigor Planning Pyramid

Examples: academies, IB program, smaller schools, more rigorous graduation requirements

Examples: increasing math instruction time, eliminating remedial courses, developing career tracks, offering summer academies, requiring PSAT or PLAN, developing dual enrollment programs

A few major tasks:

Selected new ventures, prototypes, projects

Many quick wins, continuous improvements, early-stage ideas

A few major tasks:

_____

Moderately difficult undertakings:

_____

Quick wins:

_____

Examples: Adding AP and honors courses, offering after-school tutoring, modifying counselor roles so that they can offer more career and college counseling, helping parents support students, taking advantage of external precollegiate academic development programs, establishing teacher talk groups

A school's portfolio of initiatives to achieve priorities can range from easy-to-launch projects to major systemic changes. This tool helps differentiate among "quick win" actions, more complex actions, and major systemic changes. It should include "high-priority" items from the Setting Priorities tool. Items will range from complex, systemic initiatives to relatively easy-to-achieve improvements. The tool is intended to help schools visualize the relative effort associated with various initiatives.

Academic Rigor: Before and After Comparison

This tool offers a model for how schools can present their progress in achieving academic rigor and support. Such a document will be useful for presentations to school boards, elected officials, parents, and the general public.

Principle	Before	After
Focus on college preparation	School offered general and vocational education programs	General and vocational education programs eliminated
More time spent on academics	196 minutes/day	270 minutes/day
Smaller academic class sizes	30 students	18 students
Students required to take academically rigorous core curriculum	General math and science met graduation requirements	English, math, and science graduation requirements increased; students must complete advanced algebra, geometry, biology, chemistry, and physics to graduate.
AP and honors courses are widely available	Opportunities limited to one AP calculus and two honors English courses	20 AP and honors courses are offered; 80% of students take at least one
Reduced teacher loads	120 students	80 students
Smaller school communities that support personal relationships	Student enrollment was approximately 1,900	Teams have 80 students for academics, schools within schools range from 225 to 400 students, student advisory groups formed
More staff focused on academic instruction	59% of teachers in core academics	68% of teachers in core academics
Significant resources spent on professional development	Staff development days devoted to diverse topics	Professional development resources doubled, multiple training opportunities, time allowed for teacher interaction, teacher talk groups formed
Teachers prepared to teach advanced courses, particularly in math and science	50% of teachers of advanced courses qualified	90% of teachers of advanced courses qualified
Availability of after-school tutoring opportunities	12 students participated in special tutoring program	350 students participate in after-school tutoring programs at school and in the community
Additional resources to academically challenged students	Students encouraged to attend summer school	Students have opportunities to participate in academies, schools-within-schools, Saturday school, catch-up classes, and summer school
Students have opportunities to participate in supplemental learning programs	100 students annually completed community service projects	The school offers internships, community service, individual research projects, and dual enrollment program with the local community college; 50% of students participate in one or more such opportunities.
Counselors encourage and support college aspirations	Counselors have college attendance as well as scheduling responsibilities	Dedicated counselor assists students and families to prepare for college
Students take PSAT and SAT or EXPLORE, PLAN, and the ACT	Students informed about dates, times, and costs of tests	Tests are free, required, and offered on site.

Appendix 2:
The Personalized Learning Plan

Self-awareness, exploration of the larger world, and setting pathways are actually part of one process: personalized learning. In short, personalized learning allows the student to understand who he or she is, what adult roles seem most desirable, and how to get from here to there in the most productive way.

Most personalized learning is designed to carry students from one phase to another: from expanding self-awareness, to understanding the demands and opportunities beyond high school, to setting a path and defining reliable steps. The process leads from the inner world where dreams are hatched, to the adult world with its very real demands, customs, and constraints; and finally, to a pathway that the student can see and understand clearly—leading to success in adult roles. Personal Learning Plans provide students with the opportunity to look at themselves, generate questions about their futures that then become goals for personal learning, and see how their talents and aspirations connect to the adult world that awaits them.

By supporting personalized learning over an extended period of time, a high school can allow student questioning, exploration, and reflection to follow its path toward resolution. The following illustrations show how the Futures Academy at Mount Abraham Union High School in Bristol, VT, designed a Personalized Learning Program to fit together over the four years of high school.

Figure 1 aims to include a wide range of different personalized learning options, beginning at the middle level and extending past graduation.

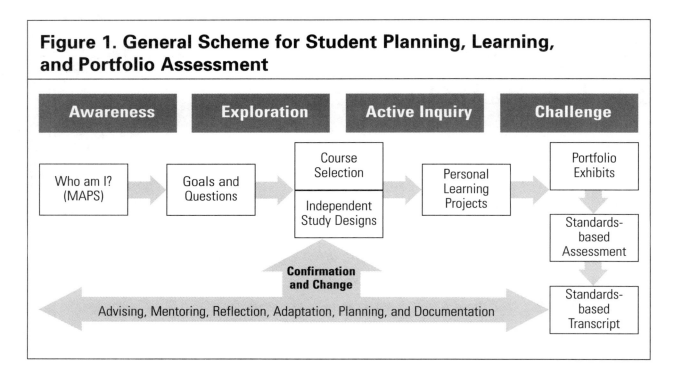

Figure 1. General Scheme for Student Planning, Learning, and Portfolio Assessment

| Awareness | Exploration | Active Inquiry | Challenge |

Who am I? (MAPS) → Goals and Questions → Course Selection / Independent Study Designs → Personal Learning Projects → Portfolio Exhibits → Standards-based Assessment → Standards-based Transcript

Confirmation and Change

Advising, Mentoring, Reflection, Adaptation, Planning, and Documentation

Figure 2 represents the same concept applied to all four high school years. Figure 3 is an example of Mount Abraham using this PLP sequence; an asterisk is attached to each element that Mount Abraham had to add to make personalized learning coherent and continuous over four years. Figures 4 shows how this sequence of work links to the school's standards-based transcript.

Sketching a pattern of PLP supports: What kinds of activities could be organized at your school to help students progress from dependence to independence in learning as they move toward graduation?

Figure 2. Sketching a PLP Sequence in the High School Years

Personal Learning	Discovery Questions	School Support Needed
AWARENESS	**Phase 1:** Who am I?	
EXPLORATION	**Phase 2:** How do things work in my areas of interest?	
ACTIVE INQUIRY	**Phase 3:** What will it take to get ready?	
CHALLENGE AND CONFIRMATION	**Phase 4:** What can I do to show how I have prepared for future challenges?	
READINESS FOR ADULT ROLES	← **Portfolio and Transcript**	

Figure 3. Courses and Advisories in a Proposed Four-Year Sequence

Purpose	Personal Learning Plans (PLP)	Credited Courses/Programs

AWARENESS

Middle Level
Grades 7–8

EXPLORATION

Grades 9–10

INQUIRY

Grade 11

CONFIRMATION

Grade 12

**READINESS FOR
ADULT ROLES**

Phase 1:
Who am I?

MAPS
Personal History
Dreams
Fears
Strengths
Needs & Aspirations

Goal Setting & Course Selection
Futures Academy Application

Phase 2:
What do I do now?

Career Advisory #1

MAPS Review
Career Interests, Preferences,
    Style & Attitude Inventories
Community-based Learning
    Projects
Reflection & Redirection

Phase 3:
How do I do it?

Career Advisory #2

Independent Studies
Internships
Dual College Enrollment
Apprenticeships
Service Learning
Senior Projects
College & Job Applications*

Team Advisories

Exploratory Activity Embedded
    in Middle Level Curriculum
Career Days

Horizons Programs:
Job Shadows

Geiger Program*
Home/school Partnerships
    (.5 cr each)*
Keyboard/Computers (.5 cr)
Futures Advisory Choice

Enterprise.com (.5 cr)
(Career Portfolio)*

Career Advisory (.5 cr)

Career Academy (1–4 cr)
    (4 at .5 credits each)*
American Studies (1 cr)
    (Vital Results Portfolio)*
Web Design (.5 cr)*
"Majors" Courses
PLP Exhibition*

Horizons Programs:

Standards-based Contracts for
    Applied and/or Independent
    Learning (.5–3.0 cr)
"Majors" Courses
E-portfolio Design (.5 cr)
Senior Project (.5–1 cr)*

Senior Exhibitions*

Standards-based Portfolio and Transcript

Standards-based transcript: A formal document listing all of the student's courses at Mount Abraham Union High School, with credits earned, grades, GPA, etc. listed under Fields of Knowledge columns on the left hand side of the document. Columns on the right hand side of the document indicate success in meeting the Vital Results. Numbers in these columns are keyed to the evidence found in the student's presentation portfolio. Additionally, Mount Abraham Union High School's standards-based transcript includes "Applied Learning" where we honor work done by the students outside of the formal school setting. Volunteer work, athletic or musical accomplishments, religious or travel experiences, etc. are linked to Vital Result Standards in this section. Figure 4 is a blank sample from the senior year.

Figure 4. Key Components of Personalized Learning

		Credit	Grade	Communi-cation	Problem Solving	Personal Development	Social Responsibility
Arts, Language, Literature							
History, Social Science							
Science, Math, Technology							
Other Courses							
	SUMMARY						
Applied Learning							

Class Rank:	Cumulative GPA	Other

Distinctions:

ADVISOR COMMENTS

FIELDS OF KNOWLEDGE	**VITAL RESULTS**
Twelfth Grade	**Notes:** Vital Results identified here are documented in the accompanying electronic portfolio. Please click on the Vital Result number to go to the sample of student work demonstrating success at meeting that standard.

All figures reprinted with permission of Mount Abraham High School.

Appendix 3: Advisories

The following discussion of advisories has been adapted, with permission, from Changing Systems to Personalize Learning: The Power of Advisories *(Osofsky, Sinner and Wolk 2003). The workbook, designed by the Education Alliance to be used in conjunction with a staff workshop to build consensus around your school's new or revamped advisory program covers the topic in depth. For more information, visit www.lab.brown.edu.*

The Power of Advisories offers five key dimensions of an effective advisory program:

KEY DIMENSION #1: Purpose. A clearly defined purpose supported by the community.

Which of the following purposes makes the most sense for your school:

- To advise students about academic decisions and monitor academic achievement
- To provide developmental guidance (both formal and informal)
- To foster communication between the home and the school and among members of the school community
- To encourage supportive peer relationships and practice conflict resolution
- To promote an awareness of diversity and tolerance
- To undertake community service both within and outside the school
- To facilitate community governance and conversations
- To prepare students for life transitions including career development and postsecondary opportunities
- To promote character development and explore moral dilemmas
- To explore the process of group development and have fun?

The following chart provides some sample activities, the goals, and the time requirements that each type of advisory might entail.

A Typology of Advisory Emphases
(for use with the card-sorting exercise)

Type	Need	Time	Goals & Focus	Advisor Skills	Sample Activities
Advocacy	Affective	Substantial implementation time	Adult-student relationship	Personal qualities— interest and concern for students	Individual student conferences
Community	Affective	Substantial implementation time	Group identity	Personal qualities— group management	Group discussions, projects, intramurals
Skills	Affective and cognitive	Substantial "prep" and implementation time	Developmental guidance	Personal qualities— group management, group facil- itation	Decision- making, stress management, race relations, values clarification
Invigoration	Affective	Minimal "prep" time	Relaxing, recharging	Personal qualities— enthusiasm	Intramurals and clubs, parties, informal "fun" activities
Academic	Cognitive	Substantial implementation time	Academic performance	Personal qualities— teaching	Study skills, silent reading, writing, tutoring
Administration	Administrative	Minimal "prep" and implementation time	General school business, "housekeeping"	Clerical, organizational	Announcements, distributing school materials, collecting money

KEY DIMENSION #2: Organization. Organized to fulfill the purpose and to ensure personalization.

The Education Alliance offers the following guiding questions as you discuss how your advisory should be organized.

People and Size

- How many advisees will each adviser have?
- Which adults in the school building will serve as advisers? What characteristics should they possess?
- If some teachers do not serve as advisers, what supportive roles can they take on? Will any advisories be cofacilitated, i.e., first-year teacher with veteran teacher?
- By what criteria will students be sorted into advisories (e.g., age, grade level, gender, race/ethnicity)?
- By what criteria will individual advisees be assigned to individual advisers (e.g., advise only students you teach, common interests, previous relationship, self-selection, random)?
- Will advisers and advisees be paired for one year or multiple years?
- What will be the specific roles and responsibilities of advisers and advisees?
- How will parents be involved in the advisory program?
- How will community members outside the school be involved in the advisory program?

Time and Space

- How often will advisories meet (e.g., once daily, twice daily, twice weekly)?
- How long will advisory meetings be (e.g., brief check-ins, longer activity periods)?
- Will there be time for individual meetings as well as group meetings?
- How will this time fit into the master schedule?
- Where will advisories meet?
- How will advisories be able to personalize their space?
- Will each advisory have its own space?

Professional Development and Support

- How do we create regularly scheduled time for advisers to meet (e.g., time for training, curriculum development, sharing successes, having kid talk)?
- In what types of configurations can advisers meet for training and support (e.g., clusters, teams, full faculty, pairs)?
- How will we identify the types of training and support that advisers need (e.g., group process and development, how to communicate with parents, listening skills, knowing when to refer advisees to others, academic advising)?
- How will initial and ongoing training be conducted and by whom?
- What resources do advisers need (e.g., a program coordinator, curriculum, parent volunteers, counselors, petty cash)?
- What additional support will be given to advisers who are new to advising?
- What additional support will be given to advisers who are struggling?
- How will advisers be observed and assessed?
- How will advisory responsibilities be dealt with in the master contract?
- What type of budget will be required for the program?

Student Ownership

- What role will students take in creating/overseeing the advisory program?
- How can advisories serve as a vehicle for empowering students, e.g., through school governance, through student-led groups, by taking on a community responsibility?
- How can students in upper-grade advisories mentor students in lower-grade advisories?

KEY DIMENSION #3: Advisory Program Content. Content based on the purposes to be achieved, on the nature of the school, and on individual advisers. Content may:

- Be organized around essential questions, themes, or skills
- Be consistent across advisories or vary based on an adviser's knowledge of his/her advisees
- Follow a common curriculum, be chosen from an advisory handbook, or be activities organized by advisers to personalize their own advisory experience.

KEY DIMENSION #4: Assessment. Assessment should be done at several levels:

- Individual students/advisees
- Individual advisers
- Advisory groups as a whole
- Overall advisory program
- School and program leadership.

Assessments should determine whether the purposes of the program are being met, and whether participants are meeting expectations.

KEY DIMENSION #5: Leadership. Strong leadership by an individual or team charged with designing, implementing, overseeing, supporting, and assessing the program

Essential leadership duties include creating buy-in among community members and ensuring that advisers have adequate training, resources, and support. Questions to be answered include:

- Who will take primary leadership of your advisory program?
- What specific barriers do you foresee in the planning, implementation, and maintenance of your program? How do you plan to avoid and/or overcome these barriers?
- What processes can be put in place to build support for your advisory program among all school community members, including consideration of the master contract? How will you ensure that consensus is achieved around the state purposes?

Appendix 4:
Instructional Practices Inventory

Specific, valid data about the instructional practices in a school are essential for school improvement. The Instructional Practices Inventory (Painter & Valentine, 2002) is a process and rubric for observing and categorizing the nature of instruction across the entire school. This rubric is used to systematically obtain a picture of instruction occurring within given schools. Observers move from room to room, taking anecdotal notes and classifying what they see into one of the six subcategories. For valid data collection, the developers of the process recommend at least 100 observations made over the course of a school day. The observers must develop a plan for scanning all classes repeatedly to ensure that representative samples of classes are being observed. Data are then collected, analyzed, and graphed in a manner that fits the needs of the school or school district.

Instructional Practices Inventory

Student-Engaged Instruction	Student Active Engaged Learning	Active mental engagement such as authentic project work, cooperative learning, hands-on learning, demonstrations, active research. Higher order thinking evident.
	Student Learning Conversations	Active conversation among students with most or all engaged. Teacher initiated but not directed. Higher order thinking evident.
Teacher-Directed Instruction	Teacher-Led Instruction	Teacher-led learning experiences such as lecture, question and answer, teacher giving directions, video instruction with teacher interaction. Discussion may occur, but instruction and ideas come primarily from the teacher.
	Student Work with Teacher Engaged	Students working on worksheets, book work, tests, video with teacher viewing the video with students, etc. Teacher assistance or support evident.
Disengagement	Student Work with/ Teacher not Engaged	Students working on worksheets, book work, tests, viewing of video, etc. Teacher assistance or support not evident.
	Complete Disengagement	Neither teacher nor students engaged in learning or teaching, such as watching video or doing activities not directly related to the curriculum.

Reprinted with permission.

Appendix 5:
School Environment Variables

Student Perceptions

Student Participation in School Activities: describes the degree to which students have participated in school activities, either as a member or an officer, in the present school year

Student Participation in Nonschool Activities: describes the degree to which students have participated in activities sponsored by groups other than your school, either as a member or an officer, in the present school year

Student Self-Concept: describes how students view themselves academically

Student Self-Esteem: describes how students feel about themselves

Academic Self-Efficacy: describes how students feel about their ability to succeed academically

Student Self-Standards: describes the academic standards that students have for themselves

Individual Student Behavior: describes the students' self-report of their behavior during the current school year

Schoolwide Student Behavior: describes the degree to which students perceive behaviors to be a problem in their school

People in Students' Lives—Friends: describes how students feel about the relationships with their friends

People in Students' Lives—Family: describes how students feel about relationships with members of their family

People in Students' Lives—Adults at School: describes how students feel about relationships with adults at school

Parent Participation: a student report of their parents'/guardians' participation in this school year

Home Study Conditions: describes students' studying conditions at home

Parent–Student Interaction: describes parent–student interactions in a typical school week

Student Homework: describes how much time students report spending on homework in a typical school week.

Source: Quinn, Greunert, and Valentine (1999, p.8).

Instructional Strategies

Planning Strategies: describes the lesson design

Instructional Strategies: describes the lesson methodology

Assessment Practices: describes the types and frequency of assessment

Parent Relationships: describes the frequency and subject of the conversation and how contact was made

Curriculum Development: describes the specific content, learning activities, teacher involvement, and student involvement in developing the curriculum.

Source: Quinn, Greunert, and Valentine (1999, p. 7).

Culture

Collaborative Leadership: describes the degree to which school leaders establish and maintain collaborative relationships with school staff

Teacher Collaboration: describes the degree to which teachers engage in constructive dialogue that furthers the educational vision of the school

Professional Development: describes the degree to which teachers value continuous personal development and schoolwide improvement

Unity of Purpose: describes the degree to which teachers work toward a common mission of the school

Collegial Support: describes the degree to which teachers work together effectively

Learning Partnership: describes the degree to which teachers, parents, and students work together for the common good for the student

Source: Quinn, Greunert, and Valentine (1999, p. 5).

Appendix 6:
Sample *Breaking Ranks II* Assessment Survey

Instructions: For each of the Breaking Ranks *recommendations noted in the first column, please indicate how important you feel the recommendation is in column 2. In column 3, please indicate to what level you believe this recommendation is practiced at our school. Remember: 1 is low and 5 is high.*

Collaborative Leadership & Professional Learning Communities

Breaking Ranks Recommendation	Rate IMPORTANCE of recommendation (1 is LOW 5 is HIGH)	Rate the Level this recommendation is PRACTICED (1 is LOW 5 is HIGH)	Difference between Perceived Level of Importance and Level of Practice.*
	1 2 3 4 5	1 2 3 4 5	1 2 3 4 5
The principal will provide leadership in the high school community by building and maintaining a vision, direction, and focus for student learning.			
Each high school will establish a site council and accord other meaningful roles in decision making to students, parents, and members of the staff to promote student learning and an atmosphere of participation, responsibility, and ownership.			
A high school will regard itself as a community in which members of the staff collaborate to develop and implement the school's learning goals.			

*Column at right for demo purposes—not to be on survey.

Source: Adapted from a survey instrument developed by the Education Alliance, based on the Breaking Ranks *recommendations. To download and customize this rubric for your school, visit www.principals.org/breakingranks.*

Breaking Ranks Recommendation	Rate IMPORTANCE of recommendation (1 is LOW 5 is HIGH)					Rate the Level this recommendation is PRACTICED (1 is LOW 5 is HIGH)					Difference between Perceived Level of Importance and Level of Practice.*				
	1	2	3	4	5	1	2	3	4	5	1	2	3	4	5
Teachers will provide the leadership essential to the success of reform, collaborating with others in the educational community to redefine the role of the teacher and to identify sources of support for that redefined role.															
Every school will be a learning community for the entire community. As such, the school will promote the use of Personal Learning Plans for each educator and provide the resources to ensure that the principal, teachers, and other staff members can address their own learning and professional development needs as they relate to improved student learning.															
The school community will promote policies and practices that recognize diversity in accord with the core values of a democratic and civil society and will offer substantive ongoing professional development to help educators appreciate issues of diversity and expose students to a rich array of viewpoints, perspectives, and experiences.															
High schools will build partnerships with institutions of higher education to provide teachers and administrators at both levels with ideas and opportunities to enhance the education, performance, and evaluation of educators.															
High schools will develop political and financial relationships with individuals, organizations, and businesses to support and supplement educational programs and policies.															
At least once every five years, each high school will convene a broadly based external panel to offer a public description of the school, a requirement that could be met in conjunction with the evaluations by state, regional, and other accrediting groups.															

*Column at right for demo purposes—not to be on survey.

Personalization and the School Environment

Breaking Ranks Recommendation	Importance	Level of Practice	Difference (not to be listed on survey)
High schools will create small units in which anonymity is banished.			
Each high school teacher involved in the instructional program on a full-time basis will be responsible for contact time with no more than 90 students during a given term so that the teacher can give greater attention to the needs of every student.			
Each student will have a Personal Plan for Progress that will be reviewed often to ensure that the high school takes individual needs into consideration and to allow students, within reasonable parameters, to design their own methods for learning in an effort to meet high standards.			
Every high school student will have a Personal Adult Advocate to help him or her personalize the educational experience.			
Teachers will convey a sense of caring to their students so that their students feel that their teachers share a stake in their learning.			
High schools will develop flexible scheduling and student grouping patterns that allow better use of time in order to meet the individual needs of students to ensure academic success.			
The high school will engage students' families as partners in the students' education.			
The high school community, which cannot be value neutral, will advocate and model a set of core values essential in a democratic and civil society.			
High schools, in conjunction with agencies in the community, will help coordinate the delivery of physical and mental health and social services for youth.			

Column at right for demo purposes—not to be on survey.

Curriculum, Instruction, and Assessment

Breaking Ranks Recommendation	Importance	Level of Practice	Difference (not to be listed on survey)
Each high school will identify a set of essential learnings—above all, in literature and language, writing, mathematics, social studies, science, and the arts—in which students must demonstrate achievement in order to graduate.			
Each high school will present alternatives to tracking and to ability grouping.			
The high school will reorganize the traditional department structure in order to integrate the school's curriculum to the extent possible and emphasize depth over breadth of coverage.			
The content of the curriculum, where practical, should connect to real-life applications of knowledge and skills to help students link their education to the future.			
The high school will promote service programs and student activities as integral to an education, providing opportunities for all students that support and extend academic learning.			
The academic program will extend beyond the high school campus to take advantage of learning opportunities outside the four walls of the building.			
Teachers will design high-quality work and teach in ways that engage students, cause them to persist, and when the work is successfully completed, result in their satisfaction and their acquisition of knowledge, critical thinking and problem-solving skills, and other abilities valued by society.			
Teachers will know and be able to use a variety of strategies and settings that identify and accommodate individual learning styles and engage students.			
Each high school teacher will have a broad base of academic knowledge with depth in at least one subject area.			

Breaking Ranks Recommendation	Importance	Level of Practice	Difference (not to be listed on survey)
Teachers will be adept at acting as coaches and facilitators to promote more active involvement of students in their own learning.			
Teachers will integrate assessment into instruction so that assessment is accomplished using a variety of methods and does not merely measure students, but becomes part of the learning process.			
Recognizing that education is a continuum, high schools will reach out to elementary- and middle-level schools as well as institutions of higher education to better serve the articulation of student learning and to ensure that each stage of the continuum understands what will be required of students at the succeeding stage.			
Schools will develop a strategic plan to make technology integral to curriculum, instruction, and assessment, accommodating different learning styles and helping teachers to individualize and improve the learning process.			

Appendix 7:
Self-Assessment for
Instructional Leaders

The following tool, developed by NASSP in accordance with the Interstate School Leaders Licensure Consortium (ISLLC) standards will help principals and other instructional leaders assess their own skills. A similar form for mentors, observers, or others you would like to see assess your skills can be found at www.principals.org/pdf/360self_obsr.pdf.

21st Century
School Administrator
Skills

NATIONAL ASSOCIATION
OF SECONDARY SCHOOL
PRINCIPALS

<u>Self-Assessment</u> for Instructional Leaders

Participant's Name _____ Date _____

Instructions: Read the definition for each skill dimension. Reflect on your current behavior and practice as it relates to the skill dimension and its definition. Read each behavioral statement below the definition and circle the number for each item that best describes your behavior. Be honest with yourself. This self-assessment is intended for your personal use. You may share it with a coach or mentor as you see fit. Copy the Observer Assessment that follows the Self-Assessment and distribute copies to as many colleagues as you like to collect their perceptions of your behavior.

For assistance or additional information, call NASSP Leadership Development and Assessment at 703 860-0200.

EDUCATIONAL LEADERSHIP

<u>Setting Instructional Direction</u>: Implementing strategies for improving teaching and learning including putting programs and improvement efforts into action. Developing a vision and establishing clear goals; providing direction in achieving stated goals; encouraging others to contribute to goal achievement; securing commitment to a course of action from individuals and groups.

1=almost never   2=rarely   3=occasionally   4=frequently   5=almost always   na=not applicable

1.	I articulate a clear vision for the school and its efforts	1	2	3	4	5	na
2.	I set high expectations for myself and for others	1	2	3	4	5	na
3.	I encourage innovation toward improvement of teaching and learning	1	2	3	4	5	na
4.	I set and clarify measurable objectives	1	2	3	4	5	na
5.	I generate enthusiasm and work to persuade others to work together to accomplish common goals	1	2	3	4	5	na
6.	I develop alliances and/or resources outside the school that improve the quality of teaching and learning	1	2	3	4	5	na
7.	I clearly articulate expectations regarding the performance of others	1	2	3	4	5	na
8.	I acknowledge achievement and accomplishment of others	1	2	3	4	5	na
9.	I seek commitment of all involved to a specific course of action	1	2	3	4	5	na
Add the circled numbers and divide the sum by 9. Enter the S.I.D. quotient here.		S.I.D. quotient _____					

Teamwork: Seeking and encouraging involvement of team members. Modeling and encouraging the behaviors that move the group to task completion. Supporting group accomplishment.

1=almost never   2=rarely   3=occasionally   4=frequently   5=almost always   na=not applicable

10.	I support the ideas and views of team members to solve problems	1	2	3	4	5	na
11.	I encourage others to share their ideas	1	2	3	4	5	na
12.	I contribute ideas toward achieving a solution	1	2	3	4	5	na
13.	I assist in the operational tasks of the team	1	2	3	4	5	na
14.	I seek input from others regarding their own ideas and solutions	1	2	3	4	5	na
15.	I assist the team in maintaining the direction needed to complete a task	1	2	3	4	5	na
16.	I seek consensus among team members	1	2	3	4	5	na
	Add the circled numbers and divide the sum by 7. Enter the T. quotient here.	T. quotient _____					

Sensitivity: Perceiving the needs and concerns of others; dealing tactfully with others in emotionally stressful situations or in conflict. Knowing what information to communicate and to whom. Appropriately relating to people of varying ethnic, cultural, and religious backgrounds.

1=almost never   2=rarely   3=occasionally   4=frequently   5=almost always   na=not applicable

17.	I deal appropriately and tactfully with people from different backgrounds	1	2	3	4	5	na
18.	I elicit perceptions, feelings, and concerns of others	1	2	3	4	5	na
19.	I voice disagreement without creating unnecessary conflict	1	2	3	4	5	na
20.	I anticipate responses of others and act to reduce negative impact	1	2	3	4	5	na
21.	I communicate necessary information to the appropriate persons in a timely manner	1	2	3	4	5	na
22.	I express verbal and/or non-verbal recognition of feelings, needs, and concerns of others	1	2	3	4	5	na
23.	I respond tactfully to others in emotionally stressful situations or in conflict	1	2	3	4	5	na
24.	I take action to divert unnecessary conflict	1	2	3	4	5	na
25.	I respond in a timely manner to others who initiate contact with me	1	2	3	4	5	na
	Add the circled numbers and divide the sum by 9. Enter the S. quotient here.	S. quotient _____					

NATIONAL ASSOCIATION OF SECONDARY SCHOOL
PRINCIPALS   © 2001 National Association of Secondary School Principals, 1904 Association Drive, Reston, Virginia 20191-1537

Judgment: Reaching logical conclusions and making high quality decisions based on available information. Assigning appropriate priority to significant issues. Exercising appropriate caution in making decisions and in taking action. Seeking out relevant data, facts and impressions. Analyzing and interpreting complex information.

1=almost never   2=rarely   3=occasionally   4=frequently   5=almost always   na=not applicable

26.	I assign appropriate priority to issues and tasks	1	2	3	4	5	na
27.	I take appropriate caution when dealing with unfamiliar issues and individuals	1	2	3	4	5	na
28.	I avoid reaching quick conclusions and making decisions with limited data	1	2	3	4	5	na
29.	I evaluate information to determine the important elements	1	2	3	4	5	na
30.	I communicate a clear rationale for a decision	1	2	3	4	5	na
31.	I seek additional information about issues and events relevant to the school	1	2	3	4	5	na
32.	I seek relevant sources of information to confirm or refute assumptions	1	2	3	4	5	na
33.	I seek to clarify information by asking follow-up questions	1	2	3	4	5	na
34.	I seek to identify the cause of a problem	1	2	3	4	5	na
35.	I seek to establish relationships among issues and events	1	2	3	4	5	na
Add the circled numbers and divide the sum by 10. Enter the J. quotient here.		J quotient _____					

Results Orientation: Assuming responsibility. Recognizing when a decision is required. Taking prompt action as issues emerge. Resolving short-term issues while balancing them against long-term objectives.

1=almost never   2=rarely   3=occasionally   4=frequently   5=almost always   na=not applicable

36.	I take action to move issues toward closure in a timely manner	1	2	3	4	5	na
37.	I take responsibility to implement initiatives to improve teaching and learning	1	2	3	4	5	na
38.	I determine the criteria that indicate a problem or issue is resolved	1	2	3	4	5	na
39.	I consider the long-term and short-term implications of a decision before taking action	1	2	3	4	5	na
40.	I am able to see the big picture	1	2	3	4	5	na
Add the circled numbers and divide the sum by 5. Enter the R. O. quotient here.		R. O. quotient _____					

NATIONAL ASSOCIATION of SECONDARY SCHOOL
PRINCIPALS

Organizational Ability: Planning and scheduling one's own and the work of others so that resources are used appropriately. Scheduling flow of activities; establishing procedures to monitor projects. Practicing time and task management; knowing what to delegate and to whom.

1=almost never   2=rarely   3=occasionally   4=frequently   5=almost always   na=not applicable

41.	I delegate responsibilities to others	1	2	3	4	5	na
42.	I plan follow-up to monitor progress of delegated responsibilities	1	2	3	4	5	na
43.	I develop action plans	1	2	3	4	5	na
44.	I monitor progress of plans and adjust plans or actions as needed	1	2	3	4	5	na
45.	I establish timelines, schedules, and milestones	1	2	3	4	5	na
46.	I am well prepared for meetings	1	2	3	4	5	na
47.	I make effective use of available resources	1	2	3	4	5	na
Add the circled numbers and divide the sum by 7. Enter the O. A. quotient here.		O. A. quotient _____					

COMMUNICATION

Oral Communication: Clearly communicating when speaking to individuals, small groups, and large groups. Making oral presentations that are clear and easy to understand.

1=almost never   2=rarely   3=occasionally   4=frequently   5=almost always   na=not applicable

48.	Demonstrates effective presentation skills, e.g., opening and closing comments, eye contact, enthusiasm, confidence, rapport, use of visual aids	1	2	3	4	5	na
49.	I speak articulately	1	2	3	4	5	na
50.	I use grammar properly	1	2	3	4	5	na
51.	I tailor messages to meet the needs of unique audiences	1	2	3	4	5	na
52.	I clearly present thoughts and ideas in one-on-one presentations	1	2	3	4	5	na
53.	I clearly present thoughts and ideas in small group presentations	1	2	3	4	5	na
54.	I clearly present thoughts and ideas in formal, large-group presentations	1	2	3	4	5	na
Add the circled numbers and divide the sum by 7. Enter the O. C. quotient here.		O. C. quotient _____					

Written Communication: Expressing ideas clearly in writing; demonstrating technical proficiency. Writing appropriately for different audiences.

1=almost never	2=rarely	3=occasionally	4=frequently	5=almost always	na=not applicable

55.	I write concisely	1	2	3	4	5	na
56.	I demonstrate technical proficiency in writing	1	2	3	4	5	na
57.	I express ideas clearly in writing	1	2	3	4	5	na
58.	I write appropriately for different audiences	1	2	3	4	5	na
	Add the circled numbers and divide the sum by 4. Enter the W. C. quotient here.	W. C. quotient _____					

DEVELOPING SELF AND OTHERS

Development of Others: Teaching, coaching, and helping others. Providing specific feedback based on observations and data.

1=almost never	2=rarely	3=occasionally	4=frequently	5=almost always	na=not applicable

59.	I share information and expertise from personal experiences	1	2	3	4	5	na
60.	I motivate others to change behaviors that inhibit professional and organizational growth	1	2	3	4	5	na
61.	I suggest specific developmental activities to assist others' professional growth	1	2	3	4	5	na
62.	I give behaviorally-specific feedback focusing on behaviors, not the person	1	2	3	4	5	na
63.	I ask a protégé what he/she perceives to be strengths and weaknesses and what he/she wants to improve	1	2	3	4	5	na
64.	I seek agreement on specific actions to be taken by a protégé for his/her development and growth	1	2	3	4	5	na
	Add the circled numbers and divide the sum by 6. Enter the D. O. quotient here.	D. O. quotient _____					

Understanding Own Strengths and Weaknesses: Understanding personal strengths and weaknesses. Taking responsibility for improvement by actively pursuing developmental activities. Striving for continuous learning.

1=almost never	2=rarely	3=occasionally	4=frequently	5=almost always	na=not applicable

65.	I recognize and appropriately communicate my own strengths	1	2	3	4	5	na
66.	I recognize and manage my own developmental needs	1	2	3	4	5	na
67.	I actively pursue personal growth through participation in planned developmental activities	1	2	3	4	5	na
	Add the circled numbers and divide the sum by 3. Enter the U.S.W. quotient here.	U.S.W. quotient _____					

NATIONAL ASSOCIATION of SECONDARY SCHOOL **PRINCIPALS** © 2001 National Association of Secondary School Principals, 1904 Association Drive, Reston, Virginia 20191-1537

Analysis

1. In the matrix below, enter for each skill dimension the skill quotient computed in your self-assessment.

2. When you have collected observer assessments from all the colleagues to whom you distributed, average the ratings for each skill dimension and enter the mean in the appropriate space in the observer average column.

3. Subtract the observer average from the self-assessment skill quotient for each skill dimension.

4. Study the results. Plus or minus differences of greater or less than 1 may indicate areas you want to focus on for professional development. In which skill dimensions do others see you performing better than you see yourself? In which ones do you see yourself performing better than your observers perceive you to be performing?

5. For differences of greater or less than one, compare your self-ratings on each behavioral indicator with the average ratings of observers on the same indicator to determine which behaviors you might seek to develop.

Skill Area	Skill Dimension	Skill Quotient	Observer Average	Difference
Setting Instructional Direction	Setting Instructional Direction			
	Teamwork			
	Sensitivity			
Resolving Complex Problems	Judgment			
	Results Orientation			
	Organizational Ability			
Communi-cation Skills	Oral Communication			
	Written Communication			
Developing Self and Others	Development of Others			
	Understanding Own Strengths and Weaknesses			

For assistance or additional information, call NASSP Leadership Development and Assessment at 703 860-0200.

NATIONAL ASSOCIATION OF SECONDARY SCHOOL **PRINCIPALS**   © 2001 National Association of Secondary School Principals, 1904 Association Drive, Reston, Virginia 20191-1537

21st Century
School Administrator
Skills

NATIONAL ASSOCIATION
OF SECONDARY SCHOOL
PRINCIPALS

<u>Observer</u> Assessment for Instructional Leaders

Participant's Name _____ Date _____

Circle the number for each item that best describes the behavior of the person named at the top of the form.

EDUCATIONAL LEADERSHIP

<u>Setting Instructional Direction</u>: Implementing strategies for improving teaching and learning including putting programs and improvement efforts into action. Developing a vision and establishing clear goals; providing direction in achieving stated goals; encouraging others to contribute to goal achievement; securing commitment to a course of action from individuals and groups.

1=almost never   2=rarely   3=occasionally   4=frequently   5=almost always   na=not applicable

1.	This person articulates a clear vision for the school and its efforts	1	2	3	4	5	na
2.	This person sets high expectations for self and others	1	2	3	4	5	na
3.	This person encourages innovation toward improved teaching and learning	1	2	3	4	5	na
4.	This person sets and clarifies measurable objectives	1	2	3	4	5	na
5.	This person generates enthusiasm and works to persuade others to work together to accomplish common goals	1	2	3	4	5	na
6.	This person develops alliances and/or resources outside the school that improve the quality of teaching and learning	1	2	3	4	5	na
7.	This person clearly articulates expectations regarding the performance of others	1	2	3	4	5	na
8.	This person acknowledges achievement and accomplishment of others	1	2	3	4	5	na
9.	This person seeks commitment of all involved to a specific course of action	1	2	3	4	5	na

Teamwork: Seeking and encouraging involvement of team members. Modeling and encouraging the behaviors that move the group to task completion. Supporting group accomplishment.

1=almost never   2=rarely   3=occasionally   4=frequently   5=almost always   na=not applicable

10.	This person supports the ideas and views of team members to solve problems	1	2	3	4	5	na
11.	This person encourages others to share their ideas	1	2	3	4	5	na
12.	This person contributes ideas toward achieving a solution	1	2	3	4	5	na
13.	This person assists in the operational tasks of the team	1	2	3	4	5	na
14.	This person seeks input from others regarding their own ideas and solutions	1	2	3	4	5	na
15.	This person assists the team in maintaining the direction needed to complete a task	1	2	3	4	5	na
16.	This person seeks consensus among team members	1	2	3	4	5	na

Sensitivity: Perceiving the needs and concerns of others; dealing tactfully with others in emotionally stressful situations or in conflict. Knowing what information to communicate and to whom. Appropriately relating to people of varying ethnic, cultural, and religious backgrounds.

1=almost never   2=rarely   3=occasionally   4=frequently   5=almost always   na=not applicable

17.	This person deals appropriately and tactfully with people from different backgrounds	1	2	3	4	5	na
18.	This person elicits perceptions, feelings, and concerns of others	1	2	3	4	5	na
19.	This person voices disagreement without creating unnecessary conflict	1	2	3	4	5	na
20.	This person anticipates responses of others and acts to reduce negative impact	1	2	3	4	5	na
21.	This person communicates necessary information to the appropriate persons in a timely manner	1	2	3	4	5	na
22.	This person expresses verbal and/or non-verbal recognition of feelings, needs, and concerns of others	1	2	3	4	5	na
23.	This person responds tactfully to others in emotionally stressful situations or in conflict	1	2	3	4	5	na
24.	This person diverts unnecessary conflict	1	2	3	4	5	na
25.	This person responds in a timely manner to others who initiate contact	1	2	3	4	5	na

 NATIONAL ASSOCIATION of SECONDARY SCHOOL **PRINCIPALS**   © 2001 National Association of Secondary School Principals, 1904 Association Drive, Reston, Virginia 20191-1537

Judgment: Reaching logical conclusions and making high quality decisions based on available information. Assigning appropriate priority to significant issues. Exercising appropriate caution in making decisions and in taking action. Seeking out relevant data, facts and impressions. Analyzing and interpreting complex information.

1=almost never   2=rarely   3=occasionally   4=frequently   5=almost always   na=not applicable

26.	This person assigns appropriate priority to issues and tasks	1	2	3	4	5	na
27.	This person is appropriately cautious when dealing with unfamiliar issues and individuals	1	2	3	4	5	na
28.	This person avoids reaching quick conclusions and making decisions with limited data	1	2	3	4	5	na
29.	This person evaluates information to determine the important elements	1	2	3	4	5	na
30.	This person communicates a clear rationale for a decision	1	2	3	4	5	na
31.	This person seeks additional information	1	2	3	4	5	na
32.	This person seeks relevant sources of information to confirm or refute assumptions	1	2	3	4	5	na
33.	This person seeks to clarify information by asking follow-up questions	1	2	3	4	5	na
34.	This person seeks to identify the cause of a problem	1	2	3	4	5	na
35.	This person seeks relationships among issues and events	1	2	3	4	5	na

Results Orientation: Assuming responsibility. Recognizing when a decision is required. Taking prompt action as issues emerge. Resolving short-term issues while balancing them against long-term objectives.

1=almost never   2=rarely   3=occasionally   4=frequently   5=almost always   na=not applicable

36.	This person takes action to move issues toward closure in a timely manner	1	2	3	4	5	na
37.	This person takes responsibility to implement initiatives to improve teaching and learning	1	2	3	4	5	na
38.	This person determines the criteria that indicate a problem or issue is resolved	1	2	3	4	5	na
39.	This person considers the long-term and short-term implications of a decision before taking action	1	2	3	4	5	na
40.	This person sees the big picture	1	2	3	4	5	na

NATIONAL ASSOCIATION
of SECONDARY SCHOOL
PRINCIPALS   © 2001 National Association of Secondary School Principals, 1904 Association Drive, Reston, Virginia 20191-1537

Organizational Ability: Planning and scheduling one's own and the work of others so that resources are used appropriately. Scheduling flow of activities; establishing procedures to monitor projects. Practicing time and task management; knowing what to delegate and to whom.

| 1=almost never | 2=rarely | 3=occasionally | 4=frequently | 5=almost always | na=not applicable |

		1	2	3	4	5	na
41.	This person delegates responsibilities to others	1	2	3	4	5	na
42.	This person plans follow-up to monitor progress of delegated responsibilities	1	2	3	4	5	na
43.	This person develops action plans	1	2	3	4	5	na
44.	This person monitors progress of plans and adjusts plans or actions as needed	1	2	3	4	5	na
45.	This person establishes timelines, schedules, and milestones	1	2	3	4	5	na
46.	This person is well prepared for meetings	1	2	3	4	5	na
47.	This person makes effective use of available resources	1	2	3	4	5	na

COMMUNICATION

Oral Communication: Clearly communicating when speaking to individuals, small groups, and large groups. Making oral presentations that are clear and easy to understand.

| 1=almost never | 2=rarely | 3=occasionally | 4=frequently | 5=almost always | na=not applicable |

		1	2	3	4	5	na
48.	This person demonstrates effective presentation skills, e.g., opening and closing comments, eye contact, enthusiasm, confidence, rapport, use of visual aids	1	2	3	4	5	na
49.	This person speaks articulately	1	2	3	4	5	na
50.	This person uses grammar properly	1	2	3	4	5	na
51.	This person tailors messages to meet the needs of unique audiences	1	2	3	4	5	na
52.	This person clearly presents thoughts and ideas in one-on-one presentations	1	2	3	4	5	na
53.	This person clearly presents thoughts and ideas in small group presentations	1	2	3	4	5	na
54.	This person clearly presents thoughts and ideas in formal, large-group presentations	1	2	3	4	5	na

NATIONAL ASSOCIATION of SECONDARY SCHOOL **PRINCIPALS** © 2001 National Association of Secondary School Principals, 1904 Association Drive, Reston, Virginia 20191-1537

Written Communication: Expressing ideas clearly in writing; demonstrating technical proficiency. Writing appropriately for different audiences.

1=almost never   **2=rarely**   **3=occasionally**   **4=frequently**   **5=almost always**   **na=not applicable**

55.	This person writes concisely	1	2	3	4	5	na
56.	This person demonstrates technical proficiency in writing	1	2	3	4	5	na
57.	This person expresses ideas clearly in writing	1	2	3	4	5	na
58.	This person writes appropriately for different audiences	1	2	3	4	5	na

DEVELOPING SELF AND OTHERS

Development of Others: Teaching, coaching, and helping others. Providing specific feedback based on observations and data.

1=almost never   **2=rarely**   **3=occasionally**   **4=frequently**   **5=almost always**   **na=not applicable**

59.	This person shares information and expertise from personal experiences	1	2	3	4	5	na
60.	This person motivates others to change behaviors that inhibit professional and organizational growth	1	2	3	4	5	na
61.	This person suggests specific developmental activities	1	2	3	4	5	na
62.	This person gives behaviorally-specific feedback focusing on behaviors, not the person	1	2	3	4	5	na
63.	This person asks the person what he/she perceives to be strengths and weaknesses and what he/she wants to improve	1	2	3	4	5	na
64.	This person seeks agreement on specific actions to be taken for development and growth	1	2	3	4	5	na

Understanding Own Strengths and Weaknesses: Understanding personal strengths and weaknesses. Taking responsibility for improvement by actively pursuing developmental activities. Striving for continuous learning.

1=almost never   **2=rarely**   **3=occasionally**   **4=frequently**   **5=almost always**   **na=not applicable**

65.	This person recognizes and communicates own strengths	1	2	3	4	5	na
66.	This person recognizes and manages own developmental needs	1	2	3	4	5	na
67.	This person actively pursues personal growth through participation in planned developmental activities	1	2	3	4	5	na

When you have completed the ratings for the person who gave you this observer assessment, please seal it in an envelope and return it to him or her. The information you give will be combined with ratings from other observers and used with other data to assist this leader in planning meaningful professional development activities. Thank you.

Appendix 8:
Keys to Teaching
Heterogeneous Groups

- Remember—every child can learn. If you make predetermined decisions about who can learn and who cannot, the students will be able to sense this and you will affect their achievement in your class.

- Provide real challenges for all kids. This means that each learning activity has intrinsic meaning for students—no busy work! It may be necessary to create additional or "honors" challenges for students who would like to go further in their learning.

- Don't ever teach to the middle—everyone loses.

- Design instructional activities and assessments for students to construct knowledge rather than simply reproducing facts and ideas.

- Choose "enduring" facts, vocabulary, concepts, theories, and skills that will help students to become responsible and informed citizens as well as self-directed lifelong learners. Help students to see how their work in school is related to the world around them.

- Use open-ended questions to challenge students and guide their inquiry during a particular course or unit of study. Open-ended questions should allow for more than one "correct answer." Inquiry and exploration will foster thinking!

- In heterogeneous groups, the "how" becomes important. Breaking the lock step of all students doing the same activities to arrive at the same end is a key to success. Although you may have a common beginning and a common end, you may have to provide alternative roads for students to achieve the learning objectives.

- In planning the scope and sequence of your instruction and assessment, attempt to address as many of the "multiple intelligences" as possible—thereby providing challenges for all students no matter what their strengths and weaknesses.

- Textbooks are designed for homogeneous groups. Don't depend on textbooks as a central focus for student learning. Use them as one of multiple resources from which students can access knowledge.

- Provide rich and varied resources. Give students opportunities to collect resources as part of the lesson/unit. Utilize a variety of resources such as guest speakers, videos, artifacts, and resources from town hall, historical societies, professionals, and local organizations.

■ Give students as many opportunities as possible to make decisions and reflect on their learning.

■ Be clear about goals and objectives of every lesson/unit. Don't keep secrets about what's going on. Post them. Share them. "Tick" them off together as they are learned.

■ Provide rubrics, product descriptors, and exemplars as early on as possible. These road maps will help students to be successful.

■ Ask that students submit multiple drafts before the final product is due so that you can give them feedback on how to improve their work.

Source: Developed by Susan H. Johnson: Reprinted with permission.

Appendix 9:
Sample Personal Learning Plan
for Faculty/Staff

This sample has been adapted from the one used by Littleton High School. Each of the Littleton learning plans has a cover page with the staff member's name, the supervisor's name, and the effective dates of the plan (e.g., 2003–2006). The cover page is followed by a table of contents specifying pages for the following: time line, philosophy of teaching and learning, collaborative professional reflection worksheet, learning plan, final thoughts, and appendices. Each of these components is covered below.

Component: Time Line		
Date	**Activity**	**Submitted to**
October 6, 2003	Inform evaluator as to your decision	Designated evaluator
December 12, 2003	Complete: Philosophy of Teaching and Learning	Designated evaluator
April 15, 2004	Complete: Collaborative Professional Worksheet and the learning plan	Designated evaluator
April 19–30, 2004	Meet with evaluator to refine plan	NA
May 7, 2004	Submit the learning plan; both parties sign the plan report	Designated evaluator
August 2004–May 2005	Execute the growth opportunities outlined in the learning plan	NA
January 20, 2006	Complete: My Final Thoughts	Designated evaluator

Component:
My Philosophy of Effective Teaching and Learning

This page would be used to allow the staff member to either list or describe in narrative form the staff member's own philosophy of effective teaching and learning. Staff members should ask of themselves:

- What are your belief statements?
- What does teaching look like in your classroom?
- How do students learn?
- What is your view of human nature as it relates to your students?
- What distinguishes you as a unique educator?
- What values/beliefs guide you in your decision making?

Time Line: Complete and submit to your evaluator by December 12, 2003.

Component:
Collaborative Professional Reflection Worksheet

Step 1: Briefly outline your potential goal(s) and the ways in which you might accomplish your goal(s).

Step 2: Identify a professional colleague (teacher or administrator) who is familiar with your instructional performance. Meet with the individual(s) to explain the concept of your goal(s), what you hope to accomplish, and how you plan to do it. Brainstorm additional ways to accomplish your goal(s) or refine the concept of the goal(s).

Step 3: Use this sheet to describe the ideas that were considered and the name of your partner(s).

Step 4: Select one goal and complete the learning plan.

Time Line: Submit to your evaluator by April 19, 2004.

Component: Learning Plan

(Enter Title of Your Goal)

Criteria for selecting the goal:

- Represents new challenges and learnings
- Inspires you to reflect on the teaching and learning process
- Doable and useful
- Aligns with a standard developed by a professional organization (such as the state Department of Education or National Council for Teachers of Math)

Goal statement:
(Prepare a statement about the concept of your goal.)

Rationale:
State your rationale for selection and the standard providing the framework for your goal. See appendix for state standards. Select a standard from a professional organization.

Expected outcomes:
Teacher outcome(s): Articulate what your expected outcome(s) will be. If the goal relates to action research, state the essential question to be answered.

Student outcome(s): Articulate how the accomplishment of the goal will positively impact students.

Growth opportunities:
Opportunity
List growth opportunities that support your goal. These are opportunities in which you engage, not students. Examples include:

Target Month, Year

- Anecdotal records _____

- Authentic teacher-made materials—designing quality work for students _____

- Individual or group action research _____

- Data collection and analysis _____

- Log entries _____

- Reflective journals _____

- Videotaped lessons _____

- Peer coaching (peer-peer) _____

Component: Learning Plan (continued)

- Cognitive coaching (peer-administrator) _____

- School visits _____

- Team teaching _____

- Assessment instruments—surveys, questionnaires, etc. _____

Resources

Documentation:
Collaboratively develop the appropriate documentation for your growth with your evaluator.

1. Artifact reflections that evidence insight and thoughtfulness

2. Self-assessment that provides insight into professional growth

3. Sharing with colleagues.

Time Line: Submit to your evaluator by April 15, 2003; meet between April 22 and 31, 2003, make appropriate revisions as agreed upon; submit a copy of your final draft to your evaluator by May 5, 2003.

Component: My Final Thoughts

Prepare a one- to two-page summary of your progress toward your goal. Possible thoughts might include responses to:

- What worked well in achieving your goal?

- How will this affect your teaching?

- In what ways was this personally meaningful?

- What would you have done differently in achieving your goal and why?

- What recommendations could you make to others on the basis of your findings?

- Based on what you have learned, what future studies would you consider doing to help your students learn?

Time Line: Submit by January 30, 2006, to your evaluator.

Component: Learning Plan Report

Teacher _____ Today's Date _____

School_____

Current Position _____

In a collaborative effort, _____ and

_____ have designed a learning plan

that is appropriate and represents new challenges for _____

_____

_____

_____

_____

Teacher's signature and date

_____

Evaluator's signature and date

Time Line: Complete after the final draft of the learning plan has been developed, by May 5, 2003.

• •

District standards as outlined in the position description meets or exceeds performance standards. Significant progress has been made toward the goal outlined in the learning plan. Attached is a copy of the professional learning plan.

_____

Teacher's signature and date

_____

Evaluator's signature and date

Time Line: Complete after the learning plan has been executed, by January 1, 2005.

Editor's note: Littleton High School also offers several tools for its teachers to help them complete the Personal Learning Plan: a list of possible interview questions one might ask of an "expert" colleague; a form for observation and peer coaching, a self-evaluation form, and a multipage delineation of standards. All forms have been designed to allow them to be completed on a computer.

References

Adelman, C. (1999). *Answers in the toolbox: Academic intensity, attendance patterns, and bachelor's degree attainment.* Washington, DC: U.S. Department of Education Office of Educational Research and Improvement.

Boyer, E. L. (1983). *High school: A report on secondary education in America.* The Carnegie Foundation for the Advancement of Teaching. New York: Harper & Row.

Camblin, S. J., Gullatt, Y., & Klopott, S. (2003). *Strategies for success: Six stories of increasing college access.* Boston: Pathways to College Network.

Carnegie Council on Adolescent Development. (1989). *Turning points: Preparing American youth for the 21st century.* Washington, DC: Author.

Clarke, J. H. (2003). *Changing systems to personalize learning: Introduction to the personalization workshops.* Providence, RI: Education Alliance at Brown University.

Clarke, J. H., & Frazer, E. (2003). Making learning personal: Educational practices that work. In J. DiMartino, J. Clarke, & D. Wolk, (Eds.), *Personalized learning: Preparing high school students to create their futures* (pp. 174–193). Lanham, MD: Scarecrow Press.

Collins, D. (1998). *Achieving your vision of professional development: How to assess your needs and get what you want.* Greensboro, NC: SERVE.

Cotton, K. (2004). *New small learning communities: Findings from recent literature.* Reston, VA: National Association of Secondary School Principals.

Dalziel, M. M., & Schoonover, S. C. (1988). *Changing ways: A practical tool for implementing change within organizations.* New York: Amacom.

Darling-Hammond, L., Ancess, J., & Ort, S. W. (2002, Fall). Reinventing high school: Outcomes of the Coalition Campus Schools project. *American Educational Research Journal, 39*(3), 639–73.

DiMartino, J., Clarke, J., & Wolk, D. (Eds.). *Personalized learning: Preparing high school students to create their futures.* Lanham, MD: Scarecrow Press.

Fullan, M.G. (with S. Stiegelbauer). (1991). *The new meaning of educational change.* New York: Teachers College Press.

Gainey, D. D., & Webb, L. D. (1998). *The education leader's role in change: How to proceed.* Reston, VA: National Association of Secondary School Principals.

Lachat, M. A. (2002). Putting student performance data at the center of school reform. In J. DiMartino, J. Clarke, & D. Wolk, (Eds.), *Personalized learning: Preparing high school students to create their futures* (pp.210–228). Lanham, MD: Scarecrow Press.

Lee, V. E., Smith, J. B., & Croninger, R. G. (1995, Fall). Another look at high school restructuring: More evidence that it improves student achievement and more insight into why. *Issues in Restructuring Schools, 9,* 1–10.

Maine Commission on Secondary Education. (1998). *Promising futures: A call to improve learning for Maine's secondary students.* Augusta: Maine Department of Education.

Marnik, G. (1997). A glimpse at today's high schools. Presented at Successful Transitions conference by the College of Education and Human Development, University of Maine, Orono.

National Association of Secondary School Principals. (1996). *Breaking ranks: Changing an American institution.* Reston, VA: Author.

National Association of Secondary School Principals. (1998). *Breaking ranks leadership: A development program for school teams.* Reston, VA: Author.

National Association of Secondary School Principals. (1999). *Using data for school improvement.* Reston, VA: Author

National Association of Secondary School Principals. (2002). *What the research shows: Breaking ranks in action.* Reston, VA: Author.

National Commission on Excellence in Education. (1983). *A nation at risk: The imperative for educational reform.* Washington, DC: U.S. Government Printing Office.

National Education Commission on Time and Learning. (1994). *Prisoners of time.* Washington, DC: U.S. Government Printing Office.

North Central Regional Educational Laboratory. (2003, Spring). *Notes and Reflections, 4.* Retrieved January 13, 2004, from www.ncrel.org/info/notes/spring03/index.html

Osofsky, D., Sinner, G., & Wolk, D. (2003). *Changing systems to personalize learning: The power of advisories.* Providence, RI: Education Alliance at Brown University.

Painter, B., Lucas, S., Wooderson, M., & Valentine, J. (2000). *The use of teams in school improvement processes.* Reston, VA: National Association of Secondary School Principals.

Painter, B., & Valentine, J. (2002). *Instructional Practices Inventory.* Columbia, MO: Middle Level Leadership Center.

Painter, B., & Valentine, J. (1999). *Engaging teachers in the school improvement process.* Reston, VA: National Association of Secondary School Principals.

Quinn, D., Greunert, S., & Valentine, J. (1999). *Using data for school improvement.* Reston, VA: National Association of Secondary School Principals.

Reeves, D. (2001). *101 Questions and answers about standards, assessment, and accountability.* Denver, CO: Advanced Learning Centers.

Schlechty, P. (1990). *Schools for the 21st century.* San Francisco: Jossey-Bass.

Sizer, T. R. (1984). *Horace's compromise: The dilemma of the American high school.* Boston: Houghton Mifflin.

Sparks, D., & Hirsh, S. (1997). *A new vision for staff development*. Alexandria, VA: Association for Supervision and Curriculum Development.

Sparks, D., & Loucks-Horsley, S. (1989). Five models of staff development for teachers. *Journal of Staff Development, 4,* 40–57.

Sullivan, C. (2004). *College readiness for all: A framework for action*. Boston, MA: Pathways to College Network.

Vermont High School Task Force. (2002). *High schools on the move: Renewing Vermont's commitment to quality secondary education*. Montpelier: Vermont Department of Education.

Webb, L. D., & Berkbuegler, R. (1998). *Personal learning plans for educators*. Reston, VA: National Association of Secondary School Principals.

Webb, L. D., and Norton, F. S. (1999). *Human Resources Administration: Personnel Needs and Issues in Personnel Administration* (3rd ed.). New York: Prentice Hall.

Westerberg, T., & Webb, L. D. (1997). *Providing focus and direction through essential learnings*. Reston, VA: National Association of Secondary School Principals.

Index

BREAKING RANKS II™:
Strategies for Leading High School Reform

NEW!

"High school reform is the next frontier of educational reform. *Breaking Ranks II* is the most powerful and practical resource available anywhere. It is chock full of realistic strategies and ideas. *Breaking Ranks II* is a must handbook for all those working on high school reform. It is superb!"

Michael Fullan
Dean, Ontario Institute for Studies in Education
University of Toronto

An acclaimed roadmap for school change, this publication outlines 31 recommendations for school leaders taking on the challenge of reforming their high schools. Each recommendation falls within the focus of three core areas:

- Collaborative leadership and professional learning communities
- Personalizing your school environment
- Curriculum, instruction, and assessment.

This handbook can be used by *all* schools, regardless of their size, geographical location, or where they are on the school improvement continuum. Middle level leaders and university professors have a stake in the changes promoted in this publication as well. Offering successful research-based practices, real-life examples, a step-by-step approach to change, obstacles to avoid, and countless resources, *Breaking Ranks II* is a must for all secondary school principals.

Share this unique guide with your colleagues—complete the order form below to purchase additional copies of *Breaking Ranks II* today. NASSP. 2004. 220 pp.

#2100401
Member $17.50
Nonmember $22.00

Check out our volume discounts!

10–24 copies	20% discount
25–99 copies	30% discount
100 or more copies	35% discount

Please apply discounts before adding shipping and handling charges.

Order Form

BRII2004RP

Member # _____ (from mailing label)

Ship to
Please note: UPS cannot send to a post office box; please provide street address.

School name _____

School address _____

City _____ State ____ Zip ____

Attention _____

Phone _____ Fax _____ E-Mail _____

Method of Payment
Payment must accompany order.

❑ Check enclosed. Make payable to NASSP.

❑ Credit card   NASSP Tax ID#52-6006937

Card type:

❑ MasterCard ❑ VISA ❑ American Express

❑ Personal ❑ Business/School

Credit card account number _____

Expiration date _____ / _____

Cardholder signature _____

Name as it appears on card _____

Credit card billing address _____

Order #	Item	Unit Price Member/Nonmember	Quantity	Total
2100401	*Breaking Ranks II: Strategies for Leading High School Reform*	$17.50/$22.00	_____	_____

Shipping & Handling*

For orders totaling:	Add:
$1–$25	$6
$25.01–$50	$7
$50.01–$75	$9
$75.01–$100	$10
$100.01 or more	9%

Subtotal _____

VA residents add 4.5% sales tax _____

Shipping & handling* _____

TOTAL _____

Send all orders to: NASSP, P.O. Box 3250, Reston, VA 20195-9864.
Credit card orders can be placed by faxing your order to 703-620-6534 or by calling 866-647-7253.

NATIONAL ASSOCIATION
OF SECONDARY SCHOOL
PRINCIPALS
promoting excellence in school leadership